DATE DUE			
Mar19 '81			

Current Issues in
Linguistic Theory

Current Issues in Linguistic Theory

Edited by Roger W. Cole

INDIANA UNIVERSITY PRESS

Bloomington & London

Published in Canada by Fitzhenry & Whiteside Limited, Don Mills, Ontario

Manufactured in the United States of America

Library of Congress Cataloging in Publication Data
Linguistic Institute, University of South Florida, 1975.
Current issues in linguistic theory.
Includes index.
1. Linguistics—Addresses, essays, lectures.
I. Cole, Roger William. II. Title.
P125.L5 1975 410 76–26427
ISBN 0–253–31608–1 1 2 3 4 5 81 80 79 78 77

Contents

CONTENTS

Preface

In 1972, when the 1975 Linguistic Institute was still in its planning stages, my (then to be) Associate Director, Thomas A. Sebeok of Indiana University, suggested that we depart from the format for the Distinguished Lecture Series that has been traditionally followed at linguistic institutes. In place of a series of "one-shot" lectures during the summer, Professor Sebeok proposed that we invite lecturers for one-week assignments, during which they would present a series of four lectures on a single topic that would later be gathered into a single manuscript for publication. For the 1975 series, we decided upon the theme "Current Issues in Linguistic Theory," and the original schedule of lectures was as follows:

Noam Chomsky, Massachusetts Institute of Technology (week of June 23), "Syntax and Semantics"

Joshua Fishman, Yeshiva University (week of June 30), "The Sociology of Language: Yesterday, Today, and Tomorrow"

Charles Fillmore, University of California, Berkeley (week of July 7), "Studies in Lexical Semantics"

Eugene Nida, American Bible Society (week of July 14), "Some New Developments in Lexicology"

Henry Hoenigswald, University of Pennsylvania (week of July 21), "Intentions, Assumptions, and Contradictions in Historical Linguistics"

Rulon Wells, Yale University (week of July 28), "An Approach to Semantics"

Wallace Chafe, University of California, Berkeley (week of August 4), "The Remembrance and Verbalization of Past Experience"

Charles Ferguson, Stanford University (week of August 11), "New
    Directions in Phonological Theory: Language Acquisition and Uni-
    versals Research"
Eric Lenneberg, Cornell University (week of August 18), "New Per-
    spectives on Aphasia"

The sudden death of Professor Eric Lenneberg just a few weeks before
the Institute began left us no time to alter the published schedule, and,
for a variety of reasons, we decided not to replace him with an alternate.

The lectures are presented in this volume in the order that they were
given during the Institute. Some contributors chose to present manu-
scripts that retain the organization and style of the lectures as originally
delivered, while others elected to make extensive revisions of their
material. As editor of the series, I made no attempt to enforce consistency
in the matter, since there are obvious advantages in both approaches.

My special thanks are due to Professor Sebeok for his invaluable
assistance in this and all other aspects of the program that made the
1975 Linguistic Institute a success; to Professor Jean Casagrande, my
Co-Director, and all other members of the Institute faculty and staff;
and, most especially, to Marilyn Engelhardt, who managed the series,
for her untiring efforts on behalf of the contributors while they were with
us, and for her indispensable assistance in preparing the final manu-
scripts for the published volume.

University of South Florida   Roger W. Cole
May 1976

Current Issues in
Linguistic Theory

Conditions on Rules
of Grammar

Noam Chomsky

In this discussion, I will assume without supporting argument a general framework that I have outlined and discussed elsewhere,[1] and I will review some recent ideas on grammatical theory within this framework.

A person who has learned a language has constructed a system of rules and principles—a grammar—determining a sound–meaning relation of some sort over an infinite domain. The linguist's grammar is a theory of this attained competence, under conventional and entirely appropriate idealizations. The general theory of grammar—call it "universal grammar" (UG)—is a system of principles that determines: (1) what counts as a grammar, and (2) how grammars function to generate structural descriptions of sentences. Thus within UG we have conditions on the form of grammar and conditions on the function of grammatical rules. Among the conditions on the form of grammar are the specification of possible base structures, grammatical transformations, phonological rules, and so on. Among the conditions on function that have been proposed are, for example, the A-over-A condition and the coordinate structure constraint. We may assume, at this point, that it is in part a matter of expository convenience how we choose to construe some feature of UG in these terms.

This chapter is based on lectures presented at the Linguistic Institute, University of South Florida, June 1975. A more detailed and extensive study covering topics discussed here and other related matters is in preparation.

Naturally, we will attempt to make these conditions explicit and as restrictive as possible. We want UG to make as strong a statement as possible about the nature of language and thus to be subject to critical tests and to provide explanations for the phenomena attested in descriptive study. We can explain the fact that linguistic competence has the property P insofar as we can show that property P conforms to UG and is, furthermore, the special case of UG determined by experience. In the most interesting cases, the role of experience is limited or even nonexistent, so that the property P simply reflects some property of UG and thus gives us direct insight into the nature of UG. We argue that a given language has the property P because UG requires that this be the case. Where it seems that speakers have been exposed to little if any relevant experience, but yet have acquired a language with the property P rather than some alternative, it is reasonable to attribute P to UG itself. The case of structure dependence of rules is a familiar simple example. If our goal is not only description of linguistic competence but also explanation, we will try to provide as restrictive as possible a theory of UG.

To restate the same commitment (in essence) from a different point of view, I assume that our aim is to assimilate the study of language to the general body of natural science. Linguistics, then, may be regarded as that part of human psychology that is concerned with the nature, function, and origin of a particular "mental organ." We may take UG to be a theory of the language faculty, a common human attribute, genetically determined, one component of the human mind. Through interaction with the environment, this faculty of mind becomes articulated and refined, emerging in the mature person as a system of knowledge of language. To discover the character of this mental faculty, we will try to isolate those properties of attained linguistic competence that hold by necessity rather than as a result of accidental experience, where by "necessity" I of course mean biological rather than logical necessity. We will therefore be particularly interested in properties of attained linguistic competence that are vastly underdetermined by available experience in general, but that nevertheless hold for the linguistic competence attained by any normal speaker of a given language, and in fact by all speakers of all languages (perhaps vacuously in some cases) on the natural assumption of uniformity across the species. The commitment to formulate a restrictive theory of UG is thus nothing other than a commitment to discover the biological endowment that makes language acquisition possible and to determine its particular manifestations. Returning to the matter of "explanatory adequacy," we can explain some property of attained linguistic competence by showing that this property necessarily results from the interplay of the genetically determined language faculty, specified by UG, and the person's (accidental) experience.

Let us assume further that a grammar contains rules that produce derivations, where a derivation D is a sequence of phrase markers $(K_1, \ldots, K_n)$, such that each K_{i+1} is derived from K_i by application of some rule. Assume further that the application of these rules is governed by the principle of the (strict) cycle. Among these rules there are syntactic transformations, lexical insertion rules, phonological rules, morphological rules of various sorts, rules that place word boundaries and that determine intonational structures, and rules that specify the class of items that are available for lexical insertion—all with their intrinsic properties. Of these various types of rules I will now consider only syntactic transformations.

A derivation will be well formed only if its "initial" and "final" phrase markers (K_1 and K_n, respectively, in the derivation $(K_1, \ldots, K_n)$) meet certain additional conditions. The initial phrase marker must be a *base structure*, that is, one of an infinite set of structures generated by the *base component* of the grammar. The final phrase marker must also meet a variety of conditions, some of which I will discuss. In a well-formed derivation, the initial phrase marker may be referred to as a *deep structure* and the final phrase marker as a *surface structure*. I should perhaps note that these terms—like other terms of grammar—have been used in varying senses as theory has evolved, a fact that may mislead the unwary reader.

The grammar determines sound–meaning relations. I will assume that the mechanism is a set of rules that associate transformational derivations with representations of sound and representations of meaning. As for the former, I have little to say here. I will assume the framework of *Sound Pattern of English* as modified by Joan Bresnan.[2] Thus surface structures contain phonetic representation, i.e., representation in terms of a universal phonetic system provided by UG.

I will be more concerned here with the relation of a derivation to semantic representation. One may ask, in the first place, whether there is a system of semantic representation analogous to phonetic representation, and if so, what its properties may be. There are various views on this matter. I will not dwell on the issue here, but will, for the moment, put the matter in a rather neutral way. Let us say that the grammar contains a system of rules that associates a derivation with a representation in a system of representation LF (logical form), but for the present, without assuming additional properties of this concept. Thus I will take LF to incorporate whatever features of sentence structure (1) enter directly into semantic interpretation of sentences and (2) are strictly determined by properties of sentence-grammar. The extension of this concept remains to be determined. Assume further that there is a system of rules that associates logical form and the products of other cognitive faculties with another system of representation SR (semantic representation). Representations in SR, which may involve beliefs, expectations, and so on, in addition to properties of LF determined by grammatical rule, should suffice to determine role in inference, conditions of appropriate use, etc. (Some would argue that LF alone should suffice, but I leave that as an open empirical question.) Thus the grammar relates LF to phonetic representation, through the medium of derivations. I will only be able to touch peripherally on the many questions that arise in this connection. See the references given in note 1 and the sources cited in these for much additional discussion.

Implicit in this presentation is a certain version of the "thesis of autonomy of syntax" (see Chomsky, 1975). Specifically, I have assumed that the rules of sentence-grammar can be subdivided into two categories, the first (call it "formal grammar") sufficing to determine representations on all linguistic levels apart from LF, the second associating such representations with LF. This empirical assumption becomes precise and substantive to the extent that we characterize the properties of the various levels of linguistic representation. It need not be correct, being an empirical assumption (though one of a rather abstract nature). I will continue to assume that it is in fact correct.

What elements of a derivation relate to LF? Several views have coalesced in recent years, in particular, the following two: (1) deep structure determines LF; (2) deep and surface structure jointly determine LF. The first is the viewpoint of the so-called standard theory. The second is the assumption of the "extended standard theory" (EST) and earlier variants of "generative semantics,"[3] which, I have argued elsewhere, simply amount to a less-restrictive variant of EST.[4] I will assume here that EST is generally correct. Thus, LF is determined by properties of both deep and surface structure. In particular, "thematic relations" such as agent, instrument, etc., are determined by the interaction of formally defined grammatical relations of deep structure and lexical properties[5] while surface structure determines all other aspects of LF: anaphora, scope of logical operators, the subject–predicate relation, focus and semantic presupposition, and so on. It may be that a suitably enriched version of surface structure suffices to determine LF fully, under a revision of EST along the lines to be discussed. See Chomsky (1976).

So much for what I will presuppose. Recall the major problem of grammatical theory, as conceived here: to restrict the class of grammars available in principle to the language learner, and thus to progress toward a solution to the most fundamental question that we can raise, namely, how people are able to acquire their vast and intricate knowledge of language on the basis of the fragmentary and degenerate evidence available to them.[6]

Within EST, the variety of grammars can be restricted at various points. We might impose conditions on the base, thus restricting the variety of possible systems. We may attempt to limit the expressive power of transformations so that fewer transformations will be available in principle; and we may limit the variety of transformational systems in other ways, say, by imposing general conditions on ordering. Further restriction can be achieved by appropriate conditions on the "interpretive rules" that associate representations in LF with derivations. Furthermore, conditions on rule application that do not in themselves directly restrict the variety of grammars may contribute to this end in an indirect but significant manner, where they permit a reduction of the expressive power of rules. In each of these categories, there has been recent research that seems to me promising.

On restriction of the base, the most promising line of inquiry, in my opinion, has to do with the "X-bar theory," which takes the base to be in its essentials a projection from the lexical features [±Noun], [±Verb], by means of general schemata.[7] I will not pursue this topic here. Rather, I would like to consider the problem of restricting the transformational component of the grammar. Some fairly natural conditions seem to me feasible, at least over an interesting range. It is these conditions that I want to explore.

In all theories of transformations that have been presented even in a semi-explicit way, a transformational rule is defined in terms of a *structural description* (SD) and a *structural change* (SC), where the SD specifies the domain of the transformation and the SC states what effect the transformation has on an arbitrary member of this domain. The domain of a transformation is a set of phrase markers, each associated with some terminal string. A transformation applies to a phrase marker K of a terminal string X subdivided into the successive *factors* $X_1, \ldots, X_n$ ($X = X_1 \ldots X_n$). The SD specifies the domain of a transformation by placing conditions on such factorization. Let us consider a few simple cases.

Assume a terminal and a nonterminal vocabulary, where the terminal symbols represent grammatical formatives and the nonterminal symbols represent categories (NP, VP, S, etc.).[8] Suppose that we also have the symbol *vbl* (variable).[9] We may then construct arbitrary strings in this full vocabulary. Let us assume the notion (1):

(1) $E(Y, \alpha, X, K)$, where Y is a substring of the terminal string X, K is a phrase marker of X, and α is an arbitrary string in the full vocabulary.

We will read (1) as: Y is an α of X with respect to (wrt) K.[10] For example, if K is a phrase marker of the terminal string *the man left*, then $E(\textit{the man}, \text{NP}, \textit{the man left}, K)$, since *the man* is a noun phrase in the sentence *the man left* wrt K.

To explain E, we have to say how it holds under various choices of α. Where $\alpha = vbl$, we will say that any string is an α; thus $E(Y,vbl,X,K)$ for any substring Y of X. Where α is a terminal string Z, then Y is an α of X wrt K only when $Y = Z$. Where α is a category symbol, then Y is an α of X wrt K only when Y is assigned to the category α by K. To make the latter notion precise, we need to elaborate the notion of "phrase marker." We may assume here any conventional theory, say labeled bracketing. If we take phrase markers to be sets of strings, along the lines of Chomsky (1955), then where α is a terminal string or a category, then $E(Y,\alpha, X, K)$ when K contains the string formed by replacing Y in X by α.

In a very simple case, we may restrict α to a terminal string, a category, or *vbl*, and represent the SD of a transformation as a sequence (2):

(2)   SD: $(\alpha_1, \ldots, \alpha_n)$.

The transformation defined by SD of (2) applies to the string X with factors $X_1, \ldots, X_n$ and the phrase marker K, where for each i, $E(X_i, \alpha_i, X, K)$.

For example, we might formulate the passive transformation in English with the SD (3):

(3)   (*vbl*, NP, Aux, V, NP, *by*, #, *vbl*)

In this formulation, the two terms *vbl* are (end-) variables, so that the first and last factors of a string X to which the transformation applies are arbitrary. The second and fifth factors must be NP's (each is an NP), the third an Aux(iliary), the fourth a V, the sixth *by*, and the seventh # (*by* and # are terminal symbols; we may think of # as an "abstract" representative of NP). In particular, the passive transformation, so formulated, will apply to the string (4), where – indicates the break between factors:

(4)   Yesterday – the boy – past – read – the book – *by* – #.

Existing transformational grammars do not restrict rules to this simple case. Nevertheless, I want to consider the possibility that only this case is permitted, and in fact, that even this case is "insufficiently simple" in that it permits too rich an expressive power for transformations.

Among the enrichments of the theory of sD's that appear in the literature, theoretical and applied, are the following: disjunctions of sequences of the form (2), meaning that the factors may satisfy any one of the disjuncts;[11] wider possibilities for α;[12] sD's defined in terms of Boolean conditions on E for a fixed sequence of factors;[13] conditions expressed in terms of quantifiers;[14] conditions involving grammatical relations;[15] sD's expressing quite arbitrary conditions on phrase markers or even sets of noncontiguous phrase markers of a derivation;[16] sD's expressing conditions not limited to a single derivation;[17] sD's involving extrasyntactic or even extragrammatical factors; e.g., beliefs.[18] These various moves toward enrichment of the theory of transformations are all distinct. Each is unwelcome (though perhaps necessary, so the facts may show), the more extreme being the more unwelcome for reasons already outlined.[19]

It would take several more lectures to discuss these and other related proposals in anything like an adequate way. I will not enter into these fundamental questions here, but will merely remark that I am not convinced by the arguments advanced, particularly for the more extreme proposals, many of which seem to me to involve nothing more than a failure to distinguish separate and quite distinct components of the full system of language that interact to determine judgments in complex cases.

Let us restrict attention to the simple case mentioned earlier, namely, sD's of the form (2). Let us inquire into the effects of other, still more stringent conditions on the expressive power of transformational rules.

The structural change of a transformation with the sD (2) will apply to a string X factored into n successive factors $X_1, \ldots, X_n$, where $E(X_i, \alpha_i, X, K)$, and K is the phrase marker of X. The structural change will in general not affect the form or position of certain factors, while others will be moved, modified, replaced, or deleted; briefly, *changed*. A factor changed by the rule, unless arbitrary or a fixed terminal string, must be assigned to a single category, under the assumptions we are now considering. For example, we cannot have a rule that moves a factor Z identified as a V + NP in the sD of the transformation. Rather, if a rule moves such a string, we must assign it to a single category, VP. Considerations of this sort have been regularly adduced in support of one or another assignment of constituent structure since the origins of work in transformational grammar.[20]

We may think of the category symbols that appear in sp's as "type variables." Thus, where NP appears as the ith term in (2), it may be "satisfied" by an arbitrary string of the type NP in factoring a string for the transformation. It is argued in Bresnan (in press, 1975) that the restriction to type variables in this sense is too narrow and that categorical terms of the sp must be generalized in terms of the X-bar system. See Fiengo and Lasnik (in press) for a similar proposal on different grounds. Suppose that X^n stands for an arbitrary category with n bars in this system. Then we might permit terms of the form X^n to appear in sp's. Cf. notes 12, 13.

It seems that factors that are truly arbitrary are never changed by rules. That is, where α_i in an sp is vbl, the ith factor will not be changed by the rule but will rather serve as a "context" for whatever changes the rule induces. Let us stipulate, then, that a factor changed by a rule must be either a fixed terminal string or a string of a constant or variable category. An unrestricted variable ($\alpha_i = vbl$) in an sp will be satisfied only by a factor that is not changed by the rule.

A radical restriction in the expressive power of transformations would be achieved if we were to impose a condition that is almost the converse of the condition imposed on factors changed in the following way. Suppose we were to insist that if a term α_i of sp is a constant or variable category, then the factor satisfying α_i must be changed by the rule. That is, categories cannot be used to define the context of the structural change induced by the transformation. Such contexts must either be arbitrary or fixed terminal strings.

Actually, the same result follows in many cases even from weaker conditions on sp's. Suppose that we were to impose a condition of *minimal factorization* that requires that the sp (2) cannot contain two successive categorial terms unless one or the other is satisfied by a factor changed by the rule. This condition in effect extends to the context of the structural change the requirement of analyzability as a single constituent that we have tentatively imposed on the factors changed by the rule. Assuming this condition, which actually is rather well motivated, let us return to the passive transformation.

In Chomsky (1972, 1973) it is suggested that there are really two components to what has been called the "passive transformation," one a rule of NP-postposing that converts (4) to (5), and another a rule of NP-preposing that converts (5) to (6):

(5)   yesterday – t_1 – past – read – the book – by [the boy]$_1$

(6)   yesterday – [the book]$_2$ – past –read – t_2 – *by* – the boy

The symbols t_1, t_2 are the "traces" left by movement of the co-indexed phrases. For the moment, we may regard this as a notational proposal, though we will see later that much more is involved.[21] NP-preposing replaces the trace t_1 by the NP *the book*.

Under the proposed condition of minimal factorization, we cannot employ (3) in the formulation of the rule of NP-postposing or NP-preposing. In the former case, the constant terms Aux, V, NP, and *by* are not changed by the rule; in the case of NP-preposing, the constant terms Aux and V are not changed (we may ignore the factors *by*, #) unless we assume that the same rule introduces *be* + *en*, adjoining it to either Aux or V, an assumption that I would like to reject for reasons discussed elsewhere (cf. Chomsky, 1976, chapter 3). Therefore, under the condition of minimal factorization, the rules must be formulated in quite a different way. Assuming now that the passive element *be* + *en* derives from an independent source, the rule of NP-preposing must be based on the SD (7):

(7)   (*vbl*, NP, *vbl*, NP, *vbl*).

Thus the transformation in question will apply to a string factored into five factors, the first, third, and fifth arbitrary, and the second and fourth NP's. Terms changed by the rule are specified as constant categories; contexts are arbitrary. The associated structural change will state that the fourth factor moves into the position of the second factor. We might formulate the rule of NP-postposing in the same manner, with a structural change indicating that the second factor moves into the position of the fourth factor.

The difficulties facing such an analysis appear at first—and may prove to be—insurmountable. Whether or not this is so is a question I would like to explore. Note that if we can go as far as this, we can take a further step, exploiting Emonds's structure-preserving hypothesis, which entails that NP can move only into an NP position in the phrase marker (Emonds, forthcoming). Thus the rules in question reduce to the following formulation:

(8)   Move NP.

This seems a natural consequence of assuming the condition of minimal factorization.

As noted, the condition of minimal factorization extends to the context of a rule the requirement of analyzability as a single constituent imposed on the factors changed by the rule. If this extension seems natural, we are then led to consider the following condition on an sd of the form (2):

(9) If α_i is satisfied by a factor changed by the rule, then α_i may be terminal or a category; if α_i is satisfied by a factor not changed by the rule, then α_i may be either *vbl* or a terminal string.

The case of terminal strings changed by a rule seems rather marginal. Perhaps we may consider such rules to be of a special type, what Bach has called "housekeeping rules" (Bach, 1965). If so, we may say that for the basic rules of the grammar, factors changed by the rule must be analyzed by the sd as categories while contexts (factors not changed) must be either terminal or arbitrary. If terminal contexts can be eliminated in general, we will have rules of the form (8).

I think that (9) is probably too strong a condition, but that the weaker condition of minimal factorization may be tenable, despite the fact that its consequences approach (9), as we have seen.

I would now like to consider a few of the problems that arise under such radical restrictions of the expressive power of transformations as those just suggested.

Evidently, a grammar limited to such rules as (7) or (8) will overgenerate massively, since intricate constraints cannot be built into specific transformations. Consider the case of NP-preposing, i.e., the leftward movement case of (7). By general conditions on recoverability of deletion (the correct formulation of which is a nontrivial matter; cf. Peters and Ritchie, 1973, the second NP can move only to an NP position that is empty of any lexical material. Assuming that the left NP position, which is to receive the moved NP, is empty, either by virtue of prior NP-postposing or for some other reason, we will have such instances of NP-preposing as the following:

(10)   (i) John is believed [t is incompetent]
         (ii) John is believed [t to be incompetent]
        (iii) John('s) was read [t book]
         (iv) John seems [t to like Bill]
          (v) John seems [Bill to like t]
         (vi) Yesterday was lectured t
        (vii) Yesterday's lecture t

In each case, t is the trace left by movement of the NP (*John, yesterday*). Of these examples, only (ii), (iv), and (vii) are grammatical, though NP-preposing has applied in a comparable way in all cases. Thus the rule overgenerates, specifically, in cases (i), (iii), (v), and (vi).

There are two general approaches to the problem of overgeneration in such cases as these: we may try to impose (I) conditions on the application of rules or (II) conditions on the output of rules, i.e., on surface structures. The latter will generally be related to rules of semantic interpretation that determine LF, under the assumptions of EST. As we will see, (I) and (II) may fall together. Both sorts of conditions may be related to perceptual strategies in some way; cf. Chomsky (1973) and references cited there.

In either (I) or (II) the conditions in question may be universal or particular; and in the case of (I), if particular, they may be language-particular or rule-particular. In the best case, of course, the conditions will be universal. That is, we try to abstract general properties of transformations that do not have to be built into specific transformations. Thus the set of potentially available grammars is reduced, and we approach the fundamental problem of accounting for the fact that language can be learned.

If we conclude that some condition is language-particular, we must find a way to account for its application in a given case. If the condition is rule-particular, we have to account for the fact that specific rules observe the condition and that speakers have knowledge of this property of the language.

Even if conditions are language- or rule-particular, there are limits to the possible diversity of grammar. Thus, such conditions can be regarded as parameters that have to be fixed (for the language, or for particular rules, in the worst case), in language learning. We would then raise the question of how the class of grammars so constituted, with rules that lack expressive power but with parameters to be fixed independently, compares with the class of grammars permitted under a theory that permits articulation of conditions on application within the formulation of the rules themselves. It has often been supposed that conditions on application of rules must be quite general, even universal, to be significant, but that need not be the case if establishing a "parametric" condition permits us to reduce substantially the class of possible rules.

We might hope to find that even if some condition C on rule application is language-particular, some general principle determines that it applies in languages of some specific type, in which case we will have again reduced the problem, indirectly, to a property of UG. Or, in the case of rule-particular conditions, we might find that they apply to rules of some specific category, say, movement rules. Such a result would be as welcome as a universal condition, in that it limits the choice of grammars in a comparable way. That is, the child would not have to learn anything about the applicability of the condition; a universal principle would determine this. Many proposals of this nature appear in the literature.

I am going to suggest that there are conditions that apply to transformational rules and interpretive rules, and other conditions that apply only to transformational rules. These conditions belong to the theory of sentence-grammar. There may be other conditions that apply to the rules that assign semantic representations to LF and elements of other cognitive structures, i.e., to rules that extend beyond sentence-grammar in their scope; for example, to "free anaphora," which may involve properties of discourse, situation, and assumed background belief.

Consider again the examples of overgeneration in (10). In work referred to above, I have suggested that we can account for these examples in terms of certain general conditions on rules. Consider a structure of the form (11):

$$(11) \qquad\qquad \ldots X \ldots [\alpha \ldots Y \ldots] \ldots X \ldots$$

Then no rule can involve X and Y in (11) where α is a tensed-S (the *tensed-S condition*)[22] or where α contains a subject distinct from Y and not controlled by X (the *specified subject condition*—henceforth ssc). (For discussion, see Chomsky 1973, 1976.) I will assume further that transformations, but not interpretive rules, meet the condition of *subjacency*, which restricts their application to a single cyclic node or adjacent cyclic nodes.[23]

The tensed-S condition suffices to explain the differences of status between (i) and (ii). ssc accounts for the distinction between (iv) and (v). To exclude (iii), we might appeal to the A-over-A condition. Note that in these cases, at least, we might reformulate the conditions in question as conditions on an enriched surface structure involving traces, instead of conditions on the application of rules.

What about the phrases (vi) and (vii) of (10)? Emonds suggests that such examples as these show that NP-preposing cannot be a unitary phenomenon, but must apply differently in sentences and noun phrases. However, we might appeal to a principle of semantic interpretation of surface structures, in part independently motivated, to make the distinction. Consider the sentences (12):

(12)   (a) Beavers build dams
              (b) Dams are built t by beavers
                   (where t is the trace left by NP-preposing).

Under its most natural interpretation, (b) is false, since some dams are not built by beavers. Thus in (b), under this interpretation, the property *built-by-beavers* is predicated, falsely, of all dams. No such interpretation is possible for (a), which predicates the property *dam-builder* of all beavers (which is not to say, of course, that all beavers build dams; rather, all have the species-property in question). Such examples indicate that the subject–predicate relation is defined on surface structures.

Of course, to understand (b) we must also know that the subject *dams* bears the same "thematic relation" to the verb *build* as it does in (a). Assuming now that traces appear in surface structure, the requisite information appears in (b) under the general convention that the trace t is under the control of the phrase *dams* that moved from the position marked by t, which we may regard as a bound variable in (b).

Let us return now to the problem of (10vi, vii), repeated here as (13a, b):

(13)   (a) Yesterday was lectured t
                        (b) Yesterday's lecture t

Assume that NP-preposing is indeed involved in each case. But the principle of interpretation that assigns the subject–predicate relation will yield nonsense when applied to (a); it makes no sense to predicate *was-lectured* of *yesterday*. We might, then, argue that (13a) is ungrammatical, but by virtue of a violation of a principle of semantic interpretation—i.e., it is "unsemantic" rather than "unsyntactic" if we regard these interpretive rules as part of semantics. In contrast, the principle of subject–predicate interpretation does not apply at all to (13b), which is not a sentence. Rather, the principle of interpretation that applies here is the one that we see exemplified in such structures as "John's kitten," which may be understood to mean the kitten that John has, or that he owns, or that he made out of clay, or that he fathered (or gave birth to, in the case of an oddly named female cat), etc. As we let factual assumptions range, the extent of possible interpretations in such cases varies widely, in a manner that has yet to be explained. It seems plausible to suppose that it may comprehend (13b) as a special case.

Thus we might try to account for the distinction between (13a) and (13b) not in terms of an enriched theory of transformations but in terms of principles of semantic interpretation that are (if this line of reasoning proves correct) independently motivated. This proposal remains a promissory note in the absence of a theory of subject–predicate and possessive interpretation. But such a theory is certainly necessary, and may well accommodate the phenomenon under consideration. It seems to me at least plausible—and perhaps quite reasonable—to adopt the working hypothesis that no enrichment of the theory of transformations is called for in this case.

The discussion of these examples illustrates the possibility of compensating for the overgeneration of a highly restricted theory of transformations in terms of conditions on transformations and on interpretation of surface structures, conditions that may be quite general, perhaps properties of UG itself.

Let us now turn to a somewhat different, though related, matter. Consider the sentences (14) and (15):

(14)   (a) The men like each other
            (b) The men like them
            (c) I like me

(15)   (a) The men want [John to like each other]
            (b) The men want [John to like them]
            (c) I want [John to like me]

Let us assume the following two rules:

(16)   Reciprocal interpretation, which assigns an appropriate sense to sentences of the form NP . . . *each other*[24]

(17)   Disjoint reference (DR), which assigns disjoint reference to a pair (NP, pronoun) (and more generally, to two NP's, under somewhat different conditions that extend beyond sentence grammar; cf. note 37)

The reciprocal rule applies to (14a), but cannot apply to (15a) by virtue of SSC. Thus, (14a) is grammatical but (15a) is not. The rule DR applies to (14b), assigning disjoint reference, but is blocked from application in (15b) by SSC. The reference of *them* in (15b) is therefore free; it can, in particular, be understood to refer to the men. In the case of (14c), DR applies, assigning disjoint reference, which is impossible in this case. In the parallel case of (15c), DR cannot apply by virtue of SSC, so that *me* and *I* may be (and must be) coreferential. Hence (14c) is "strange" (whether ungrammatical or not is a matter that need not concern us here; it depends on what status we assign to DR), in a sense in which (15c) is not.

In these examples, as before, SSC functions so as to permit a very simple formulation of rules. Thus such examples as (14) and (15) do not compel us to depart from the simplest possible formulation of the rule of reciprocal interpretation and DR, a formulation that simply asserts that they hold for any NP and an anaphoric element (reciprocal, pronoun).

I suggested before that (10v) is blocked by SSC, but without explaining how. Let us consider two interpretations of this suggestion. We assume now that (10iv) derives by NP-preposing from the underlying structure "X seems [John to like Bill]," where X is some terminal "placeholder" for NP, the exact character of which need not detain us now. On one interpretation, SSC prevents the rule from preposing *John* in "X seems [Bill to like John]" to give (10v). Thus, SSC blocks a certain transformational rule. Alternatively, we might construe SSC as a condition on surface structure interpretation but not transformations. Thus, the NP-preposing rule applies freely, giving both (10iv) and (10v). But we must surely regard the relation between NP and the trace that it controls as a special case of bound anaphora (cf. Fiengo, 1974; Chomsky, 1976); that is, as a relation just like the one that holds between antecedent and reciprocal. Thus, SSC will block the rule of bound anaphora exactly as it blocks reciprocal interpretation and disjoint reference in the cases just described. It is in this sense that we can regard SSC, in such cases, as a condition on surface structures applying quite generally to anaphora (hence to the NP-trace relation), rather than a condition on transformations. In principle, the two interpretations of SSC have distinct empirical consequences, but the issue is complex and it is not easy to sort out the consequences.

Were it not for SSC, the rules as formulated would overgenerate (in the case of (16)) and undergenerate (in the case of (17), since when it applies it rules out certain sentences and interpretations). Thus SSC compensates for certain instances of mis-generation. The same is true of the tensed-S condition. Consider (18):

(18) (a) The candidates expected [that each other would win]
     (b) The candidates want [each other to win]
     (c) The candidates expected [that they would win]
     (d) The candidates want [them to win]
     (e) I expected [that I will win]
     (f) I want [me to win]

The condition blocks the reciprocal rule in (a) but not (b). It blocks DR in (c) but not (d), so that the pronoun may refer to the candidates in (c) but not (d). It blocks DR in (e) but not in (f), which is therefore "strange" or ungrammatical, depending on our conclusion concerning violation of DR.

Now consider the examples of (19), (20):

(19)   (a) The men seem to John [*t* to like each other]
          (b) The men seem to John [*t* to like them]
          (c) I seem to John [*t* to like me]

(20)   (a) John seems to the men [*t* to like each other]
          (b) John seems to the men [*t* to like them]
          (c) John seems to me [*t* to like me]

The examples of (19) are analogous to (14). Thus in (a), *each other* is anaphorically related to *the men*; in (b) the pronoun cannot refer to the men; and (c) is strange or ungrammatical. In short, the rules of reciprocal interpretation and DR apply in (19) as in (14).

The examples of (20) are correspondingly analogous to (15). Reciprocal interpretation is blocked in case (a). DR is blocked in case (b), so that the pronoun can refer freely, in particular, to *the men*. And (c) is fine.

These examples are analogous to those discussed earlier, and should fall under the same principle. But SSC does not seem to apply, since there is no subject in the embedded sentences of (20) as there was in (15) to put it into effect.

The examples of (19) behave as though there is no specified subject in the embedded sentence; the examples of (20), in contrast, are treated as though there were a specified subject in the position marked by the trace *t* left by NP-preposing of the subject of the matrix sentence. In the case of (20), a "mentally present" subject blocks application of the rules by SSC, just as the physically present subject *John* in (15) blocks the same rules. In the case of (19), the mentally present subject does not block application of the rules.

To extend SSC to all of these cases, it is necessary to define "specified subject" as above, p. 14. Though not logically necessary, this is entirely natural. It amounts to regarding the trace as a bound variable, with all of the (relevant) properties of its "controller," the noun phrase to which it is bound. Let us now stipulate explicitly what we have been tacitly assuming: movement of a phrase by a transformation leaves behind a trace controlled by the moved phrase; the trace will be interpreted as a bound variable along lines to which we will return. The trace is a zero morpheme—phonetically null but morphologically on a par with any other terminal symbol of the level of phrase structure. Just as the lexical string *John* serves as a specified subject in (15), blocking any rule that relates Y of (11) to X, so the trace *t* serves as a specified subject in (20), blocking any rule that relates Y of (11) to X unless t is bound by X. In all cases, then, the rules apply as though the noun phrase binding the trace t were actually present in the position of t. The trace theory thus permits otherwise valid conditions to apply, again overcoming cases of misapplication of rules: overgeneration in the case of the reciprocal rule, undergeneration in the case of disjoint reference (DR).

Observe that there is no plausible semantic reason for the inapplicability of the rules in (20). Consider the reciprocal rule. The pair (*each of the men, the other(s)*) is similar in meaning to the pair (*the men, each other*). Thus corresponding to (14a), (15a), (19a), and (20a), repeated here as (21a-d), we have (22a-d) respectively:

(21)   (a) The men like each other
       (b) The men want [John to like each other]
       (c) The men seem to John [t to like each other]
       (d) John seems to the men [t to like each other]

(22)   (a) Each of the men likes the other(s)
       (b) Each of the men wants [John to like the other(s)]
       (c) Each of the men seems to John [t to like the other(s)]
       (d) John seems to each of the men [t to like the other(s)]

The sentences of (22) are fully grammatical. (22a) is similar if not identical in meaning to (21a), and there seems to be no independent semantic principle that explains why (21b-d) should not be correspondingly related in meaning to (22b-d). The effect of SSC in (21) cannot be explained in terms of semantic incoherence or complexity of processing or the like because any such consideration should apply as well to the corresponding examples of (22). Or to put it differently, suppose that a language were like English except that SSC did not apply. In this language, (21b-d) would be near synonyms of (22b-d) just as (21a) is a near synonym of (22a). The language would be none the worse for that on any general "functional" grounds of comprehensibility, interpretability, and so on. The same would be true of a hypothetical language just like English except that SSC applied only when the specified subject is physically present, so that (21b) would be excluded but (21c,d) would be quite grammatical with (roughly) the meanings (22c,d). It seems to be an empirical fact that SSC applies to physically present subjects and mentally present ones (trace). But there is no a priori reason why this should be so. It is a principle of English grammar—and, it is fair to postulate, of UG, since it is difficult to imagine that each person capable of these discriminations has been given explicit evidence or training that bears on them.

There is, in fact, an appearance of paradox here. Thus, we might ask why ssc blocks the reciprocal rule and DR, but not the rule that relates *each of the men* to *the others* in (22b-d). It seems that we are compelled to formulate ssc as a rule-particular principle, this giving the unwanted (though not intolerable) theoretical consequence discussed before. In fact, this consequence is forced on us unless we can find a principled difference between the two cases. Is there such a difference?

The answer is obvious. Reciprocal interpretation and DR are rules of sentence-grammar; the rule interpreting *the others* is not. Thus compare the paired cases of (23):

(23)   (a)   Some of the men left today. The others will leave later.
       (a′)   Some of the men left today. Each other will leave later.

       (b)   Some of the articles are incomprehensible, but we each expected John to understand the others.
       (b′)   Some of the articles are incomprehensible, but we expected John to understand each other.

Examples (a′) and (b′) are ungrammatical. The rule of reciprocal interpretation, being a rule of sentence-grammar, is inapplicable in case (a′) and is blocked by ssc in (b′). The rule assigning an interpretation to *the others*, however, is not a rule of sentence-grammar at all, as (a) indicates. Thus it is not subject to the conditions of sentence-grammar, so that (23a,b) are as grammatical as (22b-d).

Note that it is strictly incorrect to imply, as I did, that (22a) is virtually synonymous with (21a). In the case of (22a), we are not required to understand the phrase *the other(s)* as referring to a set related through reciprocal interpretation to the set of *the men*. Thus consider the context (24):

(24)   Each of the women likes some of the books; each of the men likes the others.

Namely, the other books. In contrast, replacement of (*each of the men, the others*) by (*the men, each other*) in (24) forces quite a different interpretation.

Returning to the basic theory outlined earlier, the rule of reciprocal interpretation and DR relates derivations (in fact, surface structures, enriched to include traces) to LF, while the rule assigning an interpretation to *the other(s)* belongs to an entirely different component of the system of cognitive structures relating LF and other factors to a full semantic representation. It would be quite appropriate to assign this rule to a theory of performance (pragmatics) rather than to the theory of grammar.

In Chomsky (1973) I pointed out that the rules of anaphora associating *he* with *John* in such sentences as (25) appear to violate otherwise valid conditions, a problem for the theory presented there:

(25)   (a) John thought that he would win.
                     (b) John thought that Bill liked him.

Others have reiterated this point, arguing that it undermines the theory outlined. But my observation was simply an error. The rule of anaphora involved in the (normal but not obligatory) interpretation of (25) should in principle be exempt from the conditions on sentence-grammar, since it is no rule of sentence-grammar at all. Cf. Lasnik (1974).

Consider again the operation of ssc. The context of application in the cases we are considering is (26):

(26)   ...NP... [NP$_s$...Y...]...

where the rule is prevented from applying to the pair (NP, Y) by virtue of the specified subject NP$_s$. Several cases can be distinguished:

(27)   (i) NP$_s$ has lexical content and is therefore not controlled by NP.
        (ii) NP$_s$ is a trace not controlled (bound) by NP.
        (iii) NP$_s$ is the interpreted subject of a complement—suppose it to be the element PRO—not controlled by NP.

Corresponding to these three cases, we have such examples as (28i-iii), respectively, where the reciprocal rule is unable to relate the italicized phrases by virtue of scc:

(28)   (i) *The men* wanted [John to like *each other*]
        (ii) John seemed to *the men* [*t* to like *each other*]
        (iii) John promised *the men* [PRO to like *each other*]

In each case, NP = *the men*; NP$_s$ is either *John* (as in (i)) or a zero morpheme controlled by *John* (trace in (ii) and PRO in (iii)). Thus in each case, the rule blocks by ssc. Note that it is a lexical property of *promise* (as distinct, say, from *persuade*) that the subject of the matrix sentence, rather than the object, controls the subject of the embedded sentence.[25]

Suppose that the subject of an embedded sentence is actually deleted, rather than assigned an interpretation as in the case (28iii). Matters become rather delicate at this point. We would expect that rules should apply over the deleted subject. There are, I think, good reasons to believe that many cases of so-called EQUI—e.g., in the complement of *want*-type verbs—involve deletion of an embedded subject. Assuming this to be true, for the moment, we would then conclude that in the case of (29), a rule relating *the book* to a phrase outside of the brackets should apply freely, there being no specified subject. But in the case of (30), (31), the phrase *the book* should be subject to a rule relating it to a phrase outside of the brackets only if this phrase is *John,* the controller of PRO:

(29)   John wants [to read the book]

(30)   John promised Bill [PRO to read the book]

(31)   Bill persuaded John [PRO to read the book]

Thus in principle we should be able to find three kinds of cases in which there is a phonetically null subject of an embedded sentence: cases (ii) and (iii) of (27) and a case like (29), where the embedded subject is deleted. To summarize, we should have the following cases, where NP_s is, again, the embedded subject and NP is the outside phrase involved in the rule:

(32)   (a) NP_s is a trace not bound by NP ($= (27ii)$)
        (b) NP_s is PRO not controlled by NP ($= (27iii)$)
        (c) NP_s is deleted by a transformation ($= (29)$)

In cases (32a) and (32b), the phonetically null subject should block application of rules, but in case (32c) it should not.

To find actual examples bearing on, let alone verifying, such predictions as these is no small task. Not only might the data be rather "exotic" and the subject's judgments, one might expect, difficult to evaluate, but furthermore, it is necessary to accept quite a few assumptions in assigning an analysis along the lines of (32) to given examples. In the present state of linguistic theory and its application, there are just too many unsolved problems and too many alternative approaches that cannot be conclusively rejected for particular proposals of such intricacy to carry a high degree of conviction. Nevertheless, I would like to try to pursue the line of argument.

We have already seen good reason to suppose that cases (32a) and (32b) operate as expected. Unfortunately, I have found no relevant examples in English to test (32c). However, some recent work of Carlos Quicoli on clitic movement in Portuguese is highly suggestive.[26] The rule of clitic movement assigns a clitic from an embedded sentence to the verb of the matrix sentence. The rule observes the tensed-S condition; thus, only infinitival complements are subject to clitic movement to the matrix verb.

Consider now the case of ssc. We have such examples as (33):

(33)   Paulo us saw [t examine the girl]
       ("Paulo nos viu examinar a garota"—"Paulo saw us examine the girl")

Here, the subject of the embedded sentence cliticizes to the matrix verb. On the other hand, we cannot have (34), in which the object of the matrix sentence cliticizes to the matrix verb, violating ssc:

(34)   Paulo us saw [the specialist examine t]
       ("Paulo nos viu o especialista examinar"—"Paulo saw the specialist examine us")

Thus lexical subjects behave as expected.

Suppose that *wh*-movement has applied, giving such structures as (35):

(35)   (i) The man [who$_1$ Maria saw [us examine t_1]] disappeared
       (ii) The man [who$_1$ Maria saw [t_1 examine us]] disappeared

Suppose we now apply clitic movement. We derive the sentence (36):

(36)   The man who Maria us saw examine disappeared
           ("O homem que Maria nos viu examinar sumiu")

In fact, (36) has the meaning of (35i) but not (35ii). Expressing the fact in terms of trace theory, we have the surface structure (37i) but not (37ii) for (36):

(37)   (i) The man [who$_1$ Maria us$_2$ saw [t_2 examine t_1]] disappeared
       (ii) The man [who$_1$ Maria us$_2$ saw [t_1 examine t_2]] disappeared

We can explain these facts in terms of ssc. The trace will block clitic movement applied to (35ii) but not to (35i).

Thus lexical subjects and traces behave as expected.

Consider now the case of an interpreted subject (i.e., case (32b)). As predicted, we do not find (38):

(38)   (i) The doctor us promised [PRO to examine t]
       (ii) Paulo us convinced the doctor [PRO to examine t]

where t is the trace left by clitic movement. That is, the zero element

PRO, just like trace, acts as a specified subject, as in English, blocking clitic movement.

Thus lexical subjects, traces, and PRO behave as expected.

As noted earlier, there is in principle another case of a phonetically null subject, the case of a deleted subject, namely, (32c). Thus in principle we might expect to find a matrix verb V with a complement sentence in which the subject is deleted, as we have assumed to be true in the case of English *want*; and in such a case, we should expect clitic movement to be possible. In fact, taking V to be *querer* (= *want*), we find just these facts. Thus, we have (39), although the superficially comparable (38i) is excluded:

(39)   The doctor us wants [to examine *t*]
        ("O medico nos quer examinar")

To summarize, lexical subjects serve to bring ssc into operation, blocking clitic movement where the clitic is distinct from the embedded lexical subject. Where the embedded subject is phonetically null, we have the three cases of (32): trace, PRO, and deleted subject. Trace and PRO block the rule, as expected. But there is a null subject that does not block the rule, namely, after *querer*. This example fills the gap in the paradigm; assuming that the subject is deleted in this case, ssc will not apply to block clitic movement.

If this analysis withstands further investigation, we will have the striking conclusion that the three kinds of mentally present, physically missing subjects permitted in principle all are exemplified, with the predicted behavior. Putting it differently, assuming ssc, we have an experimental probe to choose among proposed analyses that postulate various choices among the various kinds of phonetically null subjects permitted in principle.

There are many questions that can be raised about these analyses. This is, however, the kind of inquiry that might be expected to give considerable insight into the formal properties of grammars and the general properties of the human language faculty that make language acquisition possible.

Before we leave this topic, a few additional observations may be relevant. I mentioned that there are some reasons for believing that in English EQUI constructions with the verb *want* actually involve deletion of the subject of the embedded sentence. A few observations may indicate why this is a plausible hypothesis. In the first place, there are phonological arguments for this conclusion. As is well known, the verb *want* followed by *to* undergoes elision, giving the form *wanna* from *want to*: thus, (40):

(40)   (i) You wanna see Bill
                            (ii) Who do you wanna see?

But as has been noted,[27] (40ii) is possible only when the *wh*-word is
understood to be the object, not the subject, of the embedded sentence.
Thus (40ii) can be derived from (41) but not from (42):

(41)   You want [X to see who]

(42)   You want [who to see]

Correspondingly, (43), deriving from (44), is impossible:

(43)   Who do you wanna see Bill

(44)   You want [who to see Bill]

In our terms, we have the surface structures (45), (46), and (47) (overlooking subject–auxiliary inversion, which is irrelevant in this particular
case):

(45)   Who [you want [X to see t]] (underlying (41))

(46)   Who [you want [t to see]] (underlying (42))

(47)   Who [you want [t to see Bill]] (from (44))

Of the structures (45)–(47), only (45) undergoes elision. Assume that
elision involves a rule adjoining the morpheme *to* to *want*, with the form
want + to then subject to elision by later phonological rules. But the
adjunction rule will be blocked by any intervening morphological material, e.g., *John* in (48) or the zero morpheme *t* in (46), (47):

(48)   You want [John to see Bill]

A zero morpheme is indistinguishable within syntax and morpohology
from other formatives. It is simply a terminal element that happens to be
assigned a null phonetic representation by later rules. Thus, elision is
impossible in (46) and (47), just as in (48). Correspondingly, (43) is
impossible and (40ii) can have only the meaning corresponding to (41).

But for this explanation to carry through, we must assume that X
in (45) is null on the morphological as well as the phonetic level; that
is, that it is not a zero morpheme but has been literally deleted. Thus we
have an indirect argument on phonological grounds for assuming that
the embedded subject is deleted after *want*, while the trace remains at
the morphological level, though it is phonetically null.

There is corroborating evidence of a syntactic and semantic nature,
though it is more complex. To sketch some relevant points briefly, it has

been noted by Howard Lasnik and Joan Bresnan that there are two
general types of verbs with complements, with some intersection between the types: *want*-type verbs (*want, prefer, hope*...) and "epistemic" *believe*-type verbs (*believe, consider, imagine*...). Verbs of the
want-type take the complementizer *for* in the complement sentence, as
in (49), a fact sometimes obscured on the surface since *for* deletes immediately after the verb, obligatorily for some (*want*) and optionally for
others (*prefer*); thus (50), (51):

(49)   I want very much for Bill to win

(50)   I want Bill to win

(51)   I prefer (for) Bill to win

Let us assume that epistemic verbs take a zero complementizer.

With regard to reflexivization and EQUI, verbs of these types are in
close to complementary distribution. Thus epistemic verbs undergo reflexivization but not EQUI (cf. (52)) while *want*-type verbs undergo
EQUI but not reflexivization, though some speakers find reflexivization
possible in some cases (cf. (53)):

(52)   (a) John believed [himself to be incompetent]
          (b) John believed [to be incompetent] [*] (EQUI)

(53)   (a) John wanted [himself to be a contender] [*,?]
          (·b) John much preferred [for himself to be candidate] [*,?]
          (c) John wanted [to be a contender] (EQUI)

Both types of verbs undergo the rules of reciprocal interpretation (16)
and disjoint reference (17):

(54)   (a) They believed [each other to be incompetent]
          (b) John believed [him to be incompetent] (John ≠ him)

(55)   (a) They wanted [each other to win]
          (b) John wanted [him to win] (John ≠ him)

The two categories are also in complementary distribution with regard
to NP-movement; thus we have (56) but not (57):

(56)   John was believed [t to be incompetent]

(57)   John was wanted (preferred) [t to win][28]

The inapplicability of NP-movement to the subject of the complement
of *want*-type verbs can be explained in terms of properties of the com-

plementizer; I believe that it follows from a general surface constraint that excludes *for–to* constructions, although the issue need not concern us here.[29]

The behavior of the two types of verbs with regard to reflexivization and EQUI can be easily explained on the assumption that reflexivization is free throughout, while there is a rule (58) that is optional or obligatory, depending in part on style and perhaps dialect:

(58)   *for X-self* → null / — VP

When (58) applies, we have EQUI. The major facts follow directly from this rule, which can be formulated as a deletion transformation.[30]

The arguments against assuming EQUI to be a rule deleting a full NP seem to me compelling. The facts just reviewed suggest that a deletion rule nevertheless explains more than an interpretation rule of the sort that has sometimes been proposed. This analysis meshes easily with Helke's analysis of base-generated reflexives (Helke, 1971), which I think is correct in its essentials. For independent arguments in support of a similar conclusion, see Fodor (1975).

Thus in addition to the phonological arguments, there are a range of other considerations in support of the conclusion that the subject of the complement sentence to *want*-type verbs is actually deleted, rather than just interpreted. We might go on to consider a general principle that NP's may be realized either as PRO or with lexical material, but not in both ways. We might think of PRO as an optional feature on the category NP; NP can be expanded by rules of the base only when it is [PRO]. This assumption would compel us to take the embedded subject to be PRO in (30) and (31) but to be an arbitrary lexically specified NP (one case being the base-generated reflexive) after *want*-type verbs, with *for X-self* deleted in the latter case to give (29). The principle might be modified to permit interpretive analysis of "gapping" and other phenomena as discussed, e.g., in Wasow (forthcoming), Fiengo (1974), but I will not pursue this question here.

Before we leave this topic, consider again examples (35)–(37), which I repeat here as (59)–(61):

(59)   (i) The man [$_\alpha$ who$_1$ Maria saw [us examine t_1]] disappeared
       (ii) The man [$_\alpha$ who$_1$ Maria saw [t_1 examine us]] disappeared

(60)   The man who Maria us saw examine disappeared

(61)   (i) The man [$_\alpha$ who$_1$ Maria us$_2$ saw [t_2 examine t_1]] disappeared
       (ii) The man [$_\alpha$ who$_1$ Maria us$_2$ saw [t_1 examine t_2]] disappeared

Recall that (60) means (59i) but not (59ii); that is, the surface structure (61i) is acceptable (giving (60)) but (61ii) is not. We explained this, following Quicoli, by assuming that wh-movement first applies, leaving a trace t_1, which blocks clitic movement by ssc. On the assumption that wh-movement is cyclic, we need not assume that wh-movement on the cycle α precedes clitic placement, since t_1 will in any event be placed by wh-movement in the internal cycle. Or, if we were to assume that wh-movement applies only on the cycle α, following clitic placement, the latter rule would in any event be blocked by ssc with who in the position of t_1 in (61ii). In this case we would have an instance of (32a).

In fact, we might once again choose to reinterpret ssc as a condition on surface structure interpretation rather than a condition on rules, along the lines discussed earlier. Then independently of any considerations involving ordering, the surface structure (61ii) is blocked by ssc.

We might also investigate the possibility of relating this interpretation of ssc to some general prohibition against anaphoric structures of the form (62) rather than the permissible (63), where items with the same subscript are anaphorically related (cf. Bordelois, 1974, for some discussion):

(62) $\ldots x_1 \ldots x_2 \ldots y_1 \ldots y_2 \ldots$

(63) $\ldots x_1 \ldots x_2 \ldots y_2 \ldots y_1$

It is not clear whether such a condition is tenable in general. Consider such examples as (64):

(64)   (i) [What books]$_1$ have [those men]$_2$ written t_1 about [each other]$_2$
        (ii) I told them$_1$ [what books]$_2$ PRO$_1$ to read t_2
        (iii) I$_1$ asked them [what books]$_2$ PRO$_1$ to read t_2
        (iv) [To whom]$_1$ did John$_2$ seem t_1 [t_2 to be referring]
        (v) Whom$_1$ did you$_2$ ask t_1 [what$_3$ PRO$_2$ to read t_3]
        (vi) Dnes mu$_1$ ji$_2$ Jana ukázala t_1 t_2
             ("Jana showed her to him today"—"Today to-him her Jana showed")[31]

But there are many unexplored possibilities, and it may be that some broader principle may be involved. For the moment, however, it seems to me reasonable to postulate ssc as a surface condition.[32]

Let us now turn to another class of cases, related to some of the examples in (64). Consider the examples (65), (66):

(65) You told Bill who to visit—you told Bill [who$_2$ PRO$_1$ to visit t_2]

(66) Who did you tell Bill to visit—who$_1$ you told Bill$_2$ [(t_1) PRO$_2$ to visit t_1]

The parenthesized trace in (66) is present under the analysis of *wh*-movement in Chomsky (1973); for ease of exposition, let us assume that it is not present, though nothing hinges on this in the present context.

The appropriate "logical form" for (65), (66) should be essentially (67), (68), respectively, assuming that an appropriate sense is given to the "quantifier" *for which person x*:[33]

(67)   You told Bill for which person x, Bill to visit x

(68)   For which person x, you told Bill, Bill to visit x

We can obtain the logical forms (67) and (68) from the sentences (65), (66), respectively, by the following rules:

(69)   (i) find the place from which *who* moved
        (ii) mark this position by x
        (iii) interpret *who* as "for which person x," controlling the free variable x
        (iv) determine control of the subject of the embedded verb (namely, as the object of the matrix sentence)

Let us disregard step (iv), assuming this to be determined by mechanisms discussed in Jackendoff (1972). As for (i)-(iii), if we consider the surface structures to be as represented in (65), (66) to the right of -, in accordance with the trace theory, then steps (i) and (ii) of (69) have already been accomplished, in effect. Thus, to interpret these surface structures it suffices to carry out step (iii) of (69), namely, to replace *who* by its meaning, *for which person x*. Hence interpretation of the enriched surface structures is direct. Thus in these cases surface structures can be directly mapped into LF merely by replacement of "quantifier words" by their meanings, with obvious notational conventions.

We might proceed in the same way in the case of simple NP-raising, as in (70):

(70) John seems to be a nice fellow—John seems [t to be a nice fellow]

The surface structure of (70) can be associated directly with the LF representation (71):

(71)   For $x =$ John, x seems [x to be a nice fellow]

We might then try to devise general rules of inference, truth conditions, etc., for such representations as (67), (68), (71).

Recall again the discussion of (12), repeated as (72):

(72)   (i) Beavers build dams
                       (ii) Dams are built by beavers

In the standard and extended standard theories, such examples were used to illustrate the fact that "thematic relations" are determined by deep structure configurations; thus to understand (ii) we must know that *dams* is the object of *build*, as in (i), just as in (70) we must know that *John* is subject of *be a nice fellow*. But under the trace theory, such examples as (70) and (72ii) do not choose between the theory of deep structure interpretation and surface structure interpretation, since the appropriate grammatical relations are also represented in the (enriched) surface structures. Since there is good evidence that some properties of LF are based on properties of surface structure (e.g., the subject–predicate relation in (72)—see above; or the logical form of (65), (66), both of which we may take as derived, essentially, from the deep structure "you told Bill [COMP PRO to visit who]") we might try to unify the theory of semantic interpretation by revising EST in accordance with the principle (73):

(73)   Surface structure determines LF.

Let us look further into *wh*-movement and its semantic interpretation, turning to some cases discussed by Postal and reanalyzed by Wasow (forthcoming), whose analysis I adapt and somewhat modify here. Consider the sentences (74):

(74)   (i) Who said Mary kissed him
                      (ii) Who did he say Mary kissed
                     (iii) Who said he kissed Mary

In (i) and (iii), the pronoun *he, him* can function as an anaphoric pronoun, referring to the person whose name answers the question: *who*? But in (ii), the pronoun functions essentially as a name, referring to someone whose identity is established elsewhere, as it may also under another interpretation of (i) and (iii). If we replace the pronoun by *John* in (74), cases (i) and (iii) keep the latter interpretation but lose the first, while case (ii) keeps its single interpretation. Thus under this replacement, we simply refer to that third person in a different way, by the name *John* instead of the pronoun *he*. To put it in a conventional but highly misleading way, in (i) and (iii) there is a relation of "anaphora" between *who* and *he–him*, while in (ii) there is not.

Consider the surface structures of (74) under the trace theory. They are, respectively, (75i-iii), ignoring auxiliary inversion:

(75)   (i)   Who [*t* said Mary kissed him]
         (ii) Who [he said Mary kissed *t*]
         (iii) Who [*t* said he kissed Mary]

Applying again the principles of interpretation for *wh*-structures already outlined (cf. (69)), we replace *who* by its meaning, deriving (76):

(76)   (i)   For which person *x*, *x* said Mary kissed him
         (ii) For which person *x*, he said Mary kissed *x*
         (iii) For which person *x*, *x* said he kissed Mary

There are familiar general principles of anaphora, the exact character of which need not concern us, which dictate that the pronoun can be anaphoric to *John* in (77) and (79) but not in (78):

(77)   John said Mary kissed him

(78)   He said Mary kissed John

(79)   John said he kissed Mary

Taking the bound variable *x* in (76) to function essentially as a name, the same principles of anaphora that govern (77)–(79) require that no relation of anaphora can hold for *he* and *x* in (76ii), though such a relation may hold in (76i), (76iii). Thus we can account for the full range of interpretations in (74) by appeal to independently motivated principles of anaphora, again on the assumption (72) that surface structure determines LF with the natural additional assumption that bound variables function (to first approximation) as names. We need not speak of a relation of "anaphora" between *who* and *he–him*, which would be strictly meaningless, since *who* is not a referring expression but a kind of quantifier; nor need we invoke any principle beyond established principles of anaphora that apply in (77)–(79).

Our revised EST now has roughly this general structure:

(80) $\xrightarrow{\text{B}}$ base structures $\xrightarrow{\text{T}}$ surface structures $\xrightarrow{\text{SI-1}}$ LF

         (LF, other cognitive representations) $\xrightarrow{\text{SI-2}}$ semantic representation

A more precise version of (80) would replace "surface structure" by another notion, abstracting away from "stylistic rules" (e.g., scrambling) that may apply to give the actual surface form of sentences. I ignore this matter here.

That is, the base rules B generate base structures that are converted by the transformational component T to surface structures enriched with trace. The latter are interpreted by rules of semantic interpretation SI-1, giving the representations LF. These along with other cognitive representations are associated with fuller representations of meaning by rules SI-2. The rules SI-1 are rules of sentence-grammar, while the rules of SI-2 generally are not. The distinction has already been discussed in connection with examples (21)–(24).

We have now discussed several rules belonging to SI-1:

(81)   (i) reciprocal interpretation
              (ii) disjoint reference (DR)
              (iii) replacement of *who* by its meaning
              (iv) conventions on control and variable binding
              (v) conditions on anaphora

The rules (v), involved in (77)–(79) and (76), are rules of sentence-grammar, which apply to such strictly sentence-internal structures as reciprocals and reflexives (but see note 23). The rules (v) apply to structures formed by rules (iii) and (iv), that is, to partially formed representations in LF. Thus we already have a degree of internal structure within SI-1.

There are other reasons for supposing that the rules of anaphora apply to (partially formed) representations in LF, rather than to surface structures. Consider the discourses (82), (83):

(82)   Every soldier has his orders

(83)   (i) Every soldier is armed, but will he shoot?
          (ii) Every soldier is armed. I don't think he'll shoot, though.
          (iii) If every soldier is armed, then he'll shoot.

Sentence (82) can and normally would be construed with the pronoun as anaphoric (bound), but in the examples of (83) the pronoun *he* must literally be construed (contrary to the obviously intended sense) as referring to someone whose identity is established elsewhere.[34] In our terms, the fact is easily explained. Quantification is generally clause-bound. Thus the rules SI-1 involving quantifiers and variables give the structures (84) for (82) and (85) for (83):

(84)   [For all *x*, *x* has his orders]

(85)   (i) [For all *x*, *x* a soldier, *x* is armed], but will he shoot
         (ii) [For all *x*, *x* a soldier, *x* is armed]. I don't think he'll shoot,
               though
        (iii) If [for all *x*, *x* is armed], then he'll shoot

As has often been observed, there is one quantifier, namely *any*, that includes within its scope a logical operator dominating it in surface structure. The rule for *any*-interpretation, which is rather complex and not fully understood (cf. note 39), thus gives (86) as the representation for (87):

(86)   If any soldier is armed, then he'll shoot

(87)   [For all *x*, *x* a soldier, if *x* is armed then he'll shoot]

In the partial logical forms (85), (87), brackets bound the phrase within the scope of the universal quantifier.

The rules of anaphora do not permit a pronoun that is outside the scope of a quantifier to be assigned an anaphoric relation to a bound variable within this scope (but see note 34). Thus (82), (86) have (88), (89), respectively, as permissible interpretations:

(88)   For all *x*, *x* a soldier, *x* has *x*'s orders

(89)   For all *x*, *x* a soldier, if *x* is armed then *x* will shoot

But in the examples of (85), such interpretations are excluded, as the corresponding interpretations were excluded in the case of (78), (74ii) (=(76ii)).

The analysis requires that the scope of quantification is determined prior to application of the principle of anaphora. In other words, here too the principle of anaphora (=(81v)) applies to partially determined logical forms, with quantifier scope and variable binding determined.

This analysis is pretty much along the lines of standard logical analysis of the sentences of natural language. A rather different approach has recently been suggested within the framework of "Montague-grammar."[35] With the motivation of relating surface structure and semantic representation more closely, it is suggested that the sentences (90), all with the surface structure NP-VP, have essentially the same logical representation (at some level):

(90)   (i) John is here
                         (ii) Every soldier is here
                        (iii) Some soldier is here

This result is achieved by associating each individual with the set of its properties (its *character*). Then we may interpret (90) as stating that the property of being here is a member of the character of John [(i)], a member of the intersection of the characters of all soldiers [(ii)], and a member of the union of characters of all soldiers [(iii)]. In contrast, a standard logical analysis might assign to (90) the analyses (91), or— taking a noun phrase to specify a type variable—(92):

(91)   (i)   Here (John)
        (ii) For all x, if Soldier (x) then Here (x)
        (iii) For some x, Soldier (x) and Here (x)

(92)   (i)   Here (John)
        (ii) For all x, x a soldier, Here (x)
        (iii) For some x, x a soldier, Here (x)

(I am ignoring here the question of specificity of indefinites.) We have essentially been assuming (92), so far. Under the interpretations (91) or (92), the sentence (90i) is given a very different analysis from (90ii, iii).

It is difficult to find an empirical test for these varying logical analyses, but if we take them literally, it seems that Montague grammar and the standard analysis should make a different prediction for the case where the sentences of (90) appear in such contexts as (83), say (93):

(93)   (i)   John is here. Will he shoot?
        (ii) Every soldier is here. Will he shoot?
        (iii) Some soldier is here. Will he shoot?

Since *John, every soldier*, and *some soldier* are understood to have the same logical status in Montague grammar, the prediction should be that they function in a parallel way in (93). But this is false. In (93i), *he* may be anaphoric, while in (93ii) it may not. And in (93iii), while there is, arguably, a relation of "anaphora," it is quite different and considerably more complex than the relation observed in earlier examples; thus, *he* does not have the semantic function of "some soldier," but rather refers to that soldier, whoever he may be, who is identified as here in the first sentence.[36]

In the "classical" theories as extended earlier (i.e., with the anaphora rule applying to partially specified LF and quantification clause-bound in the case of *every* and *some*), the discourse (93i) has an entirely different status from (93ii) and (93iii). In (93i) the pronoun *he* simply refers to John, and under one central interpretation can be replaced by *John* without change of meaning.[37] In the other two cases, such an anaphora relation cannot hold, because *he* is outside the scope of the quantifier. It is strictly meaningless, in the classical approach, for *he* to have an anaphoric relation to *every soldier* or *some soldier* (nonspecific). This conclusion seems to me correct so far as it goes (it does not yet account for (93iii) or the examples of notes 34, 36). Thus there would seem to be empirical confirmation for the classical analysis over Montague grammar in the rather small area where they have different predictions, if taken to have empirical content. The behavior of anaphoric pronouns indicates that the logical structure of (90i) is quite different from (90ii, iii), and also that the principles of anaphora apply to a partially developed logical form, not to surface structures.

Returning now to the main theme, let us consider some of the more complex examples of *wh*-movement and anaphora discussed by Postal and Wasow. Consider the sentence (94):

(94)   Who did the woman he loved betray?

By the principles so far proposed, this should be assigned the representation (95) which can be converted to the LF (96):

(95)   For which person *x*, the woman he loved betrayed *x*

(96)   For which person *x*, the woman *x* loved betrayed *x*

Conversion of (95) to (96) does not appear to violate the conditions (81v) on anaphora; compare (97), where *he* may be anaphoric to *John*.

(97)   The woman he loved betrayed John

But (96) is not a possible interpretation of (94). Why not?

Wasow notes that while the general "precede-and-command" conditions of anaphora do not require that the pronoun be nonanaphoric in (97), nevertheless some constraint prevents an "anaphoric" relation from holding between the italicized phrases of (98):

(98)   The woman *he* loved betrayed *someone*

Suppose that we establish a subsidiary principle of anaphora that prevents a phrase X from serving as antecedent to a pronoun to its left when this phrase is "indeterminate," where *someone* is indeterminate. Then it will follow that an anaphoric relation cannot hold in (98), though it can in (99):

(99)   Someone was betrayed by the woman he loved

Returning to (94), it has often been noted that there are striking similarities between *wh*-questions and indefinites. Pursuing this analogy,

Wasow suggests that the trace left by *wh*-movement should share with indefinites the property of indeterminateness. Then, it will follow that (95) cannot have the interpretation of (96), as required.

There are some problems with this suggestion. As in the case of (74), it is misleading to speak of an "anaphoric relation" between *someone* and *he* in (98) since *someone*, like *who*, is not referential. Furthermore, the property of determinateness is not an easy one to characterize, as Wasow points out. The cases to be covered are fairly clear—indefinites (apart from specific and generic), the trace left by *wh*-movement in questions and relatives—but it is not clear just what semantic property these cases might have in common. Thus, in the case of relatives, the analogy between *wh*-structures and indefinites breaks down and the *wh*-element even seems to have something of the character of a definite noun phrase (see Kuroda, 1968). But the trace behaves as in questions. Cf. (100), which cannot have the interpretation (101), just as (94) cannot have the interpretation (96):

(100)   The man *who* the woman *he* loved betrayed—is despondent

(101)   the man *x* such that the woman *x* loved betrayed *x*—is despondent

Wasow does give some reason to believe that in restrictive relatives the head is indeterminate, but the matter is quite unclear, as is the question how this property, whatever it may be exactly, inheres in the trace.

We can overcome all of these difficulties by revising Wasow's theory along the lines of our earlier discussion. Again, let us assume that the rules (81i-iv) of SI-1 apply to the surface structures of (94) and (100) to give (102) and (103), respectively.[38] Assume also that (98) is analyzed by a familiar rule, to give (104):

(102)   For which person *x*, [the woman he loved betrayed *x*]

(103)   The man *x* such that [the woman he loved betrayed *x*] is despondent

(104)   For some *x*, [the woman he loved betrayed *x*]

Whatever the rules of anaphora may be, they should treat the bracketed phrases in (102)–(104) in the same way, since they are identical. Thus, (94), (100), and (98) should have parallel interpretations, as in fact they do. It remains only to determine the subsidiary principle of anaphora that is involved in all of these cases. Assume it to be(105):

(105)   A variable cannot be the antecedent of a pronoun to its left.

Suppose that *someone* in (98) is replaced by *anyone*. The sentence as it stands is not well formed. It becomes well formed in the context (106):

(106)   If the woman he loved betrayed anyone, he will be despondent

By the *any*-rule mentioned earlier, the scope of *any* includes *if*, so the "first-stage" logical form should be (107):[39]

(107)   For every person x, [if the woman he loved betrayed x, then he will be despondent]

If principle (105) is correct, then the leftmost occurrence of *he* cannot have x as antecedent, though the rightmost may. Thus, apart from the reading in which neither occurrence of *he* in (106) is anaphoric, the only interpretation of (106) should be (108), where x is not the antecedent of *he*; that is, an interpretation analogous to (109):

(108)   For every person x, if the woman he loved betrayed x, then x will be despondent

(109)   For every person x, if the woman John loved betrayed x, then x will be despondent

I think I can convince myself that this is correct, but without much faith in the conclusion.

We may think of the principle (105) as part of a rule replacing a pronoun by a variable at some level of the derivation that will ultimately specify LF. We have given insufficient evidence to determine the rule in detail. Let us take it to assert that a pronoun P within the scope of a quantifier may be rewritten as the variable bound by this quantifier unless P is to the left of an occurrence of a variable already bound by this quantifier. This rule will be one part of a more comprehensive convention specifying anaphora relations in partially developed logical forms. For ease of reference, let us call the rule in question A (anaphora). The rule A applied to (110), underlying (112), will give (111) (optionally):

(110)   For some x, x was betrayed by the woman he loved

(111)   For some x, x was betrayed by the woman x loved

(112)   Someone was betrayed by the woman he loved

But A cannot apply to the pronoun *he* in the structures (113):

(113)   (i) For which x, the woman he loved betrayed x (underlying (94))

(ii) For some x, the woman he loved betrayed x (underlying (98))

(iii) The man x such that the woman he loved betrayed x—is despondent (underlying (100))

The reason is that A obeys condition (105).

Note that the rule A is oblivious to the source of the variable in (113) that prevents it from applying. In the case of (113i) and (113iii), the variable is introduced by a syntactic movement rule, under the trace theory. In (113ii), the variable is introduced by a rule of semantic interpretation belonging to SI-1. The sentences for which these are the underlying structures are quite different in form and in surface structure, but alike in semantic representation at the stage following the rule that assigns to *someone* its meaning. It is at this stage, it appears, that A applies. Thus A is "local," like other rules of grammar, in that it applies to the last step of the derivation so far constructed, paying no heed to the original source of the elements that determine how the rule applies.

We noted earlier that a bound variable, as in (113), behaves quite differently from a name in the same position, as in (114) (=(97)):

(114)   The woman he loved betrayed John

Thus in (114), the rules of anaphora A can associate *he* and *John*. But a qualification is necessary. In (114), the rule A can associate *he* and *John* only if the main stress is on *betray*. If the main stress is on *John*, then the word cannot serve as the antecedent of *he*. Thus stress on *John* gives the word essentially the status of a bound variable. What is the explanation for this fact?

A possible explanation is the following: Consider the rule of SI-1 that determines the focus of a sentence. Consider the simplest cases, e.g., (115), (116), where capitalization indicates main stress:

(115)   Bill likes JOHN

(116)   BILL likes John

Let us say that a rule FOCUS assigns to (115) the representation (117) and to (116) the representation (118):

(117)   The x such that Bill likes x—is John

(118)   The x such that x likes John—is Bill

We may take (117) and (118) to be partially developed logical forms, informally presented. As such, they seem to give an accurate representation of an important aspect of semantic representation in a natural way.

The rule FOCUS applied to (114) with main stress on *John* gives (119):

(119)   the *x* such that the woman he loved betrayed *x*—is John

But observe that the rule A that replaces *he* by *x* cannot apply to (119); it is blocked by the principle (105), exactly as in the examples of (113). In contrast, the rule would not have been blocked had main stress been on *betray* rather than on *John* in (114). Thus we find still another instance of (105): it applies in the case of the trace of a movement rule (e.g., (113i, iii)), the variable introduced by interpretation of existential and universal quantifiers (e.g., (113ii)), and the variable introduced by the rule FOCUS (e.g., (119)). Thus, a number of disparate phenomena fall together, giving an interesting range of empirical evidence bearing on the nature of LF.

Note that it makes quite a difference what notation we choose for representing phenomena in LF, just as it matters what phenomena we take to belong to LF. It appears that these are by no means questions of convention to be resolved by fiat or convenience for one or another purpose. Rather, I believe, they can—and should—be interpreted as empirical questions that can be subjected to test.

The examples just reviewed give independent support for the general conclusions proposed earlier. The rules of SI-1 apply to an enriched surface structure, including trace, giving an analysis in terms of quantifiers and bound variables. Further rules of SI-1 (those of anaphora) assign these representations a specific range of more explicit representations within LF.[40] These examples enhance the general plausibility of the conception sketched in (80), and in particular, the trace theory of movement rules, which we have motivated quite independently in earlier discussion. I cannot review here other evidence bearing on these assumptions.[41]

The preceding discussion illustrates some of the ways in which we might hope to overcome the difficulties that immediately face a theory of transformations that is radically limited in expressive power. We may try to discover narrower conditions on base structures, conditions on application of rules, and conditions on surface structure. Under EST, principles of semantic interpretation, at least those of SI-1, would be expected to relate very closely, in many cases, to conditions on base and surface structures; particularly, surface structures, if the revision of EST suggested here proves to be essentially correct. It may be that conditions on transformations can be assimilated to conditions on surface structures and (in the best case) to independently motivated rules of semantic interpretation under the trace theory.

I do not mean to suggest that the problems that lie in the way of developing a theory with restricted expressive power, along the lines sketched at the outset, have been overcome. But I think that there has been encouraging progress. I am inclined to think that the program outlined is feasible and that the general approach I have been reviewing may prove to be well founded.

If we pursue this approach further, we find, I believe, that the rules of sentence-grammar fall into several distinct types. At the core of syntax we have the two rules of (120), each of considerably broader scope than has hitherto been imagined:

(120)   (i) NP-movement
                         (ii) *wh*-movement

The rule of NP-movement appears superficially to violate subjacency (cf., e.g., "John seems to be likely to win") while it observes SSC, the tensed-S condition, and other constraints. The explanation is that the rule is cyclic and bounded (observes subjacency).

The rule of *wh*-movement, which may involve several subtypes, seems superficially to violate subjacency, SSC, and the tensed-S condition while observing the complex noun phrase constraint and other island conditions. The explanation is that the rule is cyclic and bounded, while movement is permitted from complementizer position in a tensed-S (depending on the nature of the matrix verb). From these assumptions, it follows that (120ii) has its familiar properties. Cf. Chomsky (1973, 1976). Included in this category, I believe, are the rules involved in formation of direct and indirect *wh*-questions, relatives, topicalization, cleft, comparatives, and a variety of infinitival complement constructions. But this proposal remains to be explained and justified.

Interpretive rules may violate subjacency, but otherwise generally observe SSC and tensed-S condition, though there are some problems (cf. note 23).

Other movement rules, such as clitic movement, prepositional phrase movement, and quantifier movement, seem to observe subjacency and other constraints, cf. Akmajian (1975), Fiengo and Lasnik (in press), Kayne (1975), Quicoli (1975, in press).

Root transformations and minor movement rules are as described in Emonds (forthcoming).

There are also "housekeeping rules," for example, those that govern deletion of complementizers.

Other rules have quite different properties, e.g., agreement rules (which have something of the character of phonological rules of matching of feature matrices), scrambling and other stylistic rules, which are not readily formulable as transformations at all, and others.

This is not intended as a comprehensive or precise analysis, needless to say. I think that (120) may constitute, in a certain sense, the core of cyclic grammar, determining an enriched surface structure that is close, in interesting respects, to logical form.

It may be possible to devise an alternative to transformational grammar in which rules of the type (120) are regarded as interpretive[42] but meeting conditions quite different from those observed by the rules here called "interpretive." Thus, we would have three types of rules for interpreting base-generated structures including traces: rules with the properties of (120i) and (120ii), with their cyclic interactions and the properties just outlined, and rules of anaphora, etc., that have the properties sketched in the foregoing analysis. If this speculation is correct, we should be able to move to a more abstract characterization of linguistic systems, adopting a point of view from which much of the core of transformational grammar will be seen to be simply one concrete realization of a set of abstract conditions that characterize the human language faculty.

The pure study of language, based solely on evidence of the sort reviewed here, can carry us only to the understanding of abstract conditions on grammatical systems. No particular realization of these conditions has any privileged status. From a more abstract point of view, if it can be attained, we may see in retrospect that we moved toward the understanding of the abstract general conditions on linguistic structures by the detailed investigation of one or another "concrete" realization: for example, transformational grammar, a particular instance of a system with these general properties. The abstract conditions may relate to transformational grammar rather in the way that modern algebra relates to the number system.

We should be concerned to abstract from successful grammars and successful theories those more general properties that account for their success, and to develop UG as a theory of these abstract properties, which might be realized in a variety of different ways. To choose among such realizations, it will be necessary to move to a much broader domain of evidence. What linguistics should try to provide is an abstract characterization of particular and universal grammar that will serve as a guide and framework for this more general inquiry. This is not to say that the study of highly specific mechanisms (phonological rules, conditions on transformations, etc.) should be abandoned. On the contrary, it is only through the detailed investigation of these particular systems that we have any hope of advancing toward a grasp of the abstract structures, conditions, and properties that should, some day, constitute the subject matter of general linguistic theory. The goal may be remote, but it is well to keep it in mind as we develop intricate specific theories and try to refine and sharpen them in detailed empirical inquiry.

NOTES

1. For example, in Chomsky (1965, 1976). The latter contains a somewhat more detailed discussion of some of the topics taken up here, some within the theory of grammar and others relating to the general framework presupposed and the ongoing debate concerning its validity.

2. Chomsky and Halle (1968); Bresnan (1973).

3. For example, Lakoff (1971). Some more recent variants seem to me to eliminate the substantive content of the theory, virtually identifying "generative semantics" with "linguistics," and thus effectively terminating the discussion of the validity of "generative semantics." Cf. Lakoff, in Parret (1974). On the course of generative semantics in recent years, see Dougherty (1975), Katz and Bever (1976), and Brame (1975).

4. Cf. Chomsky (1972, chapter 3). Cf. Bresnan (1975, in press) for discussion of some of the issues involved.

5. Chomsky (1972, chapter 3). For much more extensive discussion, see Jackendoff (1972), Katz (1972), and more recent papers by these authors.

6. Just how degenerate is this experience? I know of no reliable evidence, but the problem appears to have been misunderstood, and some incorrect statements have been made about what has been asserted. As for the problem, suppose that a scientist were presented with data, 2% of which are wrong (but he doesn't know which 2%). Then he faces some serious difficulties, which would be incomparably more serious if the data were simply uncontrolled experience, rather than the result of controlled experiment, devised for its relevance to theoretical hypotheses. The fact that these difficulties do not seem to arise for the language learner, who is, of course, faced with degenerate data of experience, requires explanation. As for false statements, consider, e.g., Labov (1970). He speaks of the "widespread myth that most speech is ungrammatical" and "the current belief of many linguists that most people do not speak in well-formed sentences, and that their actual speech production or 'performance' is ungrammatical." As his sole source, he cites a statement of mine that asserts nothing of the sort. Labov also alleges that "in a number of presentations" I have "asserted that the great majority of the sentences which a child hears are ungrammatical ('95 percent')." He cites no source; there is none. No such statement appears anywhere, to my knowledge, and surely not in my writings. I have discussed the matter "in a number of presentations" but without quantitative estimates

(since I know of none) and surely without the estimate that he places within quotes.

7. In addition to the references cited in Chomsky (1976, chapter 3), see now Bresnan (1975, in press) and Hornstein (1975).

8. Thus, categories are nonterminal atomic (prime) elements in the X-bar system.

9. In the earliest work on transformational grammar (e.g., Chomsky, 1955), the terms of sd were restricted to constants. The effect of variables was achieved by the device of constructing "families of transformations" with a fixed structural change and sd's meeting a fixed condition. The reason had to do with a requirement that transformations be single-valued mappings. This requirement followed, in turn, from the theory of T-markers as a linguistic level. Cf. Chomsky (1955, 1965, chapter 3); Katz and Postal (1964).

10. For precision, we should distinguish occurrences of Y in X. Cf. Chomsky (1955). For a more careful presentation of the notions sketched here, see Chomsky (1961), Chomsky and Miller (1963). See Peters and Ritchie (1973) for a full formalization of a fairly rich theory of transformations.

11. Consider, for example, a rule of cleft-formation that asserts that NP's or PP's can be clefted; or, the rules of Chomsky (1955) and later work involving the verbal auxiliary. On disjunction, cf. Bresnan (1975, in press).

12. Thus, it is plausibly argued in Bresnan (1975, in press) that α may be of the form $C+vbl$, where C is a constant terminal (e.g., *wh-*) or category. To achieve the same results within the framework of (2) it might be necessary to assume that *wh-* is a feature of categories, as suggested in Chomsky (1973), and comparable modifications would be required in other cases discussed. This course raises problems that would carry us too far afield here.

13. Bresnan's theory, discussed in note 12, has this property. Or, suppose that (3) is inadequate for the passive, in that we must also require that the string consisting of the sixth + seventh factors is an NP. Or, consider a rule of extraposition of an S-complement of an NP, which maps a structure [NP N S] VP into N VP S. We might want to say that the transformation applies to three factors, the first an N, the second an S, and the third a VP, and the first + second an NP. For a formalization of a theory of this sort, which is standard in descriptive practice, see Peters and Ritchie (1973). Cf. Kayne (1975) for many examples, in a very careful and extensive study.

14. For example, we might want to say that a rule applies to an NP only if it is directly dominated by S (i.e., if it is a subject, in the framework of Chomsky, 1955), of if there is no PP dominating it, etc. Similarly, quantifiers would be needed to formulate the A-over-A condition as a property of particular rules.

15. Cf. Postal (in press) for an argument that the rule of quantifier movement requires reference to the grammatical relation "subject of," and Fiengo and Lasnik (in press) for a counterargument, which I think is correct, showing that the data rule out any such analysis and require rather a simple posi-

tional theory of the sort outlined here. For more discussion of the issues mentioned here, see the latter paper.

16. So-called derivational constraints. Cf. Lakoff (1971) and Postal (1972). On technical difficulties in this proposal, cf. Soames (1974). On the empirical issues, see Brame (1975) and references cited there.

17. So-called transderivational constraints.

18. Cf. Ross (1973, 1975).

19. Postal (1972) argues to the contrary, but I think he is mistaken for reasons given in my remarks in Parret (1974).

20. For discussion of the logic of the argument, see Chomsky (1955). In more recent work, the condition was made explicit, perhaps first in Ross (1967).

21. Cf. Chomsky (1973, 1976), Wasow (forthcoming), Fiengo (1974).

22. In the case of a transformational rule, we may understand "X is involved in the rule" to mean that X is changed by the rule or is a constant context for some change (see Fiengo and Lasnik, in press, for an interesting case of the latter sort). Thus the terms involved in the rule are the factors that are not arbitrary strings, in accordance with the SD. In an interpretive rule, we may say that X and Y are involved if the rule establishes a relation of anaphora or control relating X and Y. Cf. Jackendoff (1972), Wasow forthcoming), Fiengo (1974). I leave other questions open, pending further investigation. The condition on α raises questions that I will not pursue. For English, tensed sentences and subjunctives fall under α. Possibly, the condition may vary within a limited range among languages; thus it might be that the condition holds for α finite only in languages that distinguish finite from infinitive complements. There is some evidence to this effect, but it is too sparse to be convincing.

23. Among the unsolved problems are some involving so-called picture-noun reflexivization, which so far resist analysis under any general theory known to me; cf. Jackendoff (1972). It may be, as suggested in Helke (1971), that English reflexivization is a complex of two processes, one a process of bound anaphora restricted by conditions on sentence-grammar, the other a more general process involving other factors that applies to "reflexives" of very different sorts. Examples of the latter can be found in such languages as Korean and Japanese, where the item that has been called "reflexive" is not bound by principles of sentence-grammar, so it appears, and thus naturally violates grammatical conditions. Note also such examples as "the men expected that pictures of each other would be on sale," where application of the reciprocal rule violates the tensed-S condition in a non-subjacent construction, as compared with "the men expected (that) each other would win," observing the tensed-S condition under subjacency. I hope to present a more comprehensive discussion elsewhere.

24. On the semantics of this construction, see Fiengo and Lasnik (1973), Dougherty (1974).

25. On this matter, see Jackendoff (1972, 1976, and references cited there), and for an analysis of a number of cases in terms of a theory of the sort under discussion here, see Chomsky (1973).

26. Quicoli's study extends to clitic and quantifier movement in other languages as well. I am indebted to him for the examples that follow, which only touch the surface of the very interesting material he is developing. Cf. Kayne (1975) for presentation of some of the basic ideas and analyses regarding ssc.

27. First noted, I believe, in Bresnan (1971). For more on the matter, see Baker and Brame (1972), Selkirk (1972), Lightfoot (1975b). Various approaches have been developed to account for the facts. It is difficult to compare these directly, since they involve somewhat different assumptions with regard to underlying theory and particular analyses.

28. Note that *want* is partially defective in this respect even as a pure transitive verb; e.g., "the book was wanted" [?], "a man who is wanted by the police—was here," "any books wanted for this course—can be obtained at the college bookstore" [?]. Other verbs of this category, e.g., *prefer*, are subject to NP-preposing as pure transitives (e.g., "this solution is preferred by most people," "the solution preferred by most people—is this one"), though examples such as (57) are impossible. The fact is easily explained on the assumption that there is no rule of raising to object position, an assumption that I will continue to adopt here (cf. Chomsky 1973, 1976). For a review of this question that seems to me generally convincing, cf. Lightfoot (1975a).

29. Bresnan, whose analysis I generally follow here, postulates instead a condition on rules involving the complementizer, but I think that there are difficulties that suggest rather that a surface filter is involved. Cf. Bresnan (1972). Bresnan also assumes no complementizer instead of a zero complementizer for epistemic verbs.

30. I suspect that rule (58) actually results from the interaction of *X-self* deletion and rules preventing *for-to* constructions.

31. This Czech example is from Toman (1975).

32. Examples such as (65) do not violate ssc for reasons discussed in Chomsky (1973). The question whether ssc must also govern transformational rules is complex. Cf. Fiengo and Lasnik (in press) for an example suggesting that it must.

33. Alternatively, for (67): "for $y = Bill$, you told y for which person x, y to visit x." And for (68): "for $y = Bill$, for which person x, you told y, y to visit x." Cf. (71), below.

34. The literal meaning is contrary to the obviously intended sense; hence, the latter may actually be assigned in discourse, as in the case of other deviant structures. But I think that the correct interpretation is as presented here. Suppose *every* is replaced by *each* in (83). Then the construal of the structures in the intended sense is perhaps somewhat easier, at least in (i) and (iii). The quantifier *each* permits us to dissociate the individuals under

consideration for the purposes of anaphora outside the scope of the quantifier, at least more readily than its near-synonym *every*. Replacement of *every* by *all* makes the structures still more deviant in the intended sense. Further complications arise as we consider other connectives. Compare "as soon as every student finishes his exam, he is to hand it in" (*he* not anaphoric) and "as soon as each student finishes his exam, he is to hand it in" (possible, with anaphoric *he*, and of course a completely different interpretation of the quantifier than in "as soon as every student finishes his exam, the lights will be put out"). In all of these cases, *his*, being within the scope of the quantifier, can be (and normally would be) anaphoric. There are many further complications, but they do not, I think, affect the central point under discussion here. Cf. Kroch (1974) for more discussion.

35. For a clear and simple exposition, see Lewis (1972), and for much more detail, see Partee (1975).

36. Complications mount rapidly as we move to sentences with two quantifiers or to plurals. Thus consider: "Some soldiers have guns. Will they shoot them?" We might want to say that *they* is anaphoric to *some soldiers* and *them* to *guns*, but the question asks whether each soldier who has a gun will shoot the gun that he has, not whether some soldiers will shoot guns.

37. The same conclusion holds in multiclause sentences, though the substitution of *John* for *he* is less natural or impossible: "John is here, but will he shoot?"; "If John is here, then he will shoot." In the latter case, and perhaps the former as well, substitution of *John* for *he* seems to me to impose disjoint reference. It seems that the rule applying here is not a rule of sentence-grammar, but is rather a rule assigning a higher degree of preference to disjoint interpretation the closer the grammatical connection. Thus, substitution of *John* for *he* is difficult in (93i). Disjoint reference is preferred, but it would be strange to use the same name, *John*, in simple successive sentences with difference of reference. In contrast, substitution of *every soldier* for *he* in (93ii) and *some soldier* for *he* in (93iii) changes the interpretation radically.

38. On rules for relativization, see Chomsky (1975), and for a detailed analysis along these lines, see Vergnaud (1974).

39. On the rule of interpretation for *any*, see Hintikka (1975). A somewhat similar proposal is mentioned in Lasnik (1972). Hintikka argues that violations of compositionality, as illustrated in (87), (107), constitute counterexamples to Fregean theories of meaning and to theories of the sort suggested by Davidson and Montague. He also points out that *any*-sentences provide counterexamples to the criterion of material adequacy for a truth definition of the Tarski type. Under his formulation of the *any*-rule, it also follows, as he shows, that the class of well-formed sentences is not recursive or even recursively enumerable. But I think that there are other formulations that cover the clear facts as well that do not lead to this conclusion, though there are, I believe, other and simpler examples that lead to conclusions similar

to his with regard to the set of sentences well formed by some plausible criterion.

40. These considerations again seem to me to support the classical logical analysis over the revision suggested by Montague, if we take these as theories with empirical import. With regard to anaphora, a good indication of referential function, the noun phrases *someone* and *everyone* behave very differently from names or definite descriptions, as the classical theory, taken literally, predicts. And furthermore the rules of anaphora apply to a logical form that contains quantifiers and variables rather than to a surface structure.

41. For discussion, see Chomsky (1976) and references cited there, particularly, Fiengo (1974). Also, van Riemsdijk (1973), Jackendoff (1975), Quicoli (1975), Lightfoot (1975b).

42. Cf. Chomsky (1973) for a brief comment.

REFERENCES

Akmajian, Adrian. 1975. More evidence for an NP cycle. *Linguistic Inquiry* 6:1.

Bach, Emmon. 1965. On some recurrent types of transformations. In C. W. Kreidler, ed., *Sixteenth Annual Round Table Meeting on Linguistics and Language Studies*. Georgetown University Monograph Series on Languages and Linguistics 18.

Baker, C. Leroy, and Brame, Michael K. 1972. 'Global rules': a rejoinder. *Language* 48:51–75.

Bordelois, Ivonne. 1974. *The grammar of Spanish causative complements*. Ph.D. diss., MIT.

Brame, Michael K. 1975. Conjectures and refutations in syntax and semantics. Mimeographed, University of Washington.

Bresnan, Joan. 1971. Contraction and the transformational cycle in English. Mimeographed, MIT.

———. 1972. Stress and syntax: a reply. *Language* 48(2):326–42.

———. 1973. Sentence stress and syntactic transformations. In K. J. J. Hintikka, J. M. E. Moravcsik, and P. Suppes, eds., *Approaches to Natural Language*. Dordrecht: Reidel.

———. 1975. Transformations and categories in syntax. Paper for Fifth International Congress on Logic, Methodology, and Philosophy of Science. London, Ontario.

———. In press. On the form and functioning of transformations. *Linguistic Inquiry*.

Chomsky, Noam. 1955. The logical structure of linguistic theory. Mimeographed. Published in large part by Plenum, New York (1975).

———. 1961. On the notion 'rule of grammar'. *Structure of Language and*

Its Mathematical Aspects. Proceedings of the Symposia in Applied Mathematics, Vol. XII. Providence, R. I.: American Mathematical Society.

―――. 1965. *Aspects of the Theory of Syntax.* Cambridge: MIT Press.

―――. 1972. *Studies on Semantics in Generative Grammar.* The Hague: Mouton.

―――. 1973. Conditions on transformations. In S. R. Anderson and P. Kiparsky, eds., *A Festschrift for Morris Halle.* New York: Holt, Rinehart and Winston.

―――. 1975. Questions of form and interpretation. *Linguistic Analysis* 1:75–107.

―――. 1976. *Reflections on Language.* New York: Pantheon.

Chomsky, Noam, and Halle, Morris. 1968. *Sound Pattern of English.* New York: Harper and Row.

Chomsky, Noam, and Miller, George A. 1963. Introduction to the formal analysis of natural languages. In R. D. Luce, R. R. Bush, and E. Galanter, eds., *Handbook of Mathematical Psychology,* 2:419–91. New York: Wiley.

Dougherty, Ray C. 1974. The syntax and semantics of *each other* constructions. *Foundations of Language* 12(1).

―――. 1975. Reflections on the Bloomfieldian counterrevolution. *International Journal of Dravidian Linguistics* 3(2):255–86.

Emonds, Joseph E. In press. Root and structure-preserving transformations.

Fiengo, Robert. 1974. Semantic conditions on surface structure. Ph.D. diss., MIT.

Fiengo, Robert, and Lasnik, Howard. 1973. The logical structure of reciprocal sentences in English. *Foundations of Language* 9:447–68.

―――. In press. Some issues in the theory of transformations. *Linguistic Inquiry.*

Fodor, Jerry A. 1975. *The Language of Thought.* New York: Crowell.

Helke, Michael. 1971. The grammar of English reflexives. Ph.D. diss., MIT.

Hintikka, Jaakko. 1975. On the limitations of generative grammar. Mimeographed, Stanford University.

Hornstein, Norbert. 1975. S and the $\overline{\text{X}}$ convention. *Montreal Working Papers in Linguistics* 4:35–71.

Jackendoff, Ray S. 1972. *Semantic Interpretation in Generative Grammar.* Cambridge: MIT Press.

―――. 1975. Tough and the trace theory of movement rules. *Linguistic Inquiry* 6(3).

―――. 1976. Toward an explanatory semantic representation. *Linguistic Inquiry* 7(1).

Katz, Jerrold J. 1972. *Semantic Theory.* New York: Harper and Row.

―――. Forthcoming. *Propositional Structure: A Study of the Contribution of Sentence Meaning to Speech Acts.* New York: Crowell.

Katz, Jerrold J., and Bever, T. G. 1976. The fall and rise of empiricism. In

T. G. Bever, J. J. Katz, and D. T. Langendoen, eds. *Integrated Theory of Linguistic Knowledge.* New York: Crowell.

Katz, Jerrold J., and Postal, Paul M. 1964. *An Integrated Theory of Linguistic Descriptions.* Cambridge: MIT Press.

Kayne, Richard S. 1975. *French syntax: The Transformational Cycle.* Cambridge: MIT Press.

Kroch, Anthony. 1974. The semantics of scope in English. Ph.D. diss., MIT.

Kuroda, S-Y. 1968. English relativization and certain related problems. *Language* 44:244–66.

———. 1973. Where epistemology, style, and grammar meet: a case study from Japanese. In S. R. Anderson and P. Kiparsky, eds. *A Festschrift for Morris Halle,* pp. 377–91. New York: Holt, Rinehart and Winston.

Labov, William. 1970. The logic of nonstandard English. In Louis Kampf and Paul Lauter, eds., *The Politics of Literature.* New York: Pantheon.

Lakoff, George. 1971. On generative semantics. In D. Steinberg and L. Jacobovits, eds., *Semantics: An Interdisciplinary Reader.* New York: Cambridge University Press.

Lasnik, Howard. 1972. Analyses of negation in English. Ph.D. diss., MIT.

———. 1974. Remarks on coreference. Mimeographed, University of Connecticut.

Lewis, David. 1972. General semantics. In Gilbert Harman and Donald Davidson, eds., *Semantics of Natural Language.* Dordrecht: Reidel.

Lightfoot, David. 1975a. The theoretical implications of subject raising. *Foundations of Language* 13:115–43.

———. 1975b. Traces and doubly moved NPs. Mimeographed.

Parret, H., ed. 1974. *Discussing Language.* The Hague: Mouton.

Partee, Barbara. 1975. Montague grammar and transformational grammar. *Linguistic Inquiry* 6:203–300.

Peters, P. S., and Ritchie, R. W. 1973. On the generative power of transformational grammars. *Information Sciences* 6:49–83.

Postal, Paul M. 1972. The best theory. In P. S. Peters, ed., *Goals of Linguistic Theory,* Englewood Cliffs, N. J.: Prentice-Hall.

———. In press. Avoiding reference to subject. *Linguistic Inquiry.*

Quicoli, A. Carlos. 1975. Conditions on quantifier movement in French. Mimeographed, MIT.

———. In press. Clitic movement in Portuguese. *Linguistic Analysis.*

Ross, John R. 1967. Constraints on variables in syntax. Ph.D. diss., MIT.

———. 1973. Nouniness. In Osamu Fujimura, ed., *Three Dimensions of Linguistic Theory.* Tokyo: TEC Company.

———. 1975. Where to do things with words. In P. Cole and J. Morgan, eds., *Syntax and Semantics,* p. 3. New York: Academic Press.

Selkirk, Elisabeth O. 1972. The phrase phonology of English and French. Ph.D. diss., MIT.

Soames, Scott. 1974. Rule orderings, obligatory transformations, and derivational constraints. *Theoretical Linguistics* 1:116–38.

Toman, Jindrich. 1975. Pronominal clitics in Czech. Mimeographed, MIT.

van Riemsdijk, Henk. 1973. A case for a trace: preposition stranding in Züritüütsch. Mimeographed, Amsterdam.

Vergnaud, Jean-Roger. 1974. French relative clauses. Ph.D. diss., MIT.

Wasow, Thomas. Forthcoming. *Anaphora in Generative Grammar.*

The Sociology of Language: Yesterday, Today, and Tomorrow

Joshua A. Fishman

During the summer of 1964 I was one of a group of ten sociologists, anthropologists, and linguists who were given visiting-faculty status at the Linguistic Institute then being held at Indiana University. Our task was to define the area of sociolinguistic endeavor, to explore its methods, and to formulate the future research and course work necessary for its growth and development. Almost all that has transpired in American sociolinguistics in the following decade can be traced back to the individuals and the concerns that interacted in Bloomington, Indiana, during that formative summer. Today, when I am once again a visiting faculty member at a Linguistic Institute, and when I have been asked to review some of the past, present, and future sociolinguistic efforts, it seems reasonable for me to begin by returning to one of the topics that had been of major interest prior to Bloomington: the Whorfian hypothesis. As one of the major pre-sociolinguistic prods requiring us to look beyond the structure of language per se and to examine the behavioral implications and concommitants of that structure, the Whorfian hypothesis is a good way of reviewing yesterday, or even the day before yesterday, en route to our more major concern with the today and tomorrow of the sociolinguistic enterprise.

The Whorfian Hypothesis: Part of Our Yesterday

It may come somewhat as a surprise today, but there is no doubt in my mind that the Whorfian hypothesis and its stress on the linguistic relativism of cognitive processes was one of the "cutting edges" of the language sciences in the 1950s and early 60s. Even in the early 60s, when the birth (or rebirth) of sociolinguistic concerns was becoming apparent to those at the forefront of theory and research in the language sciences, it did not strike me as surprising to hear the prediction that "one of the major topics of sociolinguistic attention will doubtlessly be the Whorfian hypothesis." I did not agree with the view at all (my 1960 paper on the Whorfian hypothesis having convinced me otherwise), but it did not surprise me still to encounter it even among the most highly informed.

Today, more than a decade later, I am even more convinced of the limited validity of the Whorfian hypothesis than I was initially. Nevertheless, paradoxically, I now see it much more clearly in relation to four other major shocks to the *amour propre* of modern man. Like Copernicus, Darwin, Marx, and Freud before him, Whorf must be viewed as a prophet of sad tidings, as a bearer of the message that man is far less free and far more insignificant than he would like to be or than he believes himself to be.

The Copernican thunderbolt brought home the message that, far from being the apple of God's eye, our planet is a mere speck in a system the center of which is occupied by a third-rate star. Three centuries later, Darwin heaped insult upon injury by demonstrating that man himself is merely a part of the entire animal kingdom, many of whose members did not escape extinction notwithstanding their various and considerable assets and distinctions. Almost simultaneously, Marx came forward to claim that human behavior was merely part of the system of economic resources and that human culture and values were really by-products of material circumstances. Finally, Freud began the twentieth century with his similarly debunking and dethroning views that make men the prisoners of their unconscious instinctual needs and of the structures into which these are systematically organized.

All four of these men powerfully changed (and dampened) our views of ourselves. Whorf, the least successful of the great detractors, must nevertheless be seen as one of their company. His ultimate message is like theirs: Man is not free. Man is not great. He is bound. He is trapped. He does not necessarily see what is there. He does not necessarily say what he thinks. He does not even think freely. Cognitively he is a prisoner of the structure of his particular language.[1] No matter how limited the validity of this claim, and several decades of sympathetic research have produced almost no convincing confirmatory evidence, Whorf deserves to be seen in the illustrious company of the other great detractors, among whom the other social and behavioral scientists (Marx and Freud) may have been no more correct, even though they became much more famous than Whorf.

The tenacity with which the Whorfian hypothesis is subscribed to must be a matter of considerable fascination for anyone interested in the sociology of science or in the sociology of knowledge. Certainly, it is an indication of the extent to which academicians, cursed as we are with "the talking disease," are ourselves fascinated by the thought that we are not fully responsible for what we are saying and thinking. Be that as it may, it is clear to me that two or more decades of research have not been particularly kind to Whorf. Even when viewed most charitably, they have revealed that the phenomenon to which he referred is, at best, a remediable or transitory one and, again at best, only a partial reflection of the truly complex embeddedness of cognitive behavior.

It may be claimed that Marx and Freud too were concerned with diseases that are both remediable and transitory. However, in their cases, they were at least as much concerned with documenting the necessary cures as with the diseases themselves. Whorf, on the other hand, was primarily a diagnostician. He left the ways and means of struggling with language relativity to others (Korzybski, Hayakawa, etc.), who made the struggle into a pseudoscience (general semantics) and recommended various types of pseudotherapy in connection with it. It seems clear to me that the pan-human struggle with linguistic relativity is generally not all that complicated, that many of us can and do overcome or counteract whatever biases our particular grammars and lexicons (and their respective ethno-typological consequences) impose upon us. All in all, we handle linguistic relativity much better than we do linguistic determinism *per se* (a much more pernicious and inescapable disease). Certainly, none of the attempts to confirm or refine the Whorfian hypothesis empirically, whether via research on memory, problem solving, classifying, or attributing (most recently see, e.g., Niyakawa-Howard, 1968), has succeeded in demonstrating that linguistic relativity is even a dependable phenomenon, let alone a powerful one, when and if encountered.

More provocatively—and this is where the sociology of language enters the picture—there is much research and ample theory to imply that the contextualization of cognition is far greater and more complex than Whorf imagined. Whorf simply makes the point that how one thinks may be influenced by *the* language in which the thinking is done. However, the sociology of language leads us away from one person–one language models. So much of mankind is bi- and multilingual and the languages utilized are so often so syntactically different that we must recognize a fundamental human capacity to escape from any one grammar and any one lexicon. Basically we all learn to work with linguistic and behavioral repertoires, even those of us who are nominally monolingual. We are not so much troubled by the differing structures of the various languages and varieties that we use as we are by the demands of communicative appropriateness across a wide variety of interlocutors, topics, and purposes. We ponder how to say (write) something the *right way* to a *particular person* because of a *particular role relationship* and *situation* impinging on our *purpose* (or cross-purpose), and we try to select adeptly and appropriately between the language and varieties we control accordingly. Far from being locked in, we are constantly weighing and choosing between grammars and lexicons in our quest to advance ourselves and our purposes more adequately (Fishman, 1972).

The sociology of language also helps us realize that whether or not language structure helps create sociocognitive reality (as Whorf would claim), this latter reality both creates and preserves language characteristics, including those of a highly systematic kind. As a result of this more complete causal system (rather than the one-way "half system" that Whorf conceived of), those planning for change need to alter not only the linguistic system (in order to foster societal change) but also—and much more basically—the social system (in order to foster linguistic change and social change *per se*). The entire system is not only far more complete but also more open and manipulable than Whorf anticipated. It can be entered at any point, but, optimally, at several points, in order to produce and consolidate the kinds of change that are desired. Further evidence of the two-way relationship that exists between the organization of language and the organization of social behavior comes from the field of "language birth." New languages or new varieties come into being simultaneously with new social facts (new interactions between preexisting language groups, new power constellations between such groups, etc.). There is simply no reason to focus only on language organization as the causal force or factor in sociocognitive behavior, as Whorf implied. The total process is of a circular or feedback nature, and the causal impact of societal organization on language organization is every bit as powerful (if not more so) as the causal impact of lingual organization on the organization of social behavior (Fishman, 1972).

Notwithstanding the above qualms and criticisms, the Whorfian hypothesis seems to be eternally capable of fascinating successive generations of students in successive disciplines. Like Marxism and Freudianism, it functions as a quasi-religious experience for some in that the enormity and the clarity of its discovery (biased though it be) is indeed breathtaking and, apparently, integratingly clarifying at a level more meaningful and more compelling than the strictly intellectual alone.

There have been mistaken scientific theories and *Weltanschauungen* that have embroiled generations of scholars and students in conflicts to no greater end than to discredit thoroughly the views advanced. The Whorfian hypothesis, or, more accurately, efforts to test, refine, or revise the Whorfian hypothesis, have done much more than that for the language sciences. It has left us at least three very vibrant legacies in the form of productive research traditions and topical concentrations that we might not have otherwise come by. These three robust by-products more than justify the time that has been invested in clarifying and delimiting the Whorfian hypothesis.

Language Universals

Whorf's stress on the endless and fargoing differences between languages ultimately prepared us to face the questions "What differences are really different?" and "Aren't there more similarities than differences?" Whorf himself realized that certain differences were not differences at all, or that they might as well be overlooked in the face of even more fargoing similarities. Thus, Whorf set up the catchall category Standard Average European (SAE) to take in all of the well-known Indo-European family whose members were viewed as differing in only unimportant ways. Whorf delighted in contrasting the basically similar SAE languages with the "really different" North and South American Indian languages. But, obviously, these too are often members of large families and, therefore, classifiable into various Standard Average groupings of their own. Ultimately, the various Standard Average groupings must doubtlessly differ in some respects but be similar in others. Thus, the question of language universals arises, and for some at least (foremost among them: Greenberg) it arose out of the phoenixlike ashes of the Whorfian hypothesis. Linguists and anthropologists long carried the burden of saving (or at least recording) all the world's languages on the strength of the view that each was a thoroughly unique reflection of the infinite, many-splendored variety of mankind. The counterbalancing view, which emphasized the pervasive underlying similarities across language, could not but make their disciplines broader and more balanced than they had hitherto been. We have the struggle with Whorfianism to thank for a good bit of this healthy development.

Ethnolinguistics

Another such development, which is even more fully derivable from Whorf-inspired directions and counterreactions, is the one that has blossomed into the various *ethno*-sciences (ethnolinguistics, ethnosemantics, ethnocognition, etc.). This fruitful field of inquiry has explored the seemingly complete and tight typological system within languages that are hardest to escape and hardest to avoid. Initially, these systems (color nomenclatures, kinship nomenclatures, status or politeness indicators, certainty indicators, shape indicators) were studied in order to test the Whorfian hypothesis, but subsequently they came to be studied in their own right, as "current ways of viewing" rather than as inescapable traps or blinders. Even if we grant, as I believe we should, that ethno-categories are far more malleable and far less tenacious sociocognitive guides than Whorf believed, they are still well worth identifying, if only in order to know (whether for purposes of intercultural or intracultural analyses) the predispositions or presuppositions that require escaping from or working on. Stripped of its Whorfian confirmatory or disconfirmatory role, this is an important contribution in its own right.

Transmitting Social Structure

Whorf held that the structured characteristics of particular languages bring about particular sociocognitive behaviors. Whatever support for this view we may find today is likely to be tied to the counterbalancing view that the structured characteristics of particular social systems elicit and preserve linguistic structures that are consonant with them and, therefore, supportive of them. Nevertheless, the directional sequence that Whorf stressed is accepted (even if its directional exclusivity is not) and is in the influential work of Basil Bernstein, among others. Certainly Bernstein believes that lower-class speech is a highly structured (restricted) code that perpetuates a way of life (of thinking and acting) as a result of its early socialization role and its subsequent function in important role relations. Unfortunately, Bernstein's work has consistently been misinterpreted as having inherent or racial or genetic implications vis-à-vis the disadvantaged (as does Whorf's work, on occasion), but that is a problem in its own right. Here it is merely appropriate to stress that there are important researchers (including recent ones who are exploring "female talk") who accept the notion that linguistic features can and do serve to freeze their speakers into normatively expected and ritualized social behaviors. Although these researchers often hold no brief at all for any deep-freeze view, nor are they unmindful of the contribution of social structure for freezing language usage, they are, at least to some degree, following in the footsteps of Whorf himself.

The Yiddish proverb "a good question begets a good answer" is applicable to the Whorfian hypothesis. Basically, Whorf asked a good question and, although the answers to his question have generally cast doubt on his own preferred answer, they have themselves been good answers and have sparked their own independent and productive research traditions—as witnessed by the three healthy offspring fields mentioned above.

There are a lot of things for which we should be grateful to Whorf, most of which he could not have anticipated. He made us more aware of linguistic relativity and, therefore, ultimately more aware of the weakness of linguistic relativity as a causal factor in sociocognitive behavior. Three robust fields, at least two of them highly sociolinguistic in character, were born out of the repeated attempts to test the Whorfian hypothesis. Our current awareness of the unsuitability of *translated* categories for indicating what is going on in the mind of the *native speaker* is much indebted to our having been forced to grapple with Whorf's English translations of Hopi verbs.[2] Similarly, grappling with Whorf has made us more resistant to the misinterpretations of language differences with respect to possible inherent superiority–inferiority implications vis-à-vis native speakers. Finally, the Whorfian hypothesis helped pave the way for three important sociolinguistic principles of today and tomorrow:

a. Language and society are associated in a two-way relationship, i.e., one of constant interdependence and feedback. It is this fact that makes the formulation "language in society" (or "language in its social setting")[3] a misnomer or, at least, a gross simplification of the true complexity of the sociology of language.

b. The relationship between language and society is not adequately represented by the Whorfian model of "one society–one language." On the contrary, a universal fact of social life is that speakers control a repertoire of varieties and/or languages that may be structurally very diverse. Their ability to use this repertoire nimbly is itself testimony to the human ability to escape from or to control the bonds of linguistic relativity.

c. The relationship between language and society is not so tightly structured that it cannot be altered via social planning and via language planning, not to mention the unplanned change to which this relationship and its component parts are amenable.

The remaining sections of this review will deal largely with points *b* and *c*. Let us remember that although we may now conclude that Whorf was substantially mistaken, he was undeniably a man of great vision. A truly great vision is always worth the price it exacts, even if it is in large part mistaken, for it stimulates worthwhile correctives and counter-visions. If only more of us in the sociology of language could be wrong like Marx, wrong like Freud, or wrong like Whorf, ultimately the sociology of language would certainly be stronger rather than weaker for our "mistakes."

Societal Bilingualism: The Bulk of Our Today and a Good Bit of Our Tomorrow

Although Whorf himself may have been bilingual[4] he unconsciously assumed, as have others before and since, that the normal model for language in society implied that each society had one language and one alone. The sociology of language, which so clearly proclaims the opposite view (and in also doing so for societies usually considered monolingual even calls into question such reifications as "the *x* language"), must, as a result, adopt others as its grandfathers. Indeed, two grandfathers come to mind in connection with the interest in societal bilingualism, Uriel Weinreich and Einar Haugen. Since they both undertook their most seminal work on this topic roughly a quarter century ago (see Weinreich's *Languages in Contact,* 1953, and Haugen's *Bilingualism in the Americas,* 1956) enough time has passed for us to ask: How far have we come and what remains to be done in this essentially post-Whorfian (if not contra-Whorfian) topic area?

As much as Weinreich and Haugen appreciated the frequency of bilingualism, it is not clear that they really understood its normality. For both of them it was a special, somewhat heightened, state of affairs associated somehow with immigrational trauma, intergroup conflict, and other expressions of man *in extremis.* Haugen wrote poignantly of the "pains and pleasures" of bilingualism precisely because it was assumed to be something special and not nearly as usual and ubiquitous as talking, breathing, and thinking. Underlying all their work is an innocence (or is it a skepticism?) with respect to societal bilingualism, i.e., that normal societies exist and function on a bilingual basis. Our view today stresses not only the normality of societal multilingualism but also its complexity and, indeed, its normal complexity across time (the centuries of recorded history) and across space (the entire world). Certainly we view it as a phenomenon infinitely more amenable to objective and quantitative analysis, as well as to integrate conceptualization, than was formerly thought to be the case.

Societal Bilingualism as a Worldwide Phenomenon

If the frequency of an event can be cited as an indication of its "normalcy," then societal bilingualism is obviously a normal phenomenon. It is *present* in almost all countries and is *dominant* in a goodly number. It is also evidenced by the spread of lingua francas such as English into non-English mother-tongue countries throughout the world.

In previous centuries lingua francas spread without official record keeping, data collecting, and professional direction of analysis. Not so today. The spread of English (and, to a lesser degree, French, Russian, Chinese, and even Arabic) is now accompanied by the search for "hard data" as to its *relative* penetration into different countries and segments of society. The volumes being published by the International Center for Research on Bilingualism on *The Linguistic Composition of the Nations of the World* (see Kloss, 1975) are replete with information on the worldwide spread of a relatively few languages of wider communication (LWC), English in particular. My own *Bilingual Education: An International Sociological Perspective* (1976) not only documents the occurrence of such education in some 110 countries (with 5,000 secondary education units and 100,000 elementary education units being involved) but also indicates the magnitude of the co-occurrence of English plus a local language as the predominant pattern of bilingual education today. This is expressly the message conveyed by Gage and Ohannessian (1974) in their very useful recent summary of ESOL enrollments throughout the world. Finally, from my work with Cooper on the "Sociology of English as an Additional Language" (MS), it is clear that the governmental, quasi-governmental, and nongovernmental use of English in non-English mother-tongue countries today is very great and still growing rapidly (particularly in the areas of technology, business, and mass media), but that the forces and factors leading to increased knowledge of English, use of English, and liking for English are usually quite different and unrelated to one another.

A host of factors have come together to foster the spread of lingua francas today, when the number of independent countries is larger than it has ever been in recorded history. Notwithstanding the proliferation of polities the number of "internationals" keeps growing, as a result of the spread of United Nations enterprises, foreign technological experts and indigenous elites, business representatives, expatriate residents, and the vastly increased tide of tourism. In city after city throughout the world these "internationals" constitute a speech community (composed of innumerable smaller networks that are often based on divergent mother tongues) and, much more often than not, English is their lingua franca, as revealed in shops, restaurants, theaters, and concerts and by parties and publications the world over. Indeed, probably not since the days of the Roman Empire has so much of the known world been so accessible via "a single language."[5]

National Bilingualism and Language Planning

The above development is not always viewed with unmitigated pleasure. International bilingualism may be well and good "in its place," but it can and may have rather unexpected and undesired intranational consequences. Since nations are currently our largest units of effectively organized consciousness it should come as no surprise that many nations have responded at a policy level to the spread of English, to define both its desired and its undesired functions and domains. Although our major attention to language planning will come in a later section, let me point out here that both status planning and corpus planning are very commonly conducted in the context of centrally controlled bilingualism involving an exoglossic LWC. Furthermore, both types of language planning are conducted in the context of a double approach–avoidance conflict, with most authorities realizing at least some of the undesirable as well as some of the desirable consequences of too much stress on English, on the one hand, or too much stress on the local/national language(s), on the other. It is precisely because of this dilemma that some kind of planned combination is pursued by most authorities, with the question normally being: which language for which purpose and for which social networks?

We now have several fine studies of such managed or controlled or planned national bilingualism, none of which were available to Weinreich or Haugen a quarter century ago. Glyn Lewis's volume on multilingualism in the Soviet Union (1972), Carol Scotton's on choosing a lingua franca in an African capital (1972), the various reports of the Survey of Language Teaching and Language Usage in East Africa (e.g., Ladefoged, 1968; Whiteley, 1975; Bender, Ferguson, and Cooper,

1976; Polome et al., forthcoming; Ohannessian et al., forthcoming), the recent volume by Harrison et al. (1975) on Jordan, all include examples of research on the national level on policy and practice with respect to national bilingualism. The concern for one or more local/national languages faced by powerful lingua francas is everywhere patently clear, even if consensus has not yet always been reached (or imposed) on the societal allocation of languages to functions. The resolutions that are sought are increasingly nonsimplistic and nontotalistic. The functions of the lingua francas, vital though they may be, are restricted so as not to erode the status of local/national languages for most speech networks in the most basic and integrative functions. Certainly no massive language shifts are being avowedly engineered with respect to nonimmigrant populations, although some may occur as lingua francas spill over the dikes and dams with which they are surrounded. It is certainly clear that a functional allocation such as that currently envisaged by the new Philippine bilingual education policy (Filipino for ethnically encumbered fields such as national literature, history, and civics, and English for ethnically unencumbered subjects such as mathematics and the sciences) is an expression of the all-too-human quest for the best of all possible worlds. Certainly it is valuable to have one or more local/ national language(s) for purposes of national integration and for mass mobilization along the road to modernity. The fact that some of the decisions have yet to be made as to which internal language(s) should discharge this function merely adds poignancy to the issue that *local/ national languages are desired.*

As Americans and as purportedly rational and objective scholars many of us cannot help expressing some impatience (if not outright opposition) with the recurring need to protect mother tongues. I have defended and studied this need many times over the past score of years (see particularly Fishman, 1968, 1973a, 1976), and, therefore, I merely want to point out here that with respect to planned national bilingualism an area in which further study is badly needed is the sociology of ethnicity. Only recently our ignorance of ethnicity was at least matched by a lack of interest in it. Today we are obviously more interested in ethnicity but almost as ignorant as before. This ignorance is not really primarily an American disease, although it does have some rather peculiarly American provincialisms masquerading as sophistication associated with it as secondary symptoms. The truth is that in three thousand years of social and sociological theory, spanning the period from the ancient Hebrew, Greek, and Roman thinkers, through the Church fathers, to the modern sociological schools, no full-fledged sociological theory of ethnicity has been elaborated, neither with respect to ethnicity as a recurring basis of human organization nor with respect to its developmental transformations *pari-passu* to more general societal development.[6] We are desperately in need of an unhurried and unharried review of ethnicity as a societal parameter, and of why it has so consistently received such brief and such negative attention from the great social theoreticians. All the social sciences will gain thereby, not least the study of planned national bilingualism with its recurring struggle to protect ethnicity and the ethnic mother tongue at the same time that the benefits of LWC's accrue to those classes and networks considered worthy of such a blessing. It is to just such a study that I propose to dedicate myself during the years ahead (Nahirny and Fishman, MS).

The Bilingual Community and Its Networks

National bilingual policy is a serious and very conscious (even self-conscious) affair. Operating at a far less conscious level is the sociolinguistic heartland of societal bilingualism: the bilingual community and its social networks. It is in this connection that the lion's share of empirical and theoretical progress has been made, particularly during the past decade, bringing us to a stage of sophistication far beyond that available when Weinreich and Haugen were reviewing and conceptualizing the field. The studies of bilingualism in the barrio (Fishman, Cooper, and Ma, 1971), of Guaraní–Spanish alternation in the Paraguayan countryside (Rubin, 1968), of diglossia in Francophone Montreal (Lieberson, 1970), of diglossia as well as its dissolution in various regions of France (Tabouret-Keller, 1972) have all provided ample evidence of the sociodynamics and sociostasis of bilingual communities. We now have rather refined accounts (and rather powerful statistical treatments yielding multiple correlations in the 90s!) of the normative societal allocation of language functions that define and predict communicative competence with respect to a bilingual repertoire. Certainly the relatively uniform and consistent individual interpretations and realizations of community norms—as well as of when and to what degree it is permitted to depart from the societal allocation of functions for metaphorical purposes—has, in recent years, been rather well represented. Students should find it progressively easier to go back and forth between individual bilingualism and the absence or presence of societal diglossia. Soon such demonstrations will become old hat.

If there is still a new frontier in the study of societal bilingualism at the community and network level it is probably in connection with the more refined explication of the change potential and change processes that may be there. As yet no one has really traced through the implications that exist for change in community bilingualism in the Labovian displacement model. We know there are consistent inter-network differences. We know that these differences imply a lack of full consensus as to the societal allocation of functions. We know that these differences are relatable to occupational, role, and attitudinal differences between networks. We know that these differences imply not merely the *potential* for change in the societal allocation of functions but that they are actually an indication of *ongoing change*, of change incarnate. Nevertheless, no one has quite put these pieces together this way in a study of community and network bilingualism. It is an exciting prospect that remains to be realized.

The Bilingual Individual in Societal Perspective

Like all societal research, the phenomenon of societal bilingualism cannot be endlessly pursued without the use of measures and observations of individuals. Just as societal bilingualism is a consolidation or compositing of individual data, so must individual bilingualism be viewed as a reflection of societal norms. Bilinguals who are equally fluent in both languages (as measured by their facility and correctness overall) are rarely equally fluent in both languages about *all possible topics*; this phenomenon is invariably a reflection of the fact that the societal allocation of functions is normally imbalanced and in complementary distribution rather than redundant. If we find an unbalanced but fluent bilingual, we can be sure that this result is due to his or her social experiences. If we find a balanced fluent bilingual we can be equally sure that the balancing is due to special schooling and studied practice rather than to the variety of social institutions (home, friendship clique, school, church, work sphere, government) upon which normal (and, therefore, unbalanced) societal bilingualism depends (Fishman, Cooper, and Ma, 1971).

Because societal multilingualism is reflected in individual behavior, sociolinguistic researchers must carefully monitor the psycholinguistic research on bilingualism as well. Every new psycholinguistic theory or measure pertaining to individual bilingualism needs to be examined for its societal implications. All motive states, personality patterns, and cognitive styles that are related to individual bilingualism must be examined for possible translatability into societal dimensions. Psychological research on bilingualism continues to stimulate the sociolinguistic imagination and to further the refinement of theory, methods, and empirical data. Our multiple correlations are already encouragingly high but there

is still sufficient unexplained variance in societally based bilingual behavior, and sufficient alternative (perhaps more manipulable) variables
to be sought to make all of us extremely attentive to the bilingualism
research and theory that colleagues are hammering out in departments
of psychology and/or in institutes of psycho-educational orientation.

I have tried to imply that the intellectual future of work on societal
bilingualism is rather good because the field is coherent, important,
and challenging. It only remains to be said that the future also seems
bright for a less-thrilling but equally vital reason, namely, that many
other basic issues in the sociology of language (and even in the language
sciences more broadly) are best and most easily handled (studied, con-
ceptualized) in societal bilingualism settings. The study of language
planning is one such topic. The study of language and ethnicity is another. This is no little thing. Indeed, it is a great asset for the intellectual
future of societal bilingualism. Since current data are now much better
than Weinreich's and Haugen's, our methods are much better, and
our theories are (though still formative) far more powerful, I am extremely confident that the study of societal bilingualism will be with us
tomorrow and will be a strong central theme in the sociology of language as a whole.

Language Planning: The Tomorrow of the
Sociology of Language

If there was little awareness of language planning among language
scientists as recently as a decade ago, then obviously Whorf must
have been largely unaware of it thirty and forty years ago. His focus on
the causal link between language structure and sociocognitive structure
was too exclusive, and his estimate of the power of that link was so
exaggerated that he could not have had much sympathy for attempts
to alter both of these structures as well as the link between them via
planned intervention. Certainly, he could not have foreseen the very
recent mushrooming of interest in language planning with more and
more courses, conferences, and research grants being devoted to it.[7] It
may be premature to attempt to integrate what is known in this area at
such an early period in its development; nevertheless, there may be a
certain benefit in doing so and thereby leaving a bench mark with which
subsequent integrative efforts can be compared.[8]

The ten conclusions or generalizations that follow are clustered into
two groups. The first pertains to *corpus planning* (CP), that is, to efforts

to alter linguistic codes. CP efforts are normally entrusted by political and cultural authorities to academies or institutes whose responsibility it is to modernize, purify, elaborate, and/or codify the language and, at times, to disseminate the products of their efforts: nomenclatures, grammars, spellers, style manuals, textbooks, teachers guides, etc. The second grouping pertains to *status planning* (SP), i.e., to efforts by political and cultural authorities to obtain (if necessary, force) acceptance of the planned corpus for particular functions: governmental, educational, technological, etc. These two aspects of language planning often go on simultaneously, attention normally beginning with printed governmental usage and branching out from there, with either CP or SP receiving greater stress as needed by successive phases of the overall plan. Obviously, without SP success, CP can become a trivial ("academic") exercise. Similarly, without CP success, SP becomes an empty declaration of intent, a language program without linguistic shape or substance. Unfortunately, at this time, much more is known (or suspected) about CP than about SP. This is a reflection of the more delimited and the more organized nature of language, with which CP deals, than of the sum total of society, with which SP deals. Ultimately, in the tomorrow of the sociology of language, the current imbalance between these two will be evened out.

Corpus Planning

1. Authorities (and not only authoritarian authorities) *can* organize effectively for CP and, indeed, can do so by some of the same methods of marshalling resources, expertise, and public opinion that are involved in agricultural planning, industrial planning, educational planning, family planning, etc. (Fishman, 1973b). The view of "language as a resource," to be shaped, augmented, and utilized productively under competent management, is, within limits, a useful metaphor for language planning. A rational society, particularly one that is faced by integrative lag, may be well advised to attend to CP (and, of course, to its counterpart SP) in conjunction with desires to make one or more local/national languages suitable instruments for modern ethnic integration and for other modern functions.

2. CP has been focused upon every aspect of language: nomenclature, phonology, morpho-syntax (including gender, tense, honorifics), writing system, number system, color system, etc. The fact that even the purportedly tight systems of language have been changed by concerted intervention must lead to the conclusion that there is practically no limit to what society can do to language structure (within the limits of available power to conceptualize and power to implement). The view

that only relatively limited, peripheral, "surfacy" aspects of language can be subjected to planning (for linguists this often means minor semantic systems) is certainly no longer tenable.

3. The model(s) of "the good language," i.e., the substantive direction that CP takes (as well as the directions that it avoids or rejects), largely derives from political, historical, and cultural considerations of considerable ideological significance rather than from objective efficiency considerations, such as those proposed by Tauli (1974). Nevertheless, innovations are most successful when they have no pre-CP rival(s) or when no strong outside (international lingua franca) influences are at play. Ultimately, disparate parts of the code, even those originally characterized by foreign markedness, come to be widely regarded as equally authentic and indigenous.

4. In view of the foregoing, three reasonable criteria of CP "success" are learning, using, and liking (as opposed to Taulian criteria, such as regularity, purity, and brevity, etc.). That is, CP must be judged by extracode rather than by intracode considerations in view of the non-linguistic pressures upon models of the good language. These criteria are neither highly nor even positively interrelated, and measures of all of them are needed, together with a large number of other social and attitudinal indicators, in order to predict any one of them.

5. At this time, the competence, performance, and attitudinal goals of CP (knowing, using, and liking) are highly predictable via cumulative multiple correlation methods that yield coefficients in the high 80s. Better attitudinal measurement would clearly boost the predictions to a much higher level (see Cooper, Fishman, et al., MS), but would not automatically result in more manipulable (practical) findings. The search for manipulable alternative or counterpart measures is an important task for the tomorrow of language planning research.

Status Planning

6. Whenever CP and SP are set in motion a large segment (indeed, the bulk) of the total target population may well be beyond its principal period of language acquisition facility. These "predates" are, nevertheless, mobilizable attitudinally and, to a lesser extent, cognitively, even though their usage patterns are only susceptible to minimal change. Attitudinal mobilization of the population over twenty years old on behalf of SP also becomes a powerful contextual factor on behalf of continued CP.

7. Those populations that have not yet passed beyond their principal period of language acquisition facility ("postdates") are most manip-

ulable with respect to the usage goals of language planning. However, younger populations often do not have the attitudinal conflict or the language conflict experiences of their elders and, as a result, more easily lose the emotional fervor in which all early sp is conducted. As a result, a generation later the typical "successful" language planning setting is one in which the most consistent "users" and best "knowers" of cp products are younger populations, who are least likely to be conscious "likers" of these products, i.e., to have any heightened emotional attachment to them or to their functional appropriateness. Conversely, older populations are most characterizable as "likers" but least characterizable as "users." This routinization process has it counterpart in other planning areas as well.

8. The implementational manipulation of rewards and punishments on behalf of language planning must also differentiate between learning, using, and liking. Because of the meager relationship between these three criteria each of them is most fully predictable on the basis of quite different primary predictors. Learning is most predictable on a socio-demographic basis; using, along occupational lines; and liking, on related ideological-attitudinal grounds pertaining to language consciousness and national consciousness more generally (Fishman, MS).

9. In the absence of sufficient power[9] to implement sp goals fully and quickly, realistic *gradual functional goals* are a useful device in the pursuit of long-term functional success. Initially modest functions are more easily expanded if they have been successfully implemented initially on pragmatic rather than on moral, ethical, ethnic, or ideological grounds.

10. In the absence of sufficient power to implement sp goals fully and quickly, realistic *nontotalistic rationales* or ideologies are a useful device in the pursuit of long-term functional success. Initially modest functions are more easily expanded if no ideological downgrading of indigenous competitor languages and their speakers has taken place. Languages of wider communication also spread effectively when a low ideological and a high pragmatic profile are maintained.

What is most needed tomorrow, in order to advance language planning significantly beyond the above skeletal decalogue, is considerably more comparative research, both at the micro and macro levels and with both cp and sp concerns. The brunt of the recent language planning research and theory derives from experiences with Hebrew, Hindi, Indonesian, Norwegian, and Turkish. Future research and theory would benefit greatly from giving similar attention to Amharic, Hausa, Khmer, Filipino, Swahili, and Vietnamese.[10] All in all, however, it will benefit most from being useful. Language planning is the (or at least a) major future field for the sociology of language precisely because it encompasses theoretical, applied, and comparative dimensions. I expect that we will hear a lot about it and learn a lot more in connection with it during the decade ahead.

Concluding Sentiments: What *Is* the Sociology of Language and What Is It Good For?

I have stressed, in most of my work and in the foregoing remarks, those aspects of the sociology of language that are derived from Whorfianism or from the stimulating dialectic with Whorfianism. The results of such an emphasis are both interesting and useful, but they do not really capture the full flavor of all of the sociology of language today. Actually, I would say that my interests and approach represent a sociological sociology of language. As such, they do not fairly sample either linguistic sociology of language (Labov, 1972; Shuy, 1972), ethnographic sociology of language (Hymes, 1974; Gumperz, 1971), or psychological sociology of language (Ervin-Tripp, 1973; Lambert, 1972).

In the dozen years since the Bloomington meeting, the sociology of language has become a discipline at the very most and a recognized area of specialization at the very least. It has two journals (*Language in Society, International Journal of the Sociology of Language*); two newsletters (*Sociolinguistic Newsletter, Language Planning Newsletter*); an international association that holds meetings every four years in different parts of the world (Section on Sociolinguistics of the International Sociological Association); sessions devoted to it at a large number of linguistic society meetings, sociology society meetings, and anthropology society meetings; doctoral programs devoted to it at a few major universities; and, finally, graduate level courses and Ph.D. dissertation supervision opportunities at universities all over the United States and Canada and in a growing number of other countries.

The fiscal crunch that has hit North American universities (and probably those elsewhere as well) in the past few years has hit the sociology of language at a very early stage of its academic development. When infants are deprived of appropriate nourishment and stimulation during certain early critical periods of development, they frequently remain retarded or disadvantaged for the rest of their lives. In the case of the sociology of language there is the danger that the field may long (or always) remain a one- or two-course area of graduate specialization, primarily for linguistic students, i.e., for students whose exposure to the social sciences (theory, findings, and methods) is also minimal at best. Indeed, there is the very definite danger that most interested students will be insufficiently trained for the amount and variety of work that there is to be done in the sociology of language today and tomorrow. Summer linguistic institutes are a good way of partly overcoming this deficiency. Indeed, just as these institutes see it as their duty to offer other specialized courses that many universities can no longer afford to sponsor individually because of their limited enrollment potential, so should they offer more advanced sociolinguistic courses, on a regular basis, for the benefit of the great majority of interested students who can never get more than one or two sociolinguistic courses at their own campuses.

Even from a brief and obviously selective review such as the foregoing, it should be clear that there are certain sociolinguistic emphases that constitute the main contributions of the sociology of language regardless of one's perspective within that field. It is these contributions, some of them to linguistics, some to sociology, and some to the world of applied concerns, that ultimately guarantee that there will be a productive tomorrow for this field, if students can only obtain the training that such contributions require.

What Does the Sociology of Language Have to Offer to the Language Sciences?

1. The concept of unitary languages ("the X language," "the Y language") is either a myth, a gross simplification, or a prescriptive value position relative to the true complexity of language use. In reality we all utilize (both productively and receptively) a repertoire of varieties (and/or languages), which may differ from and interpenetrate each other quite radically, and which are normatively allocated to recognized functions.

2. The characteristics of the varieties we utilize (their "purity," standardization, elaboration, and even their most structural traits) are socially influenced as well as socially evaluated and, therefore, subject to further social influences.

3. The (alterable) functional allocation of varieties (relative to roles, situations, domains, etc.) defines the range of the generally unconscious communicative competence of the native speaker and, therefore, the (alterable) social grammar of his language use.

4. Languages and varieties are best learned and taught when fully contextualized, i.e., via real communication involving real roles, situations, domains, etc. Native languages and second languages, lingua francas and local/national languages, all are learned best and most

fully when they are put to real (i.e., to contextualized) communicative use.

What Does the Sociology of Language Have to Offer to the Social Sciences?

5. Languages and societies are multiply (even though not tightly) interdependent. They do not change at similar rates or to similar degrees but their interdependence involves them in both basic processes of human grouping and human self-identification.

6. Language boundary definitions are very worthwhile clues as to network or community boundary definitions. Changes in the one are often indicative of changes in the other. Similarly, societal definitions of the routines of daily life and their role boundaries often also have language usage counterparts that are important aids both to members and to researchers.

7. Group identity and group membership are manipulable and influenceable factors. They can both be consciously influenced, broadened, narrowed, and altered. Language can be similarly influenced with respect to its group-symbolic validity and inclusivity.

8. Change in functional allocation of languages and language change *per se* represent powerful untapped fields for social science inquiry into community diversity, change in power relationships, and social change more generally.

What Does the Sociology of Language Have to Offer to the World of Applied Affairs?

Many of the basic topics of the sociology of language correspond to important applied areas: native language teaching, second language teaching, bilingual education, status planning (for change in functional allocation of languages), corpus planning, nationality or ethnicity planning, and sociocultural planning more generally. All of these are areas of social need, occupational opportunity, and intellectual promise. In conjunction with them and with the parental basic disciplines, the sociology of language will not only be around tomorrow but will be put to good use.

NOTES

1. I have indicated extensively before (1960, 1972) that this line of thinking was by no means original to Whorf and that it stems very directly

from at least a century of prior Herderian, Humboldtian, and Boazian influences in social philosophy, folkloristics, linguistics, and anthropology. Certainly, it can also be traced back far earlier in the West (to Classical Greek and Hebrew sources) as well as in the East (to Indian and Chinese sources). In Whorf's day linguistic relativism was certainly also subscribed to and articulated by Sapir and Benedict, and it fit in harmoniously with then current emphases on cultural relativism. Nevertheless, to dub the stress on causal linguistic relativism as the *Whorfian* hypothesis is no more incorrect than to acknowledge that "Columbus discovered America." Regardless of the significant contemporaries who aided and abetted him in his views and formulations and who simultaneously advanced such ideas themselves, and regardless of the very substantial earlier intellectual tradition out of which these views and formulations doubtlessly grew, it was primarily Whorf, rather than others, who articulated, developed, organized, and presented these views in sufficiently telling fashion during the 1930s and 40s so as to leave an intellectual legacy with which the language sciences of the 50s and 60s (including their nascent sociolinguistic component) had to deal.

2. There is now much evidence that Whorf's understanding of Hopi was often quite deficient, but that is quite beside the point. Even if his English translations of the embedded desiderata of the Hopi verb system or noun system had been correct, there would still be absolutely no reason to assume that such translations accurately reflect what is "going through the native speaker's mind." The fact that the Spanish (and the Yiddish) for "I dropped the book" literally translates into English as "The book fell out to me from the hands" is no indication at all of the complexity–simplicity (let alone of the active–passive nature) of that sentence for the native speaker.

3. The view that language structure must be investigated more broadly, as is implied by "language in society" and similar figures of speech, may also be considered a healthy by-product of Whorfianism. Certainly there are exciting efforts within linguistics proper, in the study of both syntax and semantics, that seek to view aspects of the social setting as part of the linguistic structure requiring explanation. Admirable and welcome as these efforts are, they must be viewed as only part of the total sociolinguistic enterprise rather than its sum and substance.

4. Here and elsewhere, I follow the American usage in accord with which *bilingualism* and *bilingual* subsume *multilingualism* and *multilingual*.

5. The work of Kachru (1975 and earlier) and several others is informative and extremely sensitive in pointing out the ways in which English is undergoing local variation as a result of its widespread use among large populations for (almost) none of whom it is the native language and (almost) all of whom share another language as a mother tongue. Further evidence on the continued development of varieties of nonstandard (or weakly monitored) English is available "in bulk" from the studies of pidginization and creolization. Although both these trends may be expected to continue, the value and the volume of reasonably standard English is sufficiently great and suffi-

ciently organized to obviate any danger of the falling apart of standard English into a variety of separately normified and mutually unintelligible new languages.

6. Anthropological theory with respect to ethnicity is certainly in a better state of repair than is its sociological counterpart. Nevertheless, what is sorely needed cannot be derived from anthropological perspective alone since that perspective is so firmly and fully embedded in ethnicity as a constant concern and context that it is difficult to conceptualize it separately from (and, therefore, to study it both when related to and when independent of) other bases of human aggregation. Anthropology at least recognizes that ethnicity is an open system and that all other bases of human aggregation (e.g., social class, occupational group, religious group membership) can become ethnicized, just as ethnic groups can become de-ethnicized and transmuted into less-"heritable," less-ascribed, and more-attained bases of human aggregation (see the work by Barth and by Depres). When, why, and how such transformations occur are things I would not expect anthropological theory alone to indicate, if for no other reason than anthropology's continued concentration on the small, pre-modern society. Certainly, we lack in the West the "institutes of applied ethnicity" that exist in the Soviet Union and in mainland China, which are engaged not only in monitoring changes in ethnic behaviors (including ethnic sentiments, beliefs, and overt behaviors) in a wide variety of populations, but also in recommending the "making" and "unmaking" of ethnic groups, at least partially on the basis of the evidence that has been gathered. While I do not regret the absence of such ethnographic institutes in the West, I do regret our relative impoverished data and theory in this area.

7. The best way of keeping abreast of this still small but rapidly growing field is to obtain the *Language Planning Newsletter* (Joan Rubin, ed.) published by the Culture Learning Institute, East-West Center, Honolulu, Hawaii. Other good introductions to this field are Rubin and Jernudd (1971) and Fishman (1974).

8. The conclusions enumerated in this section flow primarily from the International Study of Language Planning Process, sponsored by the International Division of the Ford Foundation and directed by Charles A. Ferguson and me (with the participation of Joan Rubin, Bjorn Jernudd, and Jyotirindra Das Gupta) from 1968 to 1972.

9. The absence or presence of force in conjunction with SP is entirely continuous within any society with its absence or presence in connection with the implementation of other central governmental or authoritative planning. Responsiveness to popular opinion, or its absence, and the utilization or disregard of genuine expertise are also very much the same in status planning as they are with respect to other important decisions and operations. Language planning in general and status planning in particular should not, therefore, be confused with thought control or totalitarianism any more than is educational planning or family planning. Each society engages in planning,

implementation, and evaluation in ways that are concordant with its own sociopolitical traditions, and language planning does not differ from other types of planning in this respect.

10. We are also still abysmally ignorant of recent Soviet and Chinese experiences with language planning. Not only is there a wealth of such experience, but also knowledge of successes and failures within totalitarian contexts are absolutely vital if truly general theory and practice of language planning are to come into being.

REFERENCES

Bender, M.; Ferguson, Charles A.; and Cooper, Robert. 1976. *Language in Ethiopia.* London: Oxford University Press.

Cooper, Robert A.; Fishman, Joshua A.; et al. MS. The sociology of English as an additional language.

Das Gupta, Jyotirindra, et al. MS. Language planning processes.

Ervin-Tripp, Susan M. 1973. *Language Acquisition and Communicative Choice.* Stanford: Stanford University Press.

Fellman, Jack. 1973. *The Revival of a Classical Tongue.* The Hague: Mouton.

Fishman, Joshua A. 1960. The systematization of the Whorfian hypothesis. *Behavioral Science* 5:323–79.

———. 1968. *Language Loyalty in the United States.* The Hague: Mouton.

———. 1971. Ein Mehrfaktoren und Mehrebenansatz zum Studium von Sprachplanungs Prozessen. In Roif Kjolseth and Fritz Sach, eds., *Zur Sociologie der Sprache,* pp. 206–13. Opladen: West Deutscher Verlag.

———. 1972. Sociocultural organization: language constraints and language reflections. In *The Sociology of Language,* pp. 155–71. Rowley, Mass.: Newbury House.

———. 1973a. *Language and Nationalism.* Rowley, Mass.: Newbury House.

———. 1973b. Language modernization and planning in comparison with other types of national modernization and planning. *Language in Society* 2:23–44.

———. 1973c. The International Research Project on Language Planning Processes (IRPLPP). In Joan Rubin and Roger Shuy, eds., *Language Planning: Current Issues and Research,* pp. 83–85. Washington, D.C.: Georgetown University Press.

———. 1975. Some implications of "The International Research Project on Language Planning Processes (IRPLPP)" for sociolinguistic surveys. In Sirarpi Ohannessian, et al., eds., *Language Surveys in Developing Nations,* pp. 209–20. Arlington: Center for Applied Linguistics.

———. 1976. *Bilingual Education: An International Sociological Perspective.* Rowley, Mass.: Newbury House.

———. MS. Knowing, using, and liking English as an additional language.

In R. L. Cooper, J. A. Fishman, et al., *The Sociology of English as an Additional Language.*

————, ed. 1974. *Advances in Language Planning.* The Hague: Mouton.

Fishman, Joshua A.; Cooper, R. C.; and Ma, R. 1971. *Bilingualism in the Barrio.* Bloomington, Ind.: Language Sciences.

Gage, William, and Ohannessian, Sirarpi. 1974. ESOL enrollments throughout the world. *Linguistic Reporter* 16: no. 9, 13–16.

Gumperz, John J. 1971. *Language in Social Groups.* Stanford: Stanford University Press.

Harrison, William, et al. 1975. *English Language Policy Survey of Jordan: A Case Study in Language Planning.* Arlington: Center for Applied Linguistics.

Haugen, Einar. 1956. *Bilingualism in the Americas: Bibliography and Research Guide.* University, Ala.: American Dialect Society.

Hymes, Dell. 1974. *Foundations in Sociolinguistics: An Ethnographic Approach.* Philadelphia: University of Pennsylvania Press.

Kachru, Braj. 1975. English in South Asia. In J. A. Fishman, ed., *Advances in the Study of Societal Multilingualism,* vol. I. The Hague: Mouton.

Kloss, Heinz. 1975. *The Linguistic Composition of the Nations of the World, Vol. I: Western, Central and South Asia.* Quebec: International Research Center on Bilingualism.

Labov, William. 1972. *Sociolinguistic Patterns.* Philadelphia: University of Pennsylvania Press.

Ladefoged, Peter, et al. 1968. *Language in Uganda.* London: Oxford University Press.

Lambert, Wallace E. 1972. *Language, Psychology and Culture.* Stanford: Stanford University Press.

Lewis, Glyn. 1972. *Multilingualism in the Soviet Union.* The Hague: Mouton.

Lieberson, Stanley. 1970. *Language and Ethnic Relations in Canada.* New York: Wiley.

Nahirny, Vladimir, and Fishman, Joshua A. MS. The Sociology of Ethnicity.

Niyakawa-Howard, Agnes. 1968. A psycholinguistic study of the Whorfian Hypothesis based on the Japanese passive. Honolulu: Educational Research and Development Center, University of Hawaii (RP: OE–3260–2–68).

Ohannessian, Sirarpi, et al. Forthcoming. Language in Zambia. London: Oxford University Press.

Polome, Edgar, et al. Forthcoming. *Language in Tanzania.* London: Oxford University Press.

Rubin, Joan. 1968. *National Bilingualism in Paraguay.* The Hague: Mouton.

Rubin, Joan, and Jernudd, Bjorn, eds. 1971. *Can Language Be Planned?* Honolulu: East-West Center Press.

Scotton, Carol. 1972. *Choosing a Lingua Franca in an African Capital.* Edmonton and Champaign: Linguistic Research.

Shuy, Roger W. 1972. The sociolinguistics program at Georgetown University. (Georgetown University) Language and Linguistics Working Papers 5:1–7.

Tabouret-Keller, Andree. 1972. A contribution to the sociological study of language maintenance and language shift. In J. A. Fishman, ed., *Advances in the Sociology of Language*, vol. II, pp. 365–76. The Hague: Mouton.

Tauli, Valter. 1974. The theory of language planning. In J. A. Fishman, ed., *Advances in Language Planning*, pp. 48–67. The Hague: Mouton.

Weinreich, Uriel. 1953. *Language in Contact, Findings and Problems*. New York: Linguistic Circle of New York.

Whiteley, W. H., et al. 1975. *Language in Kenya*. London: Oxford University Press.

Topics in

Lexical Semantics

Charles J. Fillmore

Lecture One

1. My task in these lectures is to offer an informal and intuitive
approach to the description of word meaning and text meaning. My
main goal is that of presenting a uniform conceptual framework for discussing the meanings of words, the construction of sentence readings,
the interpretation of texts, and the processes of expression and comprehension.

I believe that the linguist, in his consideration of a number of issues
in semantic theory, can profit from the exercise of examining these issues
within a larger view of language production and language comprehension. Previous traditions of semantic analysis have tended to be limited
in their subject matter because of their commitment to lesser goals.
Some linguists—Coseriu, for example—have gone to great pains to
ensure that they are limiting themselves to what is exclusively and
purely linguistic, free of contamination from knowledge about cultures,
belief systems, or facts about the world. The anthropological or so-called
cognitive semantics tradition has concentrated on the discovery and
display of systems of discriminations in taxonomies, and their effort at
finding the simplest representations of such systems has presumably
been motivated by the desire to capture the culturally unique basis of a
given taxonomy in a given linguistic community. Those structuralist tra-

ditions in which the emphasis was that of finding a core meaning for any given linguistic form seem to have had as their motivation that of accounting for the maintenance of a single linguistic form through time. In the generativist tradition, the concern has been largely a notational one, motivated by the desire to have, in the end, exactly the right number of features (or abstract predicates, depending on which branch of the tradition you are considering) that would simultaneously serve as counters in a system of semantic rules for the language—rules about truth and synonymy, for example—and as the basis for theorizing about the language-universal foundations of semantics. By contrast, the task I am taking on is that of locating a concern with meaning within a larger theory of language processing; the aspect that I will concentrate on here is that of text comprehension.

I would like to begin my discussion with an examination of the various steps in the comprehension process. One pastime indulged in by people working in text interpretation is that of choosing or inventing some text that offers particularly serious problems for the theory and challenging each other to show what can be done with it. The result of such demonstrations is usually—and justly—a sense of gloom about the prospects of an ultimate theory of texts. Since my interest, for now, is in discovering the steps in the interpretation process, without worrying too much about how in the end everything can be accounted for, I offer my example of a particularly troublesome text in good conscience. I do not pretend to be ready to talk about the final form of the correct theory.

My text is easy to understand; its complexity is in the description of the understanding process. It is taken from a recent issue of *Signature*, a magazine sent every month to holders of the Diners Club credit card. The article, clearly intended to be humorous, dealt with the public-speaking career of a professional baseball player named Pete Rose. It was mainly a collection of funny things that had happened in Rose's off-season public life. I will concentrate on just one sentence from the article, but I will tell you something about the preceding context.

Rose was giving a speech at an athletic club in Cincinnati. Since Cincinnati is Rose's home, his four-year-old son was in attendance. While Rose was speaking, unknown to him, the child moved up to the speaker's table and stood next to him. Rose told a joke, there was laughter, and after the laughter there was a moment of silence. Here, now, is the sentence I wish to bring to your attention:

> At precisely that moment a small but amplified voice notified the entire room, in the most lucid of idioms, of a common childhood emergency.

All mature native understanders of current English will know, of course, that the small voice was the child's; that there must have been a microphone at the table, which was responsible for amplifying the child's voice; that it was because of this amplification that the entire room got "notified"; that it was not, in fact, the "entire room" but rather the people in the room who heard the child's utterance; and that the author is not really using the word "notified" in strict literalness, given what we believe about the possible intentions of four-year-old children. We know furthermore, from personal experience, what this childhood emergency must have been; and from the phrase "in the most lucid of idioms" we even have a fairly good idea of the actual words the child might have used.

That is not all that we know about this piece of text. On another level, we have an idea why this episode was included in the article. That is, we know why people might consider it funny. We know what kinds of experiences are embarrassing; we know that when they are somebody else's experiences rather than our own, we find them amusing; and we know that the embarrassment is not serious, and that therefore our pleasure is forgivable if the embarrassing act is performed by a small child.

On yet another level, we know why the author described the episode as indirectly as he did. He did not come right out and tell us what the child said; he made us figure it out for ourselves. The effect here is accounted for by what Berkeley graduate student Robert Gaskins refers to as the Little Jack Horner theory of wit. Young Horner, on discovering the plum, was delighted mainly with himself, and only secondarily, if at all, with the baker. ("He put in his thumb, And pulled out a plum, And said 'What a good boy am I!'") If the plum had been sitting right on top of the pie, discoverable without any cleverness or effort on the diner's part, the experience could not have been half so rewarding.

2.   As this exercise has taught us, whenever we are interpreting what somebody has said or written, there are four questions we have to answer for ourselves:

> (I)   What did he say?
> (II)   What was he talking about?
> (III)   Why did he bother to say it?
> (IV)   Why did he say it in the way that he said it?

Only the first of these questions—"What did he say?"—is among the traditional concerns of linguistics. Linguists professionally pay attention to what people have said, and they can more or less feel that their work is done when they have devised a system of categories and contrasts, a notation, and, possibly, a generative theory, which will enable them to make systematic statements about each part of what has been said.

The third question—"Why did he say it?"—brings us into the province of speech-act theory and the logic of conversation. (If the speaker said something, there must have been a reason for him to say it. He may have wanted us to know the information he was giving us, for example. If so, he must have assumed that we did not already know it. Since he said it at the time that he said it, it must have been relevant to something that was just then in the air. Thus goes the kind of reasoning that one engages in in the various versions of speech-act theory.) The fourth question—"Why did he say it in the way that he said it?"— brings us to one of the concerns of rhetoric.

I wish to focus on the second question—"What was he talking about?" By that I mean, not simply what was the topic of the discourse, or of the portion of the discourse in question, but rather, what can we say about the "scene" or "history" or "situation" or "world" or "image" or whatever the speaker intended the hearer to create at this point in the discourse.

In giving an informal analysis of the interpretation process for our sample sentence, we might say the following. The preceding part of the text mentioned an athletic club banquet and identified our hero as the guest of honor, the after-dinner speaker; and we know something of what this must have been like from our own experiences in the world. A sentence in the text brought our attention to the child. We know about children's voices, so our awareness of the presence of the child makes it possible to know right away whose "small voice" the author identified. Our knowledge of microphones and their use helps us make sense of the reference to amplification; and we know that loud noises can be heard at greater distances, and hence potentially by more people, than soft ones. Our expectations about the possible intentions of four-year-old children and about the kinds of relationships a small child can hold with other people enable us to guess reliably that the verb "notify" in the text is being used in a nonserious way. Our experience of childhood embarrassments and their urgency, a part, surely, of our general belief systems about very young children, lets us readily know what the child's problem was; and our knowledge of alternative ways of talking about human body functions, and their different social valuations, makes us aware that some of these locutions are more straightforward, more "lucid," than others; and hence we can guess something about what might have been said on this occasion.

3. A question we need to consider at this point, of course, is whether there is any way of talking about such things within linguistics; that is, whether, within linguistics proper we have any business talking about settings, beliefs, expectations, memories of personal experiences, and the roles these matters play in the process of figuring out what somebody is talking about.

The argument that such questions are proper questions for linguistics can be based on the following facts: first, that some of the judgments and interpretation strategies that make up a part of this process are related in clear ways to choices of specific linguistic forms and categories; second, that there are sometimes differences from language to language in the ways in which linguistic material maps onto detailed images or experiences; and third, that it is possible to make use of many of these notions in formulating generalizations about the text interpretation strategies that people use. The arguments are, then, that the facts are lined with the choice of linguistic material, that they can vary from language to language, and that they sometimes permit summarizing generalizations—matters that linguists, if not "linguistics" in some narrowing definition, ought to be able to deal with.

We make use of many kinds of judgments and awarenesses whenever we interpret a language text. We need to be aware of the nature of the ongoing communication act. We need to make use of our knowledge of whether the communication is urgent or playful, whether or not it is accompanied by actions on the part of the participants, and so on. In the present case, for example, we make critical use of the knowledge that the text is a report of supposedly humorous events, is intended to entertain, and is meant to be read at leisure.

At any point in the discourse the interpreter needs to be aware of scenes or images or memories that are, so to speak, "currently activated," a point argued at some length by Wallace Chafe in his recent work on consciousness and language.[1] We were told early in the *Signature* article that the child was at the banquet; just before our target sentence, however, we are told that the child was standing next to Rose, and that Rose was unaware of his presence. We have in our minds a kind of outline image of an after-dinner speech setting, with the relatively clear parts out of the outline being the father and son standing next to each other.

We sometimes have to appeal to memories of experiences, sometimes to ongoing experiences, sometimes to procedures for acquiring experiences. Memories of inconvenient childhood experiences and the attendant sense of helplessness and dependence have to be available to us for understanding what is going on in this story. Awareness of current experiences is necessary for the understanding of sentences like "Put this one over here and that one over there." We have to notice what the speaker is doing while he is talking in order to know what he is telling us to do. And procedures for acquiring experiences are necessary for understanding a sentence in James McCawley's cookbook, which instructs the reader to knead a certain pastry dough "until it has the texture of an earlobe."[2]

We often have to have knowledge of what a number of workers in artificial intelligence call "scenarios" or "scripts,"[3] conventional or familiar routines or behavior sequences in terms of which we analyze and individuate larger events by seeing smaller events as parts of them. We have a scenario, for example, for the kind of after-dinner speech that is most likely to be given before an athletic club. We know that most commonly it would consist of, or at least include, lots of jokes, that the jokes would be followed by pauses during which the audience would laugh, that the general mood, for the ideal after-dinner speech at any rate, is one of jovial good humor, and so on.

And we have to have available to us certain strategies for constructing, from the pieces of a text, from our knowledge of the world, and from our estimates of the author's or speaker's purposes, some single coherent view of what is going on, some possibly complex but unified scene or story or world that we would recognize has been matched to this particular text.

4. This series of lectures, somebody is surely eager to remind me, has been given the title "Topics in Lexical Semantics." My emphasis, in fact, will be on the use of some of the notions I have been talking about in the description of individual lexical items. Lexical items will have to have their meanings described, if I am right, in ways that will show something of their contribution to a process of the kind I have been talking about. I can begin to show you what I mean by that by examining some of the things we have to know about the English verb *write* in order to understand sequences containing it, knowledge on the basis of which we can construct text meanings and make judgments about text coherence.

The verb *write* in what we might call its "prototype" meaning depicts an activity in which somebody is guiding a pointed trace-leaving implement across a surface. I suggest—and I think that there will be a general agreement on this—that this prototype scene associated with the verb is more or less what is basically understood when other information is not provided. Skywriting and writing in the air with one's fingers are departures from this prototype and would be understood as the intended scene for a text only if there was explicit information to that effect in the text or if the interpreter had very special knowledge about the context.

The prototype scene associated with *write*, then, contains the individual that does the writing, the implement with which the individual writes, the surface on which the writing is done, and the product of a writing act—that is, some configuration of marks on the surface.

If the only thing we know about a text is that it contains the verb *write*, then the only associated scene we can construct for it is a kind of simple outline scene with positions for the entities I mentioned but with none of the details filled in. We never, of course, have only one word to go on: the word is embedded in a text.

Suppose that I say to you, "Harry has been writing." You will know that the scene I have asked you to create is being presented as an event in the real world, and that I expect you to know who Harry is. And so the writing scene you create in your mind is one in which Harry is the one who is doing the writing, the one who is guiding the trace-leaving implement. A part of this depends on the fact that I used a progressive form. If I had said, "Harry wrote," you would feel that I had not quite finished saying what I had planned to say, because with the preterit we have the idea of a completed act rather than a time-extended activity, and you have the right to expect some indication of what it is that Harry wrote. If I had said, "Harry writes," you would have the right to assume that I thought I was answering a question about what Harry does for a living. As these observations indicate, the knowledge that users of a language have about individual words may create different scenes for different linguistic contexts—differences illustrated here by choices of tense and aspect. And, elements that are within specific grammatical relations with the word—such as the subject of the verb—contribute in specific ways in providing details to the scene that the interpreter constructs for himself.

It may well have been, of course, that the knowledge that we already share about Harry will give you a framework for fitting in this new information about Harry's having been writing. Suppose you know, for example, that Harry is in the middle of his dissertation and that he always does his writing at a typewriter. Then, if you know a few other things about him, it might be quite appropriate for you to give the responses that show up in the following dialogues: I say to you, "Harry has been writing," and you say, "Has he finished chapter seven yet?"

Or I say to you, "Harry has been writing," and you say, "I thought his typewriter was broken." These second-speaker responses can be seen as showing how the outline scene presented with the sentence can get fitted into specific kinds of belief-worlds on the interpreter's part.

If we do not have ready-made scenes into which to integrate the outline scene provided by a text or piece of text, then there are many "positions" in the text-associated "scene" that are left blank, so to speak. I believe that one way of exploring the meaning of a word is to consider what questions are relevant at the point when we have received and processed the latest bit of text, and the extent to which these questioning possibilities are determined by the presence and the selection of the word in question. The questions of the sort I have in mind are those designed to fill in the blanks of the outline scene that is in the process of being created. If *write* has the interpretation I have given it, then it follows that we would need very special contexts before we could believe we were talking coherently in the following examples: Somebody says to me, "Harry has been writing," and I say, "What time is it?" or I say, "When do you think I should go home?" Questions that do make sense, however, are questions like, "What did he write?" or "What was he writing on?" or "What was he writing with?" These are questions that identify positions in the schematic scene activated by *write*.

The points that I have made so far, I am sure, do not quite ring true, and that is because something has been left out of the description of this verb that is absolutely essential to its interpretation. The prototype scene associated with writing does indeed involve somebody guiding a trace-leaving implement across a surface, but it carries more with it than just that. Whenever we use the verb *write*, it is also understood that the *product* of the act of writing is something *linguistic*—that is, is something that represents linguistic forms. Since that is a necessary part of the scene associated with *write*, it follows that we could also ask, coherently, when told that Harry has been writing, such questions as: "What language was he writing in?" or "What does what he wrote mean?"—in short, we can ask about anything that is a necessary part of any scene in which a sample of written communication is a part. This last aspect of *write* distinguishes the English verb from the Japanese verb *kaku*, which is the usual—and usually correct—translation of *write*. The Japanese verb does not dictate the same assumptions about the nature of the product. The result of an act of *kaku*-ing can be a word or sentence or letter, or, just as well, a painting or sketch or doodle.[4]

I suggest that the first two tests I proposed for the relevance of talk about text/scene correspondences are satisfied. The first was that the choice and character of particular scenes could be related to the choice of particular elements; the second was that languages could be shown to differ from each other in ways that can be made clear by appealing to scenes and properties of scenes. For the first of these there was the choice of the verb and a given tense and aspect, with a particular grammatical subject; for the second we have the difference between the English and the Japanese verb.

5.   The slogan that goes with the approach to semantics that I am taking is this: Meanings are relativized to scenes. I am using the word *scene* in this discussion in a technical sense that includes its familiar visual meaning, but much more as well. I mean by it any coherent individuatable perception, memory, experience, action, or object. Some scenes are made up out of other scenes; others cannot be analyzed, but must merely be known, that is, can only be demonstrated or experienced, not explained. The point I am making is that for a great many words and phrases in our language, we can only understand them if we first know something else, and this something else may not be analyzable. If you know what birds look like, then I can identify a certain part of a prototypic bird and tell you that part of it is called its "beak." To understand what is meant by such verbs as *wink, crawl, sneeze, yawn*, etc., you have to know about bodies—especially human bodies—and what kinds of things their owners can do with them, and what kinds of internal things can happen to them. To understand what is meant by *heartburn* you have to have had certain kinds of body experiences; to understand what is meant by *déjà vu* you have to have had certain mental experiences.

A word appearing in a text that is being interpreted by someone who understands the word can be thought of as activating a scene and pointing to a certain part of that scene. *Beak* induces the scene of a bird, and identifies a particular part of the bird.

So far my "scenes" have been static, or nearly so. For many kinds of verbs, or for adjectives indicating temporary states, the word will focus on a single period or stage of a history, but this single period must be understood as a part of a larger scene. It is as if we are looking at a single frame in a filmstrip, but our view takes in, at least in outline, the rest, or part of the rest, of the filmstrip too.

With respect to this last point, consider the following situation: Two identical twins—let us call them Mark and Mike—are patients in a hospital. They are staying in adjacent rooms, and as we walk by their rooms, accompanied by their nurse, we notice that each one is seated on the edge of his bed, in exactly the same position. By coincidence they have both assumed the same postures and they are wearing absolutely identical gowns. Photographs of the two scenes could not be told apart.

The actual visual scenes, then, are indistinguishable. Yet, as the nurse walks by Mark's room, she says, "I see that Mark is able to sit up now"; and as she walks by Mike's room, she says, "I see that Mike is able to sit down now."

To say of Mark that he is sitting up places the scene we have just observed in a history, and a preceding period of that history has Mark lying down; to say of Mike that he is sitting down places what we have observed of Mike in its separate history, and in a preceding period of that history, Mike was standing up.

If we know everything about Mark and Mike that the nurse knows, then we will take her utterance as merely expressing a judgment that we might have made too. If, however, we are merely overhearing her remarks, then we will probably find ourselves exercising our text-processing strategies by passing to the question "Why might she have said that?" We guess that the boys are in the hospital because of some kind of health problem. We know that in a hospital it is more or less taken for granted that the patients' conditions will change, and it is hoped that their conditions will change for the better. These bits of knowledge induce us to create larger scenes in which we see the present scenes as parts. We might conclude that the present positions of these two boys represent improvements in their conditions; and that would get us to believe that Mark was sick with something that made it difficult for him to sit up, and Mike with something that made it difficult for him to sit down. We end up with fairly detailed, but still in outline only, opinions about the hospital stays of these two boys and of the significance of their present states. When later on we learn that one of them has been suffering from mononucleosis and the other from hemorrhoids, we have ready-made frameworks within which to integrate this new information, and we are not likely to be confused about which boy had been suffering which of the two disorders.

Here is another example. The same two brothers, many years later, spend a few hours in San Francisco, separately, but doing essentially the same things. Later that day, Mark writes home, "I spent three hours on land this afternoon," and Mike writes home, "I spent three hours on the ground this afternoon." The actual observations we might have made of these two boys while they were in San Francisco could not have given us a basis for choosing these particular descriptions, yet we know that one of them expressed the outing as an interruption of a sea voyage and the other as an interruption of a period of air travel. We know this because we know that for the sea voyage scene English provides a pair of expressions, "at sea" and "on land," for a particular two-way contrast. Since this is a contrast between mutually exclusive alternating states, since we know that Mark is talking about himself, and since the sentence about his having spent three hours on land is in the past tense, we can assume that he was once again at sea when he wrote the letter. Similar reasoning is appropriate for the two-way contrast "on the ground" and "in the air," expressions relativized to scenes of air travel.

Once again, the comprehension process involved knowing what larger scene the expressions were relative to, what parts of those larger scenes were being focused on, and what further "computing" could be done in creating the larger scene, by considering such things as the use of tenses.

6.   I need to introduce the concepts that I think are necessary for discussing the communication and comprehension processes. I am still finding it difficult to give precise definitions of these notions—and I am appropriately embarrassed by the conclusions that *that* state of affairs invites—and so I will merely try to show you some samples of how I talk about meaning and comprehension.

The meanings of individual lexical items can best be understood in terms of their contributions to the process of interpreting a text. This involves, as I have suggested, much more than the processing of meanings directly provided by the text, but also memories, knowledge, and current perceptions of the interpreter, as well as the application of a set of procedures for determining the basis of the coherence of the text. A word or phrase or sentence or text identifies a scene, and it foregrounds, or highlights, some portion of it. It is to be understood that the identity of a scene can be established at any number of levels; an event, for example, can be seen as composed of a number of subevents and as being a part of some larger event or situation; I allow myself to use the word *scene* for each of these.

Sometimes we can be said to have a scene at the ready, made up of our general knowledge, memories, imaginings, and whatever is currently a part of our conscious awareness; and we can also speak of constructing a scene, and in the act, making sense of what we are reading or what somebody is telling us. The scenes to which the meanings of linguistic forms are said to be relativized are individuated in ways that are partly natural, partly convention, partly idiosyncratic. At any rate, we can speak of the individuatability of scenes in terms of their fit with certain prototypes or paradigm instances. (Much of the work of the Berkeley psychologist Eleanor Rosch can be thought of as being directed toward the discovery of the mechanism of scene formation in my sense; her early research concerned prototype notions of natural kinds, colors, shapes, and basic level artifacts; she is currently considering the question of the ways in which the character and the boundedness of events and situations are determined in the categorization process.[5])

A given real-world scene is perceived according to the degree to which it matches some paradigm or prototype outline scene. Prototype scenes can be thought of as scenes from simple worlds, worlds whose properties simply do not take in all of the facts of the real world. Prototype scenes account for the clearest cases, the best examples. Much of our use of language, however, requires us to use words that activate a prototype scene even though we are talking about something that departs from the prototype. A widow is a woman whose husband has died. The prototype "scenario" for widow does not cover the case of a woman who murdered her husband, or of a woman who had three husbands and now has only two left, or of a woman whose divorce became final on the day of her husband's death. If we do not know whether to use the word *widow* in these cases, it is not because we are unsure of the meaning of the word, but because the prototype scene that provides the setting for our knowledge of the word *widow* simply does not cover all these cases.

A final concept in this survey is what I will be calling "perspective." At any point in a text we are viewing a scene from a particular perspective; that is, while we have the whole scene in view, so to speak, we are focusing on just some portion of it.

The words I intend to use in this discussion, then, include *scene*, *prototype*, *activation*, and *perspective*. A few others will be introduced in some of the later lectures.

7. Earlier I identified a scene in which somebody was acting in such a way as to leave traces on a surface. The English verb *write*, I pointed out, is one that adds to that scene the information that the product is something linguistic. The word *sketch*, by contrast, adds the information that the product is something representational—a sketch, drawing, or diagram of something—and includes the information that the implement used is of a particular kind: it is not, for example, a brush. *Draw* seems to be more or less like *sketch*, but both are different from *paint* since to *paint* (in the use with which the direct object names the *product*) is to produce an artistic object, but not necessarily something

that is representational. And the verb *paint*, as we know, brings special assumptions about the medium. *Printing*, as it is closely related to our prototype scene—as opposed to what one does with a printing press— requires the understanding that the product is made up of alphabetic elements of a particular form. There is a general verb *write*, but in two-way contrast between *printing* and *writing* the word *write* refers to the act of producing a product of the cursive or nonprinted form.

Only when the product is a representation of the writer's name, in a written rather than a printed form, and in an individualized form, can the verb *sign* be used. Further, only when the action is that of producing a sample of one's signature for the sake of somebody who wants it as a souvenir can the verb *autograph* be used.

The product of an act of writing can be named with a noun, and when this is done a new scene is introduced, the scene associated with the product. It can be the name of any of a number of linguistic-product units, such as word, phrase, sentence, paragraph; or book, article, poem, essay; or letter, preface, dedication, obituary, or confession, and a very large number of others; or it can be a *signature*, that is, an individualized rendering of the writer's name, or an *autograph*, that is, a signature that has been written as a memorabilium.

There are verbs that increase the detail of the dynamic aspect of the scene, that bring along some understanding, for example, of the manner of writing. These will include *scribble* and *scrawl*, which indicate a messy or careless manner of writing; *print*, which indicates a careful manner of writing plus the notion mentioned earlier of the nature of the product; and *jot down*, which indicates the brief recording of a short text.

Other verbs make specific the kind of implement that is being used. This is true of verbs taken directly from the names of the implements, such as *pen* and *pencil*, as well as the verb *type*, which indicates the use of a typewriter.

Some verbs activate scenes with the necessary presence of a source or model of what is produced. With *transcribe* the model is spoken; with *copy* the model is graphic, and not necessarily linguistic; with *trace* the model is understood as being directly beneath a translucent surface.

For all of these verbs the grammatical subject in the underlying form is the Agent, the person who performs the trace-leaving act. In many cases the direct object is some description of the product; thus: "He penned his answer," "He scribbled a poem," "He drew a picture," "He signed his name," and "He wrote his name." In the case of *write* it is possible to use the verb without an explicit product name if the product is understood to be a letter and as long as it is understood that the letter is intended to be sent to some person; in that case the indirect object phrase can stand as the only explicit complement to the verb. Thus, in "She wrote to me twice" or "I'll write you more about this later on," it is understood that the product of the writing is a letter. This choice is not possible for "He drew me" or "He scribbled to me" or any of the others we have considered.

In the case of *sign*, the direct object can be the name of the document that in some way becomes official as a result of the signing act. In this case the product is understood to be a signature, but a further aspect of the total scene is that the writing of a signature onto a particular document made that document valid. Thus I can say, "I signed the contract," "The king refused to sign the treaty," and even—since an autographed book is something special—"He signed my copy of his book." Notice that in each case the product is the writer's signature.

The verb *autograph* is one with the notion of signature built in. In the case of *sign* you can say "He signed his name" but not "He signed his signature"; with *write* you can say either "He wrote his name" or "He wrote his signature." In the case of *autograph*, however, there is no way of expressing the nature of the product, but only the name of the object onto which the signature was written. Thus we can say "He autographed my football" or "the menu" or "my copy of his book."

Sometimes the purpose of writing one's signature is extremely specific, and in that case there may be a separate technical term just for the act of signing. An example is *endorse*, as in the phrase "endorse a check."

One highly specific writing-act verb is *address*, which can take as its direct object only nouns naming things that can be mailed, like letters, packages, and postcards. It means, of course, to write on each of these the destination of the thing. *Addressing* something is specific not only with respect to the content of the product, but also with respect to the purpose: thus I am not *addressing* an income tax form or a job application when I fill in my name and address.

8.   These examples tell us something of what is required of a notation system for the lexicon. We need to know for each word what scene, or cluster of linked scenes, is to be activated by it; how, with a given meaning relative to a given scene, it is to be combined with other lexical elements, and what grammatical relations these will hold with each other. And this, as we have seen in the simple case of *write*, must have added to it some account of the effect of the choices of particular tenses

and aspects. For example, there is a sense of *write* which designates an activity; it is this that is compatible with the progressive aspect. There is another sense of the verb in which it designates an act; it is this that is compatible with the preterit tense. There is another sense of the verb in which it designates a profession or avocation; and this is compatible with, among others, the simple present tense. This sort of information, I suggest, is to be given in connection with the description of the linguistic choices available for individual scenes. From that it will follow, through an understanding of the semantic force of the tenses and aspects, which of these are compatible with which senses of the verbs.

The theory of the lexicon will specify for each verb, with respect to each scene to which it is relevant, what we might call, following Tesnière and a number of European lexicologists,[6] its "valence," the concept of valence being extended to include simultaneously reference to the surface form of sentences containing the verb and to the elements and aspects of the associated scenes. In the writing scene, for example, there are the writer, the implement, the surface, and the product. For all of these verbs, the writer appears as the subject. For some the product is realized as the direct object; for others the direct object is the name of the receiving surface. The implement is introduced into sentences related to the writing scene, if at all, by means of a *with*-phrase. For a number of special scenes, in which the writing act serves some larger purpose having its own, dominating scene, the structuring of the sentence can depend on facts about this larger scene: here I have in mind the indirect object structure with *writing* understood as *letter writing*.

Another part of the details of a "valence" description corresponds to what are sometimes called "selection restrictions." That is, some words are limited to highly specific scenes, and for that reason the other words in the structure have to be of a limited sort. I would introduce such information as a description of the scene rather than as a special kind of relationship holding between words or word classes in given grammatical constructions. I will have more to say about this in the next lecture.

9. In later lectures I will say something about the semantic role of subjects and objects associated with a verb; the relative saliency of aspects of scenes that determine which parts of a scene get realized as which kinds of grammatical constituent; the relation of lexically determined scenes to immediate context, and hence to questions of deixis and pragmatics; the performance of this kind of semantics in the de-

scription of traditional semantic notions; a survey of lexical domains; and some concluding predictions and confessions about the future of semantic research within this framework.

Lecture Two

1. Jeffery Paige and Herbert A. Simon, in their paper "Cognitive processes in solving algebra word problems,"[7] have pointed out three different strategies by which students interpret and 'solve' algebra problems formulated in words. I believe that from their results we can see something of the ways in which ordinary discourse is understood. This will be a fairly clear illustration, though with a slightly unnatural text, of some of the points I was making in Lecture One.

Here is an example of one of the problems discussed in their article. Pay close attention.

> A board was sawed into two pieces. One piece was two-thirds as long as the whole board and was exceeded in length by the second piece by 4 feet. How long was the board before it was cut?

The various strategies that Paige and Simon found students using for solving this problem drew differently on the scene-constructing principles I spoke about in the first lecture.

Students' responses to this problem were of four kinds, one being, of course, to give up. The three more interesting responses came from people who, in their opinion at least, knew what to do. Students in the first of these groups gave the answer as *minus twelve feet*. They formulated the set of relationships given in the text as a linear equation, with x as the unknown length of the original board, and then solved for x. One of the pieces, the text tells us, is two-thirds the length of the original board; its length is $2x/3$. The other piece, then, is $x/3$. Since the piece that is two-thirds the length of the original board is four feet shorter than the other one, the equation we need must be

$$2x/3 + 4 = x/3$$

Solving for x gives us -12.

The students who followed this first strategy did what they learned to do in mathematics lessons, and they were able to do so by suspending any inclination to interpret the text in an ordinary, everyday way. Mathematicians, of course, need to develop precisely that ability. A young student who took this first approach may become a fine mathematician some day, but maybe not a particularly good engineer.

The second strategy was to take the text as a description of some possible scene, and to see how things work out in the mentally constructed world containing this scene. This process cannot be carried out, since it requires that there be two board segments each of which is longer than the other. The response made by students who used this strategy was that the problem was unsolvable. The problem supposes things that cannot be. The user of the second strategy is a careful reader and a visualizer. He may become a good philosopher. In philosophy you have to learn to read carefully and to consider whether what you read is believable.

The third strategy is to assume that the teacher or experimenter is presenting the problem in good faith, free of tricks and deceit, and therefore assume, perhaps without even noticing the contradictions in the text, that the words "is exceeded by" were intended to be "exceeded." The answer given by the follower of this strategy is *twelve feet*. The strategy is to figure out what the speaker is driving at, to construct the scene you think he wants you to construct, and to proceed accordingly. A person who does so—whom we can call a cooperative visualizer—will make a good engineer. A good engineer can figure out what you need even if your description of what you need is flawed.

It is this last strategy—one that in this case gives a "wrong" answer—that is characteristic of the kind of comprehension process that is most typical for language understanding in normal settings. You hear what a person says, you try to figure out what he is talking about, you guess what his reasons are for saying what he is saying, and you let these beliefs influence your interpretation of what he said. (You may even let these beliefs influence your perception of what he said.) Actually, of course, the person who gives the correct ("unsolvable") answer uses this third step, too. In his case, instead of assuming that the interaction is completely in good faith, he assumes that he is in a testing situation and senses that one of the things he is being tested for is his ability to read carefully.

2. The scenes we construct for texts are partly justified by the lexical and grammatical material in the text and partly by the interpreter's own contributions, the latter being based on what he knows about the current context, what he knows about the world in general, and what he assumes the speaker's intentions might be.

The lexical information we need in a description of the workings of a language includes more than information about the nature of the associated scenes; it includes information about the grammatical form of the sentences in which the lexical item is free to appear. In particular, if the lexical item is a verb, we need to know which of the possibly many separate entities in the associated scene is to get realized as the subject of the verb, which is to appear as the direct object (if there is to be one), and in what grammatical guise the others will appear.

Some years ago I came up with a proposal on how this problem should be dealt with.[8] It was in the form of a representation of sentence meanings that was deeper than deep structure, which had labels for the roles entities could have in a situation or event—roles like Agent, Patient, Instrument, Goal, Experiencer, Location, and so on. It defined a ranking or hierarchy among these notions, together with a set of principles that I referred to as the Subject Selection Rules. I referred to the role notions as deep structure cases; I claimed that any clause could be represented as a verb, indicating the nature of an event or situation, together with a collection of noun phrases marked with indicators of the case roles of each entity realized as the noun phrase; and I hoped that the subject-and-object structuring of a sentence, at the surface level, could be provided by rules of subject formation and rules of direct object formation. What I proposed assigned one kind of organization to sentences at a semantic or conceptual level, another kind at the surface structure level, with no intermediate level corresponding to Chomsky's 'deep structure' notion.

Of the many pages that have appeared in the journals and in my mail deploring Case Grammar, which was what I called this system, the one that hit hardest was a piece written by Stephen Anderson on the semantic role of deep structure.[9] Anderson pointed out a number of semantic generalizations that could only be given a simple formulation at a level of deep structure, since they involved the semantic roles of deep structure subjects and objects. Anderson's point was that noun phrases that function as subjects and objects in deep structure have holistic interpretations that are missing in nouns that are sentential complements or adjuncts other than subjects or objects. I will have occasion to mention some of his examples later on.

In the meantime, an underlying structure for grammar has been proposed by Paul Postal and David Perlmutter and by David Johnson. In it the notions subject, object, and indirect object are to be taken as primitive grammatical relations, assigned initially in a fixed way to underlying representations and modifiable by rules. They call their system Relational Grammar.[10] In their terminology, elements that are subjects,

objects, or indirect objects are called Terms (other noun-phrase constituents of clauses being Non-Terms), and terms are given ranks—namely,
1, 2, and 3 for Subject, Object, and Indirect Object, respectively. They
have proposed a great many generalizations about grammar that they
claim can be formulated most easily as operations on terms; these operations include the reranking of terms and the removal of termhood. Their
system, too, recognizes a distinction between underlying subjects and
objects and surface subjects and objects. Other scholars, especially
Edward Keenan and Bernard Comrie,[11] working independently, have
proposed a number of typological principles as well as a great many
language-universal processes and constraints on grammatical rules in
which the notions subject, object, and indirect object play a central role.

I find much of this work compelling, and I am willing to reintroduce
something like the notion of deep structure representation—at least a
notion of the assignment of subjects and objects in a particular way to
underlying predicates. Anderson's observations can, of course, be
formulated in a relational grammar; that means that the form of grammar we ultimately decide on does not have to be one in which grammatical relations are defined solely in terms of tree structure configurations,
which I take it as what Anderson himself, following Chomsky, would
prefer.

3.   Since, as I have been arguing, we can talk about the scenes underlying a text—in particular, the scenes underlying single-clause sentences
in a text—we ought to be able to examine the principles according to
which aspects of scenes map onto grammatical representations and
determine the subject/object structure of clauses.

I will refer to the part of a sentence that contains a predicating word
and the grammatical terms that are linked with it as the Nucleus, the
remainder as the Periphery, of the sentence. We need to ask two questions concerning the relationship between scenes and the clauses that
activate or are activated by these scenes. The first is, "Which of the
entities in a scene get realized in the associated sentence as members of
the nucleus?" Simplified, the question is: "What enters the nucleus?"
The other question is, "When two or more elements from a scene get
realized in the associated sentence as members of the nucleus, are there
general principles that determine which of these is the subject, or first
term, and which is the object, or second term?" (I disregard here the
indirect object, or third term.) Put differently, our second question is,
"What determines the ranking of terms in a nucleus?"

It is conceivable, of course, that the answers to these questions will be different for different languages. If that turns out to be the case, we must ask ourselves to what extent the terms of relational grammar can be thought of as semantic primitives, which is what Postal and Perlmutter have in mind. Can it be that language-universal properties—of the kind Postal, Perlmutter, Keenan, and Comrie have been suggesting—are to be found in categories that are themselves defined in language-specific ways? On its face, that possibility is not ridiculous, since apparently kinship semanticists find universally valid principles across kinship systems even though the most basic relationship within such a system, the parenthood relationship, may be conceived of differently in different cultures.

4.   Answers to the first question involve mainly the problem of the semantic import of the direct object function. English requires every sentence to have a subject, and so the question of whether or not a sentence will have a subject is less interesting than the question of whether or not it will have an object. And this question, obviously, becomes relevant only in the case in which it is clear from the meaning of the verb that there are two entities in the associated scene, one of which must become the subject, the other of which may or may not become the direct object.

Jespersen writes that "The notional relations between verbs and their objects are so manifold that they defy any attempt at analysis and classification."[12] The task of finding generalizations about the semantic import of the direct object is a difficult one, to be sure, but maybe not a hopeless one as long as we are willing to see the problem in a slightly different light. I suggest that we ask, not what kinds of relationships there are that link objects with their verbs but what properties of scenes determine whether or not something will be realized as a direct object. Some of the examples that most interested Jespersen can be thought of as resulting from fairly superficial amalgamational processes and can probably be ignored. I, at least, would not particularly trouble myself with sentences like "She laughed her thanks" or "He nodded his acquiescence" until I see whether they can be made to fit principles that seem to govern the clear cases.

5.   In exploring the second question, we should consider four situations: (1) That of verbs that can realize either of two things as direct object, the leftover element becoming a peripheral element, expressible in a preposition phrase. An example of this first situation is *blame*: We can say either, "He blamed the accident on me" or "He blamed me for

the accident." (2) That of verbs that can realize either of two things as direct object, but with constraints on whether the leftover element can be expressed at all. An example of this second kind is the verb *sign*. We can say, "He signed his name" and "He signed the contract"; but while we can say, "He signed his name on the contract," we cannot say, °"He signed the contract with his name." (3) That of verbs that can include a nonsubject noun either in the nucleus or in the periphery. An example is *shoot*: We can say either, "She shot him" or "She shot at him." (4) That of pairs of verbs that have related meanings but that differ from each other in the choice of what is in the nucleus and what is in the periphery. Verbs exemplifying the fourth situation are the pair *put* and *cover*: We can say either, "He put a towel over the alarm clock" or "He covered the alarm clock with a towel." Expressing the same situation, *towel* is the direct object in one sentence, *alarm clock* in the other.

The question I am asking is different from, but possibly related to, the question of the reasons for creating *surface* subjects and objects. Surface subjects can be created by passivization, raising into subject position, applications of tough-movement, and so on; and surface objects can be created by dative movement, raising into object position, reduction of range complements, and so on. The question I am asking is what assignment of terms is available to lexical verbs prior to any application of grammatical processes of the kind that restructure sentences.

The verb *hit* fits scenes in which something comes into abrupt contact with something else, including those in which some agent manipulates the first of these objects. In the three-element hitting scene, the agent or causer of this event appears as the subject, but apparently either of the other two entities can be realized in the direct object position. That is, we can say either, "I hit the cane against the fence" or "I hit the fence with the cane." (Incidentally, this example demonstrates the need to distinguish what is in the nucleus of a sentence from what are the obligatory constituents of a sentence. *Hit*, it appears, must be accompanied by some mention of the subject against which something moved, even though that object need not be realized as the direct object. In other words, while we can say either, "I hit the fence with the cane" or "I hit the fence," with the same real-world scene in mind, we can say, "I hit the cane against the fence," but not just, "I hit the cane," for that same scene. The contrast between nuclear and peripheral elements is not the same as the contrast between obligatory and optional sentence constituents.)

Using semantic case notions for talking about these sentences, we can say that the things that ended up in the nucleus included the Agent in each of the sentences; some included the Patient, others the Goal; and we say that some representation of the Goal entity is obligatory in the active form of any of these sentences. One intuitive way of thinking about what is going on is to assume that the decision to include things in the sentence nucleus is the decision to take a particular Perspective on a scene. When I spoke of perspective before, I spoke of focusing on a part of a scene, possibly because of some special salience of that part, while being fully aware of the rest of the scene. It is difficult, however, to see how this notion fits the examples we are considering now, since it is not easy to imagine contexts in which we can have the cane in focus but not the fence, and vice versa.

It may be possible to see, at least, what it would mean to let the Agent be out of perspective. Suppose we have a scene in which the Agent swings the cane against the fence. Consider the two sentences: "Harry swung the cane wildly. It hit the fence." Here, even if we understand that Harry was still hanging on to the cane at the time of impact, we have succeeded in putting the Agent's action into the background in the second sentence and are somehow focusing on the contact between the cane and the fence. Here, the two physical objects are in the Nucleus, but the Agent is not.

Let us consider what it would take for us to increase the relative saliency of either the Patient or the Goal in a scene that has the Agent in perspective. This time let us use the word *beat*, which is like *hit* except that it requires the belief that the Agent holds on to the implement throughout the action, whereas *hit* is compatible with a scene in which the Agent lets go. (Consider "Standing on the ground, I hit the third-story window with a brick." Here we get either the scene of a very tall man or of a man who lets go of the brick.)

Since as humans we are more interested in human beings and in human reactions than in what happens to inanimate objects, one way of showing a difference in perspective is to involve another human being in the scene. Consider the sentences "I beat the stick against Harry" and "I beat Harry with the stick." The scene for the first might well be one in which the speaker regards Harry as a nonperson; the second is more compatible with a scene in which Harry says "Oof!" It seems, in other words, that when the goal of a hitting or beating act is a human being, that is, something or someone that is clearly affected by the event, that fact gives the Goal entity sufficient saliency to be included in the Nucleus. If this explanation is correct, it should follow that if the Patient noun designates a human being and the Goal noun does not, the choice of Patient as direct object is the more natural choice. I believe this is true, though with the verb *beat* it is a little difficult to separate out purely linguistic from other kinds of reactions to the test sentences. The point is that it sounds more, let us say, respectful, to say, "I beat Harry against the corner of the building," than to say, "I beat the corner of the building with Harry."

It seems, in short, that one of the conditions favoring inclusion within the nucleus is the condition in which an element is a sentient being who is affected, in the event that is being depicted, in ways we can empathize with. It should follow that if there are two human beings involved, that fact alone yields no basis for choosing one or the other. Thus, the two sentences "I hit Harry against Bill" and "I hit Bill with Harry" ought to be and are, I think, equally bizarre.

For situations in which a given noun can be either in the nucleus or in the periphery, one condition favoring inclusion in the nucleus is that of the affected object's undergoing some kind of change. Thus, if I act against something, and if as a result of my action, that something changes, it thereby acquires the saliency to merit inclusion in the nucleus of the sentence.

Suppose, for example, that I am pulling at something and the thing does not budge. In that case I can say that I pulled "at" it or, of course, that I "tried" to pull it, but probably not simply that I "pulled" it. If I pulled at it and it moved in my direction, that is, if it moved closer to me as a result of my pulling at it, then I can say, "I pulled it." Or suppose, to take a similar example, that I am pushing against something and the thing does not budge. I can say that I pushed "against" it, or that I "tried" to push it, but not simply that I "pushed" it. If, however, the thing moves in the direction of my push, as a result of my pushing against it, then I can rightly say, "I pushed it." If you act against something and as a result of that action, the thing moves, that, to repeat myself, gives it the saliency to deserve realization as the direct object.

There seems to be a kind of 'markedness' quality here. If I say, "I pushed the table," you more or less have to believe that I succeeded in getting it to move; if I say, "I pushed against the table," I have not committed myself—except, maybe, in context, by rules of conversational cooperation—to any claims about whether or not the table actually moved.

The verb *break* can be used for a three-entity scene in which someone brings something into contact with something else and *one of those two things breaks*, that is, acquires some discontinuity as a result of this impact. Either the Patient or the Goal noun can appear as the direct object, but only if it stands for the thing that breaks. Suppose, for example, that I swing a hammer against a vase and the vase breaks. I can then say, "I broke the vase with the hammer." As with the *hit* and *beat* sentences earlier, the manipulated object, when it is in the periphery, is marked with the preposition *with*. But now suppose that I swing a hammer against a vase and the *hammer* breaks. This time I must say, "I broke the hammer on the vase." And this time the Goal noun, now out of the nucleus, is marked by a preposition that gives directional information.

The verb *cut* illustrates the same point, though with this verb it is impossible to imagine two things having properties that will allow either one to cut the other; examples with *cut*, in other words, cannot be parallel with those for *break*. Anyway, I can say, "I cut my foot with a rock," regarding my foot as the thing against which a rock was used or manipulated; or I can say, "I cut my foot on the rock," regarding my foot as having acted against the rock. In each case, whether Patient or Goal, the entity that gets cut is the entity that is realized as the direct object of the verb.

Here is a different kind of example. Suppose I take a gun and with it send a bullet toward Harry. I can take the Agent and Source into perspective and say, "I shot the gun"; I can take the Agent and Patient into perspective and say, "I shot the bullet." But if all I did was shoot the bullet in Harry's direction, then I cannot bring Harry into perspective. In such a case I can say, "I shot at Harry," or "I shot the gun at Harry," or "I shot the bullet at Harry"; but only if I succeed in hitting Harry with the bullet can I say, "I shot Harry." That is, only the scene that includes hitting Harry as a consequence of the shooting act is one in which Harry has the saliency to be included in the nucleus of the sentence.

This is the place to make clear that this speculation about saliency and the nature of the development of scenes is not in itself an explanation of, for example, why *Harry* can be a direct object in "I shot Harry," but rather an attempt to account for the conditions under which a verb is allowed to take a Goal noun as its direct object. There is still the lexically specific information to contend with. A verb very similar to *shoot* is *fire*, but *fire* does not have the same set of options with the Goal noun phrase. We can say, "I fired a gun," or "I fired a bullet," or "I fired at Harry," but not, with the same scene in mind, "I fired Harry."

Sometimes a Source, Goal, or Range constituent completes the sentence in such a way that the action described by the sentence acquires in total some special salience that allows the associated nonsubject nounphrase to become the direct object. If it were no particular accomplishment to swim across the English Channel, we would only speak of the deed as "swimming across the Channel" not as "swimming the Channel." If leaping or jumping across something is not taken as any kind of special feat, we will speak of leaping across the thing; if the deed takes on some special salience, by virtue, say, of the fact that the thing across which one leaps is an obstacle, then we speak of leaping the thing. Thus, as Jeffrey Gruber has pointed out,[13] we can talk about either "leaping across the wall" or "leaping the wall," since leaping across a wall can be viewed as an accomplishment of some importance; but while we can speak of "leaping across a line" (drawn on the sidewalk), it is hard to imagine a scene appropriate to the sentence "He leaped the line."

I mentioned earlier that the verb *sign* can take as its direct object either a noun designating the product of the writing act—as in, "He signed his name on the contract"—or a noun that designates something that acquires some new importance by virtue of the signing act—as in, "He signed the contract" or "He signed the check." Here again the acquired validity of the thing gives it the needed saliency. Notice that although we can say, "He signed his name on the men's room wall," it would be odd to say, "He signed the men's room wall."

Let me turn now to the examples Anderson used in his arguments in support of the standard theory's level of deep structure. They have to do with familiar pairs like, "I loaded the truck with hay" as compared with "I loaded hay onto the truck," and "I sprayed paint on the wall" as compared with "I sprayed the wall with paint." There is a natural or unmarked choice of direct object—namely the Patient noun—only when there is nothing special to say about the Goal. However, if the action with respect to the Goal acquires saliency by virtue of being in some sense 'complete,' then the Goal noun comes into the nucleus. Thus, for these sentences, the act of "loading the truck with hay" is most naturally seen as "filling" the truck with hay, and the act of "spraying the wall with paint" is most naturally seen as "covering" the wall with paint. This is Anderson's holistic interpretation. Anderson's way of saying it is that we start out with subjects and objects defined by phrase structure configurations, and the semantic component then assigns a holistic interpretation to certain nouns, in certain contexts, only when they are in subject or object position. My way of saying it is that a verb is sometimes capable of having its subject/object structuring accomplished in more than one way, and that such saliency properties as totality or completion justify bringing certain nouns, depending on their underlying case role, into the nuclear structure.

It should follow, then, that there can be verbs matching scenes that have the totality or holistic interpretation built in. This is true, for example, of the verbs *cover* and *fill*, the verbs I used in explaining the saliency conditions mentioned in the last paragraph. Thus, "He covered the alarm clock with the towel" is English, while "*He covered the towel over the alarm clock" is not; and "He filled the jar with ink" is acceptable, while "He filled ink into the jar" is not. By contrast, the verbs *place* and *pour* require focus on the object-manipulating rather than the resulting-state parts of their scenes. They allow expressions like "He placed the records on the shelf" but not "*He placed the shelf with records," and "He poured ink into the jar" but not "*He poured the jar with ink."

It should be emphasized that idiosyncratic lexical properties are at play here too. There is no noncircular way of describing a verb as necessarily focusing on, say, the Agent-manipulating-Patient part of a scene. Judging from the meaning of the verb *hang*, one would expect that it might require such a focus; yet it is possible to say things like "He hung the wall with drapes." And in Hungarian, which allows many of the same valency changes as I have been illustrating for English, the verb *tölt* translates as both "pour" with Patient as direct object, and English "fill" or "stuff" with Goal as direct object.

It seems, in short, that the decision to include nouns in the nucleus of the sentence or to leave them in periphery is guided, at least in part, not so much by any understanding of the action itself, but by some notion of the saliency of the action as a whole or the saliency or importance of the specific entities involved in the scene that make one portion of the scene specially deserving of focus. I feel sure that there must be some random historical forces at work here too, but I frankly do not know of any completely noncircular way of showing what I mean. (David Justice has brought to my attention Baugh's[14] report that in South African English the verb *throw* can take as direct object a person hit by the thrown missile; thus it is possible to say, "I threw Harry over the hedge with a rock." Niels Ege has told me that the Danish verb meaning "shoot" takes an animate Goal as direct object only if the result of the shooting is that the being that was hit actually dies. And I have found in the current class of students in Berkeley that there is a fairly common use of the verb *win* with a human direct object referring to the opponent in a competition. These young people can say not only "I won the game" and "I won the prize," but also "I won Harry," meaning "I defeated Harry.")

6.   The second problem for the mapping from scenes onto underlying structure was that of determining the ranking of elements put in the nucleus. For this I suggest that there might be a Saliency Hierarchy

that serves several purposes in a grammar. In the first place, since every sentence has to have a subject, the scene entity that has the highest rank will be realized as the subject; in the second place, if two entities are in the nucleus, that is, are in perspective, the roles of the first and second terms will be allocated according to relative position in the hierarchy. In the third place, the hierarchy imposes a constraint on what can appear in the nucleus and what in the periphery for the same verb. If it is a verb that can take either of two things as direct object, the one that outranks the other on the Saliency Hierarchy wins out.

At present this is sheer speculation.[15] What I have in mind is something to replace the Case Hierarchy of my work on case grammar. Now what I say is that we have a scene, with some part of it put in perspective. A saliency hierarchy that provides a mapping principle between this perspective and the structure of the sentence in terms of grammatical relations will look something like this:

1. An active element outranks an inactive element.
2. A causal element outranks a noncausal element.
3. A human (or animate) experiencer outranks other elements.
4. A changed element outranks a nonchanged element.
5. A complete or individuated element outranks a part of an element.
6. A 'figure' outranks a 'ground.'
7. A 'definite' element outranks an 'indefinite' element.

The intention is that this hierarchy is to be consulted in the order in which these statements are listed. Thus, an active element outranks everything else; a causal element outranks everything but an active element; and so on.

If two elements in a scene are of equal rank by the Saliency Hierarchy, then it is possible to put either one of them into perspective. Thus, in a commercial act, it is possible to take either the buyer or the seller into perspective, but only by regarding the other as the Source or Goal, rather than as an Agent. In locating something with respect to something else, it is possible to take either one as the figure and the other as the ground. Thus, we can speak of the map on the wall being under the picture, or the picture being over the map. The actual physical scene does not determine this choice, only the speaker's need to take one of the objects as the reference object.

7.   Let me turn now to the commercial event, and make some initial proposals on a notation for scenes, perspectives, and grammatical rela-

tions. The elements in a prototypic commercial event scene are the buyer, the seller, the money that changes hands, and the goods that change hands. Let us regard as the prototype scene for the commercial act one in which a seller sells what he owns, rather than, as a salesman, what somebody else owns; that the buyer buys by rendering money, not services or favors; that what is exchanged is goods, not services; and that the transaction occurs as a single, completed event, with no I.O.U.s or down payments.

Let us use as an example a scene in which our friend Harry buys a puppy for $60. Here are some of the things we can say about this event.

> Harry bought the puppy.
> Harry bought the puppy from Mr. Smith.
> Harry bought the puppy for $60.
> Harry bought the puppy from Mr. Smith for $60.
> Harry bought the puppy with the $60 that his
>   mother gave him.
> Mr. Smith sold the puppy.
> Mr. Smith sold the puppy to Harry.
> Mr. Smith sold the puppy for $60.
> Mr. Smith sold the puppy to Harry for $60.
> Mr. Smith sold Harry the puppy for $60.
> Mr. Smith sold Harry the puppy.
> Harry spent $60 on the puppy.
> Harry spent $60 for the puppy.
> Mr. Smith charged $60 for the puppy.
> Mr. Smith charged Harry $60 for the puppy.
> Mr. Smith charged Harry for the puppy. (He
>   didn't give it to him.)
> The puppy cost $60.
> The puppy cost Harry $60.
> Harry paid for the puppy. (He didn't get it free.)
> Harry paid Mr. Smith for the puppy.
> Harry paid $60 for the puppy.
> Harry paid Mr. Smith $60 for the puppy.
> Mr. Smith priced the puppy at $60.

Let Fig. 1 stand for the commercial event as a whole; and let the strip in Fig. 2 represent an analysis or unpacking of Fig. 1. In Fig. 2 the left-to-right order of the boxes indicates change in time, and vertical stacking indicates simultaneity. A and D are the buyer and the seller, respectively; B is the goods; C is the money. The figure is intended to

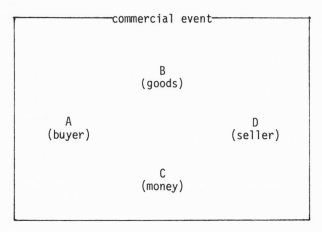

Fig. 1

show that in one time slice, A owns a certain amount of money C (he may own more than that too, of course), D owns B, and it is agreed between A and B that an exchange between them of these things will result in a transfer of ownership. In the next time slice A gives D the money and D gives B, whatever that is, to A. In the final time slice, A owns B and D owns the money.

Since there is nothing in Figs. 1 or 2 indicating perspective, they represent a scene schema rather than the meaning of some linguistic form. The labels on the boxes indicate scenes that either have to be simply known by experience or need to be explained or defined by more detailed diagrams of the sort given here.

With the larger diagram in Fig. 2 taken as a kind of definition of the commercial act, we can now construe Fig. 1 as a schema for a commercial act taken as a single situation, and identify the participants as A, B, C, D, according to their roles in the scenes specified in the definition. In the diagrams given below as Figs. 3 through 9, the part of the scene that is put in perspective is in an enclosed curve; the grammatical relations are indicated with the numbers 1 and 2; peripheral elements that are expressible as complements to the verb are marked with their appropriate prepositions; and elements from the scene that cannot be included in a simple clause whose main verb is the label of the box are put in square brackets. A Goal element that is obligatorily made into an indirect object is marked with the number 3.

8.   What I am after, of course, is a representation that is informal and

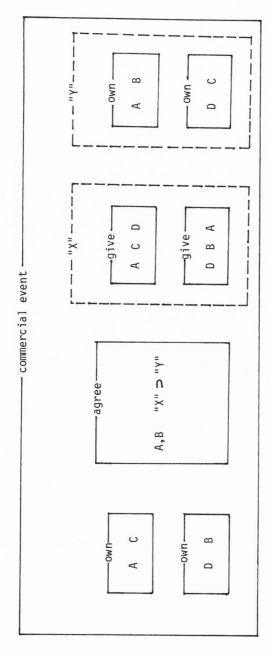

Fig. 2

easy to work with, so that lexical differences can be displayed in a fairly straightforward fashion. The complications are many, but taking this as a goal is one way of discovering just what the complications are. They include the necessity of defining the larger scene (and that includes being clear about the temporal relationships); the difference between

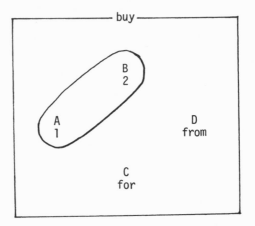

Fig. 3

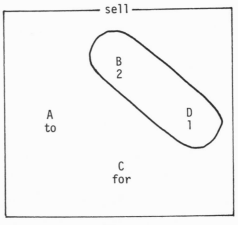

Fig. 4

obligatory and optional elements; the difference between nuclear and nonnuclear elements; the grammatical relations of the elements in the nucleus; the grammatical markings of the elements in the periphery; and—something that is disguised here—the aspects of other scenes that

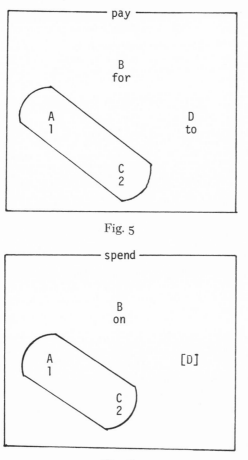

Fig. 5

Fig. 6

must also be integrated with these scenes, or ways in which the lexical item being displayed here refers to a larger scene than the one being discussed.

A detailed description of these verbs will have to point out that with *buying*, prepositions distinguish reference to the actual cash and reference to the value of the money; thus, we can say, "I bought it with the silver dollar I found in the attic," or "I bought it for a dollar." With *selling*, on the other hand, the preposition *for* is used in both cases: "I sold it for a dollar" and "I sold it for this silver dollar." *Spending* can name a relationship between a person and money over a series of purchases, as in, "I spent seventy dollars last week," as well as the relation-

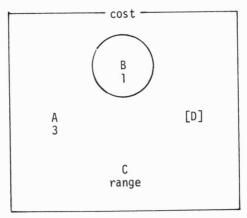

Fig. 7

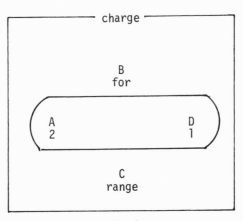

Fig. 8

ship between a person and the money spent in a single commercial event. *Paying* can involve any prearranged required transfer of money, as in paying debts, paying a child his allowance, etc., and is not limited to commercial event scenes. *Charging* can be used without any notion of an exact money amount, indicating simply a contrast with giving something for nothing, as in, "He usually gives it to me free, but today he charged me for it." *Costing* can refer to a static relation between an object for sale and its price, independently of any actual or specific buying/selling act. This can be seen in a sentence like, "If it didn't cost so much money, maybe somebody would buy it."

By taking a kind of simple prototype commercial event, we can

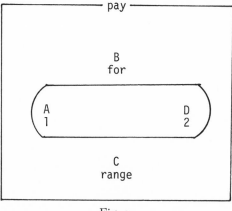

Fig. 9

examine, one by one, the lexical items that activate or are activated by scenes of such an event. By comparing, intuitively, what we know of the use of these words with the properties of the scene as we have set it up, we have a framework for discussing the words that require more information—more complicated scenes—as well as those that are actually more general, that require less detailed scenes, than the prototype we set up.

I have only scratched the surface with this collection of verbs. In the next lecture I will explore money giving with a little more detail, I will suggest some more possibilities with the notation, and I will end by saying something about how cognitive scenes of the type we have been considering can be seen to integrate with scenes found in the current context of interaction in a conversation.

Lecture Three

1. In my second lecture I proposed a simple method of diagramming certain properties of what I referred to as the 'scenes' that 'activate' or 'are activated by' given linguistic expressions. I intended these to represent aspects of what people have in mind when they comprehend texts containing the expressions.

My hope was that this kind of diagramming will make it possible to present in an intuitively graspable way simple aspects of word meaning and text meaning. It remains to be seen whether or not the result will still be satisfying after we have devised the abbreviations and conventions that will surely be necessary for displaying subtler aspects of meaning than those I will be illustrating. In any case, I believe that by exploring this method for what it is worth, we can gain some clarity on the nature of some of these subtler factors. In that sense our notation can serve as a kind of 'discovery procedure' for semantic exploration.

Where time development is relevant in characterizing a scene, the notation has some resemblances to a comic strip. Thus our method begins by representing in a fairly simple way something that would require in most other notations cumbersome formulations of the type

> Event e occurred at or during time t and event e′ occurred at or during time t′, and t is earlier than t′.

In addition to mere sequence in time, of course, we need to know what aspect of a complex scene is being focused on by the speaker through his use of a particular linguistic form at a particular point in the text. For this we can add an arrow to our comic strip notation. Recall that in order to understand our earlier sentence about the hospitalized Mark *sitting up* we needed to have in mind an earlier state during which Mark was lying down. Thus, using the arrow for the focus, we can represent *sitting up* in a way suggested by Fig. 10. The sentence is saying

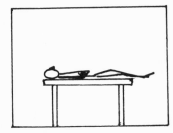 

Fig. 10

something about the state pointed to by the arrow; but the person who understands that sentence understands that the state being pointed to is a stage in a history; and he knows something about the nature of that history—the rest of the strip represents that knowledge.

A second property we need to be able to represent for natural-language semantics is simultaneity. If left-to-right order of scenes is used for showing temporal sequence, then the most natural way to indicate simultaneity is vertical stacking. This was something we needed for talking about the various stages in the commercial event. The resulting state in that event, for example, was one in which the seller owns the money and the buyer owns the goods. That state of affairs is indicated by the stacked boxes given here again as Fig. 11. Comic strips, of course, do not have anything corresponding to our vertical stacking. Instead of thinking of the separate boxes in our notation as representing individual frames in a comic strip, we can think of them as providing instructions to an artist concerning the objects and the relationships that ought to be depicted in the total scene that occupies that part in the strip. For our example, the artist merely needs to know that the scene must show A as the owner of B and D as the owner of C. As the amount of stacked information increases, however, as is the case in the development of a large text, the resulting picture becomes more and more Breughelian.

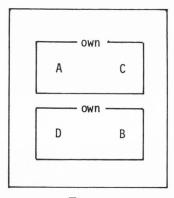

Fig. 11

I hope, by the way, that my appeals to visual imagery are more helpful than misleading. I obviously do not mean what I say literally, so that is why, instead of trying to draw a picture of somebody owning something—that, after all, is impossible—I merely provide each scene or subscene with a label that identifies the property or situation or relationship, listing variables standing for the entities in an order dictated by the saliency hierarchy.

2.   In addition to sequence and simultaneity, a third aspect of scenes that we need to represent I will call "selection." I have not had anything to say about it so far. Sometimes a meaning is relative to a scene that offers a selection from two or more possibilities; and sometimes individual words are understood as identifying one choice within just such a contrast set. The meaning of the word requires, then, an understanding of the nature of the contrast within this particular scene.

For example, there is the scene connected with the kind of commercial event that takes place in a store. At least two situations provide for the use of the word *cash*. In one of these, the contrast is between paying in currency as opposed to paying by some other means. In this setting, the word *cash* rules out the possibility of payment by personal check. In another situation the term opposed to *cash* is *credit*. Within this setting the choice of credit requires the clerk to write up the sale on a special form, to ask for the customer's signature, and perhaps to check the customer's credit rating; here the word *cash* can be taken as including the possibility of payment by check. By knowing something about the nature of these two contrast sets, we can know that the corner tobacconist who does business for cash only will not accept a check; and at the same time we know that if a clerk in a large department store asks, "Will that be cash or charge?" the correct answer, if we intend to pay by a check is "cash."

In each case the important difference is between what is particularly salient or troublesome, and its opposite. In the one setting, payment with currency is safer than the alternative; in the other, payment with a credit card is the more troublesome. In both cases these 'marking' properties are determined from the merchant's or salesperson's point of view. The word *cash*, in other words, designates different possibilities for payment depending on which contrast set it belongs to. One way of representing this state of affairs, in the cash/charge contrast case, is by means of a diagram like that shown in Fig. 12, which is to be presented in a simultaneity relationship to a commercial event. We can insert a variable representing the commercial event in the appropriate cell.

3. Some scenes involve understandings about contracts, conventions, laws, expectations, etc., and these may require cross-references linking one part of a scene to another. To indicate these cross references, I propose using the late letters in the alphabet (W, X, Y, Z) as variables, in quotes, both within the statement about the agreement (or whatever) and as indicators of the portions of the scenes to which they refer.

For example, something counts as a commercial event, not just by virtue of an exchange of a sum of money and some goods resulting in ownership changes; that situation, after all, is compatible with a simple coincidence of two gift-giving acts. There has to be an agreement, in advance of the act, on the part of both parties, that the exchange will in fact result in the ownership changes.

A part of the notation for the commercial event presented in the last lecture is given here again as Fig. 13, which indicates that at one

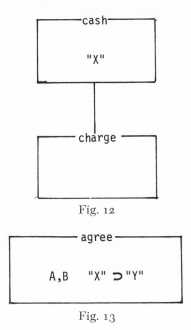

Fig. 12

Fig. 13

stage in this history, A and D agreed that after the event labeled "X" occurs, the state labeled "Y" will necessarily obtain.

Here, too, it is necessary to repeat that what I have in mind when I talk about 'the commercial event' is a prototype instance of such an event. A sign in a china shop that reads, "Break it and you've bought it," identifies a situation that departs a little from the prototype. Most cases of buying and selling, in fact, do not involve explicit agreements made by the two participants in the transaction but rather agreements that are implicit in the situation. If there is a price tag on the bar of soap you are about to buy, there is no reason, in most parts of the English-speaking world, at any rate, for you to make any on-the-spot agreements with the clerk on the amount of money he requires in exchange for the soap. (The terms of the prototype I have set up are perhaps more directly appropriate for primitive markets than for supermarkets.)

4. Another aspect of the diagram for the commercial act was the presentation of conditions that have no temporal position in the scene at all, but that simply hold throughout. Information of that kind includes what we might think of as the 'cast of characters' and general descriptions of the larger setting for our scene. For the representation we

devised for the commercial event this was the information that C was money, B was goods, and A and D were people. We can put such information in a box that stretches through the whole strip.

5.   So far I have spoken mainly of scenes associated with verbs. Remaining within the money realm, I would like now to examine an application of this notation for describing the meanings of the various nouns that speakers of English use when talking about sums of money exchanged in specific money-transferring scenes. Suppose we know that on a particular occasion, one person gave another person some money. Consider what must be assumed about the larger scene of which this scene is a part, once we know what the money, on this occasion, was called. A metaphor that fits the view of semantics I am proposing is that when you pick up a word, you drag along with it a whole scene. The insight beyond that metaphor might become particularly clear if you try to imagine, for each of the following nouns, something about the nature of the larger scene. Consider them one at a time.

tip	bonus
ransom	rent
allowance	fare
refund	child support
honorarium	bus money
bounty	salary
tuition	reward
retainer	alimony

The list could go on, of course.

Any semantic notation needs to account for the scenes introduced by nouns, too. More often than not, the richness and detail of the large scene we eventually construct for a text may be more dependent on scenes introduced by nouns than on those introduced by verbs.

Consider for a moment the word *alimony*. If A pays alimony to B, we know that at one time A and B were married, we know that that marriage ended in divorce, and we know that roughly at the time of the divorce an agreement was made between the two participants to the effect that one of them would pay money to the other. The prototype, which these days may be losing its prototype, has it that the ex-husband is the one who pays money to the ex-wife.

We know that this history must have included more than that, too, so that if we were to dwell on this example to fill in more of the details, we might have images of bitter disagreements, lawyers, court appearances, court fees, public notice, and a host of other things.

The part of this larger scene that seems to be necessarily assumed whenever some exchange of money is correctly referred to as the payment of alimony is represented here as Fig. 14. The diagram is a representation of the meaning of the word *alimony:* we see in the diagram that the lexical item *alimony* is linked by an arrow to the entity C, a fixed sum of money, in the rightmost box. Other aspects of the total scene we

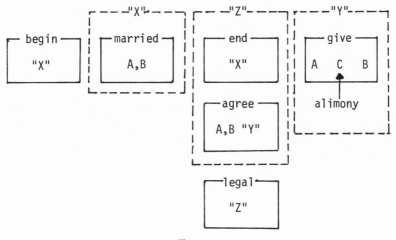

Fig. 14

were able to imagine are associated with the concept *alimony* only indirectly, by means of prototype scenes associated with legal acts and with the marriage relationship.

As a second example, let us take the noun *ransom*. If what A pays B is called *ransom*, we have the right to assume that B had illegally taken possession of some person or object C that is important to A, that B had offered to return C on condition that A give B some money, and that A had accepted this offer. A comic-strip representation of *ransom* would include the information that at one stage B took illegally something valued by A; at a later stage B offered to return what he took on condition that A would agree to give B a certain sum of money; at a third stage A gives B the money, which is then properly called *ransom*, and B takes on the obligation to restore what he took.

6.   In my discussion of nouns like *alimony* and *ransom* I have so far been talking as if what we were dealing with was merely a matter of choosing a noun for referring to some amount of money that changed hands. These examples allow me to make another point about scenes

and texts. The expressions that we need to embed these nouns in are not uniform. Some situations call for an indefinite determiner, some for the definite determiner, and some for a possessive pronoun; and some allow the verb *pay*, others only *give*.

If it is clear that A is expected or obliged to give the money to B, the possessive pronoun is appropriate. Thus: "I gave him his allowance, his salary, his change." If the presentation is not expected or obligatory, the indefinite article can be used. Thus: "I gave him a tip, a bonus, a reward." Sometimes before a money-exchange agreement is made, one can talk about it with the indefinite article; once the agreement is complete, a possessive or definite article might be necessary. Thus I can say in advance, "I'll give you an honorarium, a salary, an advance," but after the agreement is made, I must say, "Here's your honorarium, here's the reward," or whatever.

These observations about determiners allow me to go to another point. The possibility of using either of two choices with the same noun shows us something of the communicative force of using a linguistic form that presupposes some specific scene or expectational set. If a waiter tells me, "You didn't give me a tip," I get the feeling that he finds me inconsiderate; if he says, "You didn't give me my tip," I get the feeling that he is telling me that I did something illegal.

What I am suggesting, of course, is that the semantics of the determiner system interacts with the semantics of the scene activated by a particular noun, in such a way that the choice of one or another article, or the choice of the possessive pronoun, will contribute in important ways to the construction of the final completed scene. One of the disadvantages of scene semantics, in short, is that it does not allow you, without embarrassment, the convenience of talking about the semantics of verbs and nouns while leaving to the future the problem of incorporating into your system information about the semantic effects of articles. Some choice from the determiner system must accompany any noun, and the scene the interpreter constructs depends in many ways on just what choice was made.

7. Still another lesson to be drawn from these examples concerns the ways in which scene schemata associated in the first instance with an individual lexical item can play a framing role in the assembly of the scene representing the meaning of a whole sentence or text. We are not going to encounter the word *alimony* only in word lists; we will find it embedded in a sentence. For example, in the sentence "Harry paid up his alimony," the scene associated with *alimony* provides the framework for

the scene that matches the whole sentence. We identify the husband in the alimony story as Harry, and we add the information that the financial agreement was fulfilled, that is, that the obligation has ended, with an arrow pointing to the box that expresses that.

But now let us illustrate that same point with a more complicated sentence, namely, "Harry paid this month's alimony with money borrowed from his stepdaughter." An analysis of this sentence will be my main demonstration of the connection between lexical semantics and text semantics.

The complex scene that we construct out of this sentence will have the marriage–divorce contract–alimony payment sequence that we have seen in association with the word *alimony*. The phrase "this month's" adds the understanding that the payments were, presumably as part of the contract agreement, to be paid in monthly installments. The noun *stepdaughter* introduces a more complicated history to Harry's life. In order for him to have a stepdaughter, he has to be married. For him to have a stepdaughter requires the understanding that his current wife was previously married and had at least one child by that marriage, and that that marriage ended. For Harry to have borrowed money from his stepdaughter means that he has entered into an agreement by which the money she gave him on this occasion must be returned at some later date. My point is, of course, that in our effort to construct a single history to fit the whole sentence, we have to fit into each other, in some satisfactory way, the various relationships and time lines that the separate parts of the sentence have introduced.

The example allows me to show something of the separate roles of linguistic and extralinguistic knowledge in an interpreter's processing of a text. We know that Harry used to be married to one person and that he is now married to another. We know these things because he is described as paying alimony and as having a stepdaughter. Our knowledge of what the world is like—at least the familiar world—includes the knowledge that a man is married to at most one woman at a time, and requires us to add to our text scene the assumption that Harry entered into his current marriage after the time of the divorce we have been considering.

There are still temporal relations that we do not know, however. This sentence, in fact, gives us a new reason for being dissatisfied with the comic-strip notation. We cannot know anything for sure about the temporal ordering of, say, the beginning of Harry's first marriage and the birth of Harry's current wife's daughter or the beginning of Harry's current wife's former marriage. It seems that what we need is a modified kind of comic strip with several tracks, printed on rubber sheets. The two sections corresponding to the two separate histories are attached at the point where their histories are known to coincide, but their beginnings are left hanging, with temporal relations between them unspecified. If later on in the same text we learn that Harry's first wife was born on the day his second wife's divorce became final, then we can stretch out the two rubber strips and staple them together at the point where the text shows a temporal coincidence of two points in these two separate histories.

The process of interpreting a text involves beginning with some sort of scene, letting that provide a framework for embedding and overlapping and connecting with other scenes. I have emphasized that the way in which this is done involves meanings of words and meanings associated with particular grammatical choices, and much more. When we interpret a text, we bring to the task more than our knowledge of the language—knowledge about the world, beliefs about human nature, assumptions about typical instances of objects, repertories of stereotypic instances of behavior, and so on. All of this contributes to the ultimate picture we get of the world that matches the text.

8.   Let us return once more to Mark and Mike in the hospital. Because of the linguistic forms *sitting up* and *sitting down* we were forced to make assumptions about their previous body positions. But there were certain other assumptions that we might have found ourselves making, too, and these had to do with our beliefs about why the boys might be in the hospital, what sorts of changes in their condition would have induced the nurse to make the remarks that she made, and so on. These details we found ourselves constructing are not strictly authorized by the text, but are added by the interpreter. Sometimes we are more aware of the part that we added than at other times; and if people's experiences are different, it follows that people differ in the sense they make out of the same text.

Highly trained and sensitive individuals, such as the ideal jurist or the ideal psychiatrist, can probably always keep in mind the difference between what a text actually authorizes and what they as interpreters have added to it. Schizophrenics, I would guess, are the least able to do this. They can believe that they have communicated to others, or that others have communicated to them, details that could only have been inferred, from what was said, by somebody with a very special set of beliefs and a very special kind of imagination. Most of us fall somewhere between these two extremes.

I have suggested that the interpreter of a text contributes to the interpretation process in ways that are independent of the meanings authorized by the text itself. There are, of course, more basic ways in which the participants in a conversation are involved in a text; and here we enter the realms of pragmatics, sociolinguistics, and deixis. Sometimes the linguistic forms found in a text themselves anchor the scenes that match the text to the world containing the conversation participants themselves. The comic strip needs to include a scene in which somebody is saying precisely the sentence that is being analyzed. Actually, the sentence we were just considering is like that to a certain extent. We have to believe that the utterance of the sentence occurred during the month that the speaker refers to in the expression "this month's alimony check."

9. The kind of analysis I have been demonstrating is text interpretation from the overhearer's point of view. In a slight fear of being misunderstood, we might think of what I have been discussing as an effort toward a 'competence' theory of discourse semantics. The task is to determine what we can know about the meaning and context of an utterance given only the knowledge that the utterance has occurred. If we know, for example, that somebody has used the sentence "You may come down out of the tree now, sir," there are many conclusions we can draw about what is being communicated, how the communicators are related to each other, socially and in physical space, and so on.

Many people regard this kind of research as evil because it ignores real-world contexts. I think the only superiority of real contexts over constructed ones is that they sometimes make you realize things you would never have thought of if you had stayed forever alone in your rocking chair. I am interested in language use, too, but I find that whenever I notice some sentence in context, I immediately find myself asking what the effect would have been if the context had been slightly different, if a different word had been used, if the sentence had been given a different intonation, and so on. In other words, I get right back to a 'competence' theory approach.

The goal in doing discourse analysis from the overhearer's point of view is that of finding the lowest common denominator among the set of possible associated scenes and contexts. Any actual use of a sentence will have some or all of the background conditions satisfied, will have some or all of the unspecified choices specified, and so on. The only uniform description that can be given to texts independently of contexts is one that characterizes in the most general way the *set* of contexts in which it could be put to use.

10.   From the point of view of the interpretation process, pragmatic knowledge can be thought of as the knowledge by which we are able to construct a scene of the setting in which the text was produced—that is, to contextualize it. If the text happens to be a conversation, then this pragmatic knowledge enables us to understand something of the setting, the conversation partners, the locations, and maybe the postures and movements of the participants.

To show the contribution of pragmatic knowledge to the scene-construction process let us consider the simple sentence "Mommy will come there tomorrow morning." The scene we construct for a sentence that contains deictic elements has to contain direct reference to the utterance being analyzed. We manage this by including in the scenes we construct the event of somebody speaking the utterance being examined.

We begin by locating the event of somebody saying "U" (= "Mommy will come there tomorrow morning") within a calendar day. Since anything at all occurs within a calendar day, that is not so significant; but we do this because we will need to refer to the *next* calendar day in the sequence. Fig. 15 is a representation of such a scene, in which A is the

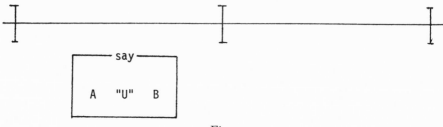

Fig. 15

speaker of "U," and B is the addressee. The time line is represented by the segmented arrow at the top; the divisions in the time line are divisions between successive calendar days.

Our sentence contains the word *come*, referring to a movement from one place to another. We could represent the movement part of this meaning as Fig. 16, in which D is to be taken as the thing that moves, E as the starting point, and F as the destination of the movement. As with the analysis of the commercial event, it would be possible to break up the movement scene into a sequence of temporally ordered subscenes representing D's location at E at one stage and D's location at F at a later stage.

The word *Mommy* is used in this text. *Mommy* happens to be a word

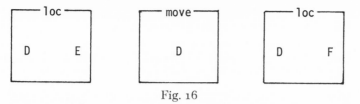

Fig. 16

used by children and by adults when speaking to children. Thus we conclude that either the speaker or the addressee is a small child, or that both of them are.

We can say, taking the competence view I have been suggesting, that the text at this point is compatible with three different scenes, depending on whether one or both persons, A and B, are in infancy. To make an arbitrary choice, I will limit my discussion to the interpretation in which A is an adult and B is a small child. The sentence "Mommy will come there tomorrow morning" is of sufficient structural complexity and maturity that somebody young enough to use the word *Mommy* in talking about his own mother would probably not be expected to form this sentence. (Here, of course, I am using information that is not completely linguistic.)

Mommy is not just a word used in a text that enables us to know something about the speaker and hearer. It is also the subject of the verb *come* and hence is the person who is going to do the traveling. The words tells us that she must be related to somebody by the mother/child relationship. The speaker did not say "your mommy" or "my mommy," but just "Mommy." A child would say "my mommy" when talking to somebody who was not in his own family, but just "Mommy" when talking to somebody who lives in his own household. We are assuming here, however, that A is an adult and that B is a child. Since we know that an adult talking to a child will tend to identify people from the child's point of view, we assume that the person intended is not the speaker's mother, but the child's mother. Since the expressions is "Mommy" and not "your mommy," we assume that the speaker and the child are members of the same household. We must keep A's identity indefinite, since we do not know from this evidence alone who in B's household A might be. A might be B's father; A might be B's mother, referring to *herself* as "Mommy"; or, of course, A could be an elder sibling, an aunt, a grandparent, or a household servant.

The result of this kind of figuring is that we can add to the description of the scene, in the version that we are working with, some 'footnote' information about the relationships among our cast of characters. Some of this is the information that D is B's mother, that A and B are members of the same household, and that B is a small child.

Now let us return to the word *come*. It presupposes movement to a destination that is in some way connected with the conversation participants. The conditions are simple, but they are hard to formulate. The possibilities include the situation where A, the speaker of the sentence, is at the destination F; this, for example, is the interpretation we would clearly get for a sentence like "Come here, please." A second possibility is that F, the destination of the movement, could be the current location of B, the addressee; this is the interpretation we would necessarily get in a sentence like "Wait for me, I'll come there right away." A third possibility is that F is the location of the speaker at the time of the mover's arrival; this is the interpretation we provide for a sentence like "I'll get there around two, and he'll come there around two thirty." The fourth possibility that I have in mind is that F could be the location of the addressee at the time of the mover's arrival; this is the interpretation forced by "As soon as you get there, he'll come and help you."

The verb *come*, in other words, allows all of these possibilities, plus a few others, all related in some way or another to the location of one of the participants in the speech act. So far, then, the description of the scene schema for our sentence will have to leave all of these as possibilities.

But now notice that the next word is *there*. For a place to be referred to as *there*, it must be a place where the speaker is not located at the time he uses the word. Therefore, one of the four possibilities that we had in mind earlier gets ruled out: the possibility that the speaker, A, is located at the destination, F, at the time of speaking the sentence.

The various possibilities depend, of course, on who A, B, and D are—in particular, on whether A happens to be D, that is, on whether the speaker is referring to herself when she uses the name "Mommy." I suggest that the scene we create for the sentence be the one that is limited to that possibility. One possible contextualization of that situation has the mother talking to the child over the telephone.

Now the word *tomorrow* locates the moving event with respect to the speaking event, the moving event being one day future to the speaking event. Furthermore, the moving event is located with respect to the "morning" subperiod of that next day. The method of communication used by A in talking to B has to be one in which they can share the kind of temporal reference point necessary for the use of deictic time words like tomorrow; as suggested before, the possibility of communication by telephone fits this condition.

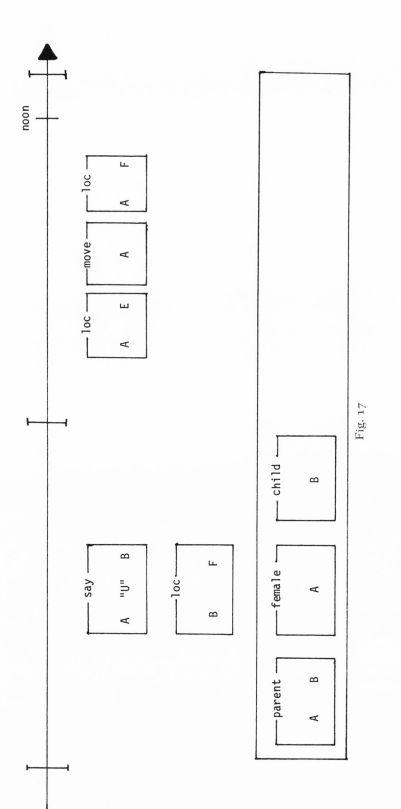

Fig. 17

Given these assumptions, then, we now know where to locate, in time, the *move* scene: in the *morning* part of *tomorrow*. But to be sure about this guess, we ought to try to unpack the notion of motion. A journey is described by specifying the starting point, the itinerary, and the destination. We need to be clear about whether the morning period includes the whole journey or only part of it; that is, we need to know whether to paste into the morning space in the strip the whole moving scene, or just the beginning or the finishing end of it.

To see if we can determine how much of D's journey is to be located within *tomorrow morning*, we can compare our sentence, which contains *come*, with similar sentences containing *go* and *get*. It seems clear, for example, that "Mommy will get there tomorrow morning" gives us a scene with the mother's *arrival* occurring during the morning, but with no commitment about the time of her departure; and it seems equally clear that the sentence "Mommy will go there tomorrow morning" locates her *departure* time within the morning period, but is compatible with a later arrival. My impression is, though I have not checked this out with more than a few speakers, that the sentence "She will come there tomorrow morning" requires the understanding that the entire journey takes place within the specified time period.

The scene that we end up with—one of the several scenes compatible with this sentence—is represented as Fig. 17.

13.   I am sure that this little exercise must have seemed extremely trivial and pointless to many of you, and must have seemed like something that concerns itself with details that a decent theory of semantics can easily postpone until certain more global and important problems are solved. I think, however, that the problems that seem important to an analyst are the problems that are hard to work out within a given model. This sentence demonstrates the ways in which the scene-construction model forces the analyst to be clear about, or at least to seek clarity about, a range of questions that can easily escape the attention of somebody working with a different notation and a different set of assumptions about the scope of semantics.

Lecture Four

0.   The notation I have been developing in these lectures is one that is capable of representing succession in time, simultaneity in time, selection from a contrast set, 'stage settings' or aspects of a scene that remain

constant through the period of the scene, conventions for cross reference in cases of agreements and contracts, and conventions for embedding in a scene a representation of the very communication act whose text the scene analyzes.

In this final, brief lecture I plan to do three things: introduce the problem of representing models of a world that are in conflict, survey some of the terminological problems these proposals give rise to, and review, in terms of these proposals, a number of traditional concepts and issues in semantic theory.

1. One of our representational problems is that of showing how one person's model of the world can include information about another person's model of the world. The representational problem is one of scene embedding. The comic-strip tradition provides conventions that might be put to use, like, for example, the balloon that represents a character's speech or thoughts, but the problem of embedding becomes serious precisely because there can be embeddings of unlimited depth. To analyze a sentence of the form "Julie thinks that her dad was honest," we will need to express the notion that the speaker's model of Julie has it that Julie's model of her father has it that her father's model of the world is compatible with the models of the world that match his speech utterances. The comprehensibility problem of a balloon over a character in a balloon over a character in a frame is probably obvious without illustration. I will say no more about that problem here.

2. The other set of cases with which I shall interest myself has to do with the vocabulary of human emotions. Some emotion words, I believe, can be captured with single scenes, in the sense that the emotional states they name are relatively simple and have conditions that can be contained in a moment in time. Some of the single-scene emotions are those named by the words *excitement, anger, peacefulness*, and *joy*.

Multiple-scene emotions are those that entail a history; for some emotion-naming words, the word is appropriately used only if it can be understood that the emotion-experiencing event is a stage in a history. One linguist who has emphasized this aspect of emotion vocabulary is Anna Wierzbicka,[16] from whose work some of these examples are adapted. Wierzbicka's paradigm emotion description takes the form "The way someone feels when . . .". In our terms, the emotion word names the final scene in a history, with the assumption that the experiencer of the emotion is reacting to this history in a normal or prototypic way.

A prototype characterization of *disappointment* might go something like this: *Disappointment* describes the way a person feels who has wanted something to happen, who has had reason to believe that it would happen, and who has discovered that it did not happen the way he expected. In our strip notation, the first frame has A wanting B to happen and expecting B to happen by the time represented in the next frame; that next frame shows A realizing that B is not going to happen; and the third frame has A reacting to this experience. The arrow links the word *disappointment* to this last frame.

Here are some other words that can be defined along these same lines. We can describe *frustration* as the way someone feels who has wanted to do something, who has tried repeatedly to do it, and who has just realized that it cannot be done. *Surprise* can be described as the way someone feels who has believed A and who has discovered non-A. *Suspense* can be defined as the way somebody feels who wants to know whether some state of affairs will come about, who realizes that he must wait longer before he can know whether or not it will come about.

In all of these cases, we have emotion words whose definitions require an understanding of conflict between the world and one's model of the world. Either the world that one desires is not the same as the world that one sees, or the world that one has believed in turns out not to be the world that one is experiencing.

3.   It is clear from these examples that my previous accounts of scene semantics have not provided all the distinctions that need to be made. In particular, I have given the word *scene* too much work to do. Here are some of the distinctions that I think are going to prove to be important.

In the first place, we need to recognize the real-world scenes in terms of which people have learned categories and distinctions, and in terms of which people have acquired their original awareness of the objects and experiences that the world has to offer, as well as the real-world scenes that are the contexts and causes of ongoing perceptions and behavior.

Secondly, there are memories and distillations of real-world scenes in people's minds, possibly restructured in ways provided by their participation in a particular community, possibly with some aspects of them forgotten or suppressed and others enhanced.

Thirdly, there are schemata of concepts, stereotypes of familiar objects and acts, and standard scenarios for familiar actions and events that can be spoken of independently of given individuals' memories of experiences.

Fourthly, there is the imagined scene of the speaker as he is formulating his text; and fifthly there is the imagined scene of the interpreter as he is trying to construct a model of the world that matches the text he is interpreting.

And lastly there are the sets of linguistic choices that a given language provides and the ways in which these activate or are activated by particular conceptual schemata.

These are fairly confusing notions, and I among many have never had a time when I felt I had a good conceptual grasp of the whole collection of concepts. The area of confusion is the area for which workers in language understanding projects within artificial intelligence have developed terms like *scene, frame, schema, description, template, scenario, prototype, module,* and *model.*

One possible set of terminological choices is the following. We can use *scene* to refer to real-world experiences, actions, objects, perceptions, and personal memories of these. We can use *schema* to refer to one of the conceptual schemata or frameworks that are linked together in the categorization of actions, institutions, and objects—such as the collection of notions we had to recognize for characterizing the commercial event—as well as any of the various repertories of categories found in contrast sets, prototype objects, and so on. We can use *frame* to refer to the specific lexico-grammatical provisions in a given language for naming and describing the categories and relations found in schemata. And we can use *model* to refer to either somebody's view of the world or the view of the world that an interpreter builds up in the process of interpreting a text. A *text model* can be thought of as the assembly of schemata created by the interpreter, justified by the interpreter's knowledge of the frames in the text, which models some set of possible complex scenes.

The integration of these concepts can be talked about in this way: from experiences with real-world scenes, people acquire conceptual schemata; in the acquisition of schemata, sometimes items from language frames are learned for labeling these and their parts; *words* from a language frame activate in the mind of the user the whole frame and the associated schema; the schemata can be used as tools or building blocks for assembling, on the basis of the words in a text, a text model —i.e., a model of the world that is compatible with the text.

We can think of a schema, as here defined, as a standard set of conditions, or as a conceptual framework, that characterizes ideal or prototypic instances of some category. As human beings, we can interpret an experience if we can succeed in assigning some sort of conceptual schema to it, that is, if we can locate the experience as an instance of the schema. In many cases this assignment is done "to a degree"—that is, the scene at hand may not match the schema exactly, but it approximates it to a degree.

We can talk about an experience if we can assign a schema to it and if we know the linguistic frame that fits that schema. People can understand our talk if their linguistic repertories activate the same or comparable schemata and if their experiences in acquiring these schemata are comparable to ours. Our interlocutors can understand what we are saying if they can assemble the schemata we have introduced into a model of a possible scene that matches the model we wished to impart to them. The process of interpreting a text, in short, can be thought of as involving a set of procedures for constructing a coherent model of a possible world.

One of the first types of objections to a world-building or image-building way of talking about text interpretation has to do with the treatment of negative sentences. How, one might ask, are we to imagine a world or scene that matches the sentence, "There are no elephants in my kitchen today." It is easy enough to imagine an elephant-free kitchen, but there is not likely to be anything about that kitchen that makes it fit the given sentence better than it will fit any of the infinitely large set of other negative sentences compatible with the same scene. My answer, of course, requires an understanding of the difference between the internal and the external contextualization of a text. The scene, in other words, has to contain an utterance of the sentence, and the understanding we seek is an understanding of the kinds of situation in which it would be appropriate to produce that particular negative sentence. These situations will involve, in the trivial case, the occurrence of the sentence as an example in a philosophy class or a linguistic class during a discussion of imagery theories of meaning, or, in the more interesting case, a situation in which somebody has already introduced into the conversation the possibility of there having been, or of there being in the future, some number of elephants in the kitchen being referred to. For some negative sentences, in other words, the scene that the interpreter constructs contains not only properties appropriate to the sentence itself but also properties connected with the context in which the sentence could be meaningfully produced.

4. My final task is to show that the way of talking about meaning that I have introduced here is capable of offering something illuminating, or at least something not clearly less illuminating than more traditional

semantic theories have allowed, about a number of traditional semantic notions.

4.1. Let me begin with *ambiguity*. We can say that a sentence is ambiguous if some linguistic form in the sentence is assigned to two different frames. The sentence "My desk drawer is ten inches deep" is ambiguous because the word *deep* is found in two different contrast sets compatible with the measurement use we find here. In one of its senses it is contrasted to *shallow*, the two making up a pair of polar opposites, with *deep* being the word used in giving measurements. In this sense the sentence can be understood as saying something about the top-to-bottom dimensions of the interior of the drawer. In the other of its senses it is contrasted to *wide*, the two making up a pair of words for measuring the front-to-back as opposed to the side-to-side measurements of any object having a roughly oblong shape. In this sense the sentence can be understood as saying something about the front-to-back dimensions of the drawer.

4.2. A sentence is *vague* in the extent to which the transition from the scenes that clearly match and those that clearly do not match the frame it activates is gradual. The sentence "My desk drawer is deep" is both vague and ambiguous: vague in that there is no clear boundary between being deep and being not deep, in either of the two senses of *deep*.

4.3. A word is relatively *general*, rather than *specific*, if the description of the associated scene is relatively less detailed than whatever word it is being compared with. It follows from this description that the number of detailed scenes that match it is greater for a general term than for a more specific term; yet that condition alone does not capture the idea of generality. The word *calf* can be used to designate the young of a cow, a hippopotamus, or an elephant; but I would not be inclined to say that it is thereby more *general* than it would be if it could refer only to the young of a cow. A single frame characterization of *calf*, if that were possible, would have to include the information that the word is not applicable to the young of horses, wolves, etc.

4.4. Two words are *synonyms* if different lexical choices are available for the same element in the same frame. Perhaps in this sense *eye doctor* and *oculist* are synonyms; and quite likely *furze* and *gorse* are, too.

More interesting than *complete synonymy* is *partial synonymy*. Words are partial synonyms of each other if parts of the frames in which they occur are identical, other parts being different. *Promise* and *guarantee* are partial synonyms. Both agree in committing the agent to the future occurrence of whatever action or event is the content of the promise or guarantee; but guarantee adds to this the understanding that the receiver of the guarantee has rights against the guarantor should the promise fail. *Signature* and *autograph* are partial synonyms, the latter differing from the former in the details of the scene having to do with the motives or interests of the person for whom the signature was obtained.

4.5. The concept of *selection restrictions* or *co-occurrence constraints* can be spoken of in terms of the linguistic frames that are associated with given schemata. Some words are limited to the kinds of schemata they activate and are constrained, therefore, to appear with the other words that belong to the frames matching such schemata. The notion of selection restriction can thus be formulated in terms of the properties of schemata and frames, and not in the usual way, i.e., in terms of the pairing of inherent features and distributional features on lexical items.

4.6. The concept of *antonymy* is more or less captured by the concept of contrast set discussed earlier in connection with what I was calling *selection*. If a frame allows one choice from a set of mutually exclusive categories, these can be thought of as forming an antonymy set. The usual sense of *antonymy* is captured by the situation in which an antonymy set contains exactly two member categories.

4.7. The concept of *category boundaries* for words can be reexamined in terms of the concept of the *prototype*. The research of Labov[18] on the boundaries of notions like *cup, bowl, glass*, etc., can be illuminatingly discussed in terms of the strategies by which subjects make use of prototype elements in schemata. The schema for the set of things one can expect to find in one's kitchen includes a prototype cup, glass, and bowl. When subjects make judgments about some sort of monster cup presented to them in an experimental setting, they are not really deciding on the boundaries of the category of cup, but rather they are trying to decide whether the new object is close enough to being a kitchen vessel to deserve comparison with the kitchen-cabinet schema in the first place, and then to decide if it is close enough to one or another of the prototypes to be classed as an instance of that type rather than of some other. Experiments of category boundaries are really experiments that test people's strategies for extending from a prototype to a nonprototypic instance of a category.

4.8. The concept of semantic field can be captured by appealing to the notion of schema, and the allied concept of vocabulary field can be identified with the notion of frame and with various linkages among frames. The human color schema identifies the semantic field of color terms; the commercial event schema underlies the vocabulary field of buying and selling. And so on.

The schema and the associated linguistic frames for the human body provide for the field of body part names and the vocabulary of body positions and body movements. I believe that the kinds of definitions that are sometimes given for certain kinds of body activities can only be made comprehensible if we assume the existence of a body schema and if the body schema is interpreted, as I have been suggesting here, in terms of *prototypes*. Eugene Nida[19] has offered analyses of certain body activities that can be adapted as follows: Let L stand for one human foot and R for the other, and let an occurrence of these symbols mean that the designated foot is on the ground; then let O stand for a period when neither foot is on the ground. Then we can define *hop* as LOLOLO . . . , *skip* as LOLOROROLOLORORO, and we can define *run* as LOROLORO . . . and *walk* as LRLRLR. . . . Now I would suggest that it is only if we accept a prototype notion of human locomotion that these definitions are acceptable. I am sure, in other words, that it is possible to meet the conditions of the definition of any one of these and yet be doing something that would not qualify as an instance of the type of locomoting named by the word being glossed. I think, in other words, that only if we already have an idea of how people typically move about, and only when we keep in mind that set of options, can these definitions correctly separate the various types from one another.

4.9.   The semantic notion of *converse* can be captured as follows: If there are two predicating words that belong to the same frame but occur in syntactic structures that require that the entities of the associated schema are mentioned in different orders, then those two words are converses of each other. *Buy* and *sell* are converses in this sense, as are *taller than* and *shorter than*, or *husband* and *wife*.

4.10.   I believe that the traditional linguistic notion of the *core meaning* (Grundbedeutung) of a linguistic form can be usefully discussed in the terms I have been setting up here. The goal for the linguist who tries to construct or discover the core meaning of a form is to find one formulation of its uses that will cover all cases. The goal is to reduce to a minimum all appearance of polysemy. My feeling is that in general this goal is not a good one for linguistic semantics. To return to the example of *calf*, I would rather say that it is a member of several linguistic frames, and perhaps add that in each of these frames its relation to the associated schema is similar, than to try to formulate as the meaning of *calf* some single statement that will exactly cover all cases of its use. I think, in other words, that the most useful information about a lexical item is the set of frames in which it plays a role and the position that it occupies in each of these frames. Whatever subregularities are lost by making this choice can be presented in the form of an historical account of the evolution of the language system, that is, in terms of the extensions of words from one frame to another in the history of the language.

Suppose, for example, that somebody decided to identify the core meaning of the word *short* independently of whether it was used as the opposite of *long* or as the opposite of *tall*. Since a semantic account of English would still need to provide the information that the word appears in just these two contrast sets, nothing could be added to our understanding of the language by this decision. Consider, as an exercise, the series of adjectives *high-low-tall-short-long-wide-deep-shallow*. It happens that each of the surrounded words in this list belongs to a different contrast set with the word to its left and with the word to its right. For example, we can speak of low and high clouds, tall and low buildings, short and tall people, long and short wires, wide and long tables, deep and wide plots of land, shallow and deep swimming pools. The decision to represent each of the internal adjectives in the list with a single statement of its meaning would completely obliterate the associations with the large number of distinct contrast sets just exemplified, and would contribute very little to our knowledge of how the English vocabulary is organized.

4.11. A frequent topic of discussion among semanticists is the issue of where and how to draw the line between linguistic information about the meanings of words and real-world information about the properties of things. This issue usually takes the form of the question "What is the difference between a dictionary and an encyclopedia?" The famous Spanish Academy definition of *dog*, as the species in which the male urinates by raising one leg, or the common dictionary definitions of *left* or *right*, which speak of the side of a person facing south or north when that person is facing west, clearly are not conceptual analyses of their definienda, but rather serve as recognition tests for people who need to make sure what kinds of things the words designate. It is frequently assumed by linguistic semanticists that the linguist's job is to determine the purely linguistic information about word meanings, and that a distinction between a dictionary and an encyclopedia can in principle be established. A more realistic view might be something like this: there are things in the world, there are typical event types that one can observe in the world, and there are institutions and cultural values that make human endeavors interpretable; for a very large part of the vocabulary of our languages, the only form a definition can take is that of pointing to these things and actions and institutions and indicating the words used for naming and describing parts and aspects of them.

I do not assume that the role of the lexicographer and that of the encyclopedist cannot be distinguished; but I also do not think that everything that a native speaker knows about the meaning and use of a word can be encapsulated in a dictionary entry. The most useful practical dictionary will in many cases simply appeal to the reader's knowledge of the world, giving enough information to enable the user to acquire further information elsewhere if he fails to understand sentences containing the word and the dictionary definition fails him.

It seems clear, at any rate, that any attempt to relate a person's knowledge of word meanings to a person's abilities to interpret texts will have to recognize the importance of nonlinguistic information in the interpretation process. We get clearly different interpretations from the sentences "The fly was on the wall" and "The cat was on the wall," just because we know different possibilities for stable positions for these two kinds of animals and because we know that the same word—*wall*—can be used to refer to a vertical surface of a room or building and to a high-relief boundary around a place. Generally this kind of disambiguation is thought of as a use of semantic competence; but in this case it surely involves information of the kind that cannot be sensibly incorporated in the definitions of the associated words.

4.12. Another semantic notion for which the difference between linguistic and encyclopedic information is relevant is the concept of *metaphor*. The act of interpreting a metaphor requires an understanding of the kind of social-interaction schema within which the speaker can expect the hearer to do some special construing of what the speaker has said, and it requires an understanding of how the detection of a mismatch between the literal meaning of what has been said and the text world that is 'under construction' can trigger these special construal efforts. If we hear something like "Harry is a pimple on the face of the community," we do not use peculiarly linguistic information to interpret what has been said. We know enough about people, pimples, and communities to know that a coherent scene cannot be constructed out of that sentence taken literally. From that detection of a mismatch, we know that we should make use of the psychocultural information that people are embarrassed by and want to get rid of a pimple, and we assume that the speaker intended us to believe that the members of the community have feelings like that about Harry.

A common approach in linguistics to an explanation of the meta-

phoring process has been to determine the criterial features of a word
and to devise a formalism for showing how the features appropriate
for one word can be superimposed on the collection of features associated with a second word or group of words in the same construction.
I believe that most cases of metaphor, including the most interesting
ones, are not like that at all.

4.13.   The concept of *abstraction* has always been a difficult one to
point out and to be clear about in linguistic semantics. Abstractions are
not names of things, but they are not simple predicates or predications
either. They are somehow to be taken as the names of larger situations,
and they frequently occur in sentences in which some comment is being
offered on that larger situation. In the kind of notation I have been
proposing here, the concept of abstraction will be represented, not by
an arrow to any particular object in a scene, but by an arrow that points
to the scene as a whole. Furthermore, in the extent to which a concept
is an abstraction, the schema that expresses it will not be fitted into the
time line that goes with the text model, but must be taken on the side
as a kind of variable.

I have no new proposals on the nature of abstraction, but I can
at least point out that it may be necessary for semantic theory to recognize many different uses for, or points of view in the use of, a single
abstract concept. For example, in the prototype abstraction *charity*, we
know independently of any specific use of the word that somebody gave
something to somebody, the giver was not under any obligation to do
what he did, the receiver as a result of the charitable act undertook
no obligation to the giver, and the giver believed that what he did was
of benefit to the receiver. Once we have characterized a situation like
that, we sometimes need to call on fairly complicated procedures for
interpreting sentences containing the word, procedures that do not
merely point to the situation as a whole.

For example, when we interpret a sentence like "Charity is a virtue,"
what we have in mind is that the giver in an act of charity is judged by
the speaker to be good. When we interpret a sentence like "Charity is
degrading," we figure out that the receiver of the gift is being described
as feeling insufficient for needing and undignified for accepting that
kind of help. When we come across a sentence like "Charity is unnecessary in an ideal society," we are saying of this 'ideal society' that there are
no situations in it that fit the charity schema. And a sentence like "He
did it out of charity" reveals something about the giver's inner life at
the time of the gift—that is, we are being told that the giver felt no

externally imposed obligation to do what he did, that he expected no reward, and that he felt that what he was doing would help someone.

4.14.   One important question that comes up frequently in lexical semantics is that of the motivation for *lexicalization*. What does it take, the question is, for something to be expressed as a single word rather than more analytically? In specific terms, when would somebody say *kill* rather than *cause to die*?

In our understanding of language in general, there seems to be a schema for lexicalization the sense of which is that the act of lexicalizing something is the act of presenting it as an established category of human thought. If a lexical item exists, in other words, it must exist as some part of a frame and must correspond to some part of a schema. The English word *vegetarian* does not merely designate a person who lives exclusively on vegetable food. If everybody did, or if all creatures on earth did, there would be no particular need for such a concept, and hence for such a word. There is such a word because there are many people who eat meat, and by contrast there are people who deliberately do not eat meat. It is by virtue of this contrast that a word like *vegetarian* can have a function in our language.

Since everybody eats, there is no word **eater*; but there is a place in our language for a word like *chicken eater*, precisely because we can easily imagine a difference between people who eat chicken and people who do not. My remark that "there is no word **eater*" can easily be challenged. But the point is that for there to be an occasion for such a word, there would have to be, or to be imagined, some situation in which being an eater was importantly distinguished from not being an eater. Presumably in a community facing starvation there can come to be certain principles for deciding who will eat and who will starve; and in such a situation a contrast between eaters and non-eaters becomes a meaningful one.

4.15.   Instances of *functional shift* can be seen as instances of a special kind of lexicalization process. There are various conditions under which, in English, a noun can acquire a verbal use. One such word is *hammer*; another is *spoon*. A simple rule for describing this derivational process might be that a noun that names the instrument with which some action can be accomplished can come to be used as a verb designating the performance of that action with that instrument. It is important to realize that the verb *hammer* does not simply refer to hitting something with a hammer, but rather to hitting something, possibly with an implement that is not actually a hammer, in the manner in which and for the purpose for which hammers are typically used. Similarly, to *spoon* something is not simply to transfer it from one place to another by means of a spoon, but to do so by using a spoon in the most typical way in which spoons are used, in particular, by using a spoon in the kinds of actions for which spoons were invented.

5.   I have tried in this last lecture to say something about what it would take to push the 'scenes' model further than we were able to in the first three lectures; I have tried to lay out a number of distinctions that a semantic theory *cum* text interpretation theory of this kind needs to take into account; and I have tried to show that this approach to semantics when compared with the more traditional formal models of semantics does not leave us obviously less able to talk intelligibly about traditional concepts and problems in semantic theory.

I would like at this time to emphasize the tentative nature of whatever conclusions I have reached in these lectures, as well as the tentative nature of my commitment to the terminology and notation that I have introduced here. In a great many conversations I have had with other scholars who use terms like *frame, schema, scene,* and *prototype*—cognitive psychologists, philosophers, linguists, and computer scientists—I have been impressed first with the variety of conceptualizations that underlie these terms, and second with the reality of subtle changes in my own use of these terms as a result of these conversations. These are not good signs. The possibility of my being misunderstood equals in seriousness the possibility of my not remembering one month what I meant one month before. Those who have come with me this far need to be given these cautions.

NOTES

Preparation of these lectures was partly supported by the National Science Foundation through Grant no. SOC75–03538.

1. Wallace L. Chafe, "Language and consciousness," *Language* 50.1 (1974):111–33.

2. Personal communication, George Lakoff (who owns an advance copy of the McCawley cookbook).

3. See, e.g., R. Abelson, "The structure of belief systems," in Roger Schank and Kenneth M. Colby, eds., *Computer Models of Thought and Language* (San Francisco: Freeman, 1973); E. Charniak, "He will make you take it back: a study in the pragmatics of language," Technical Report, Istituto per gli studi semantici e cognitivi (Castagnola, Switzerland, 1974); M. Minsky, "A framework for representing knowledge," in P. H. Winston, ed.,

The Psychology of Computer Vision (New York: McGraw-Hill, 1975); and Roger Schank, "The structure of episodes in memory," in Daniel G. Bobrow and Allen Collins, eds., *Representation and Understanding: Studies in Cognitive Science* (New York: Academic Press, 1975).

4. It should be pointed out that the Chinese characters used in writing the word in these two senses are distinct.

5. Eleanor Rosch, "Natural categories," *Cognitive Psychology* 4(1973): 326–50.

6. Lucien Tesnière, *Elements de Syntaxe Structural* (Paris: Klincksieck, 1959); and Gerhard Helbig and Wolfgang Schenkel, *Wörterbuch zur Valenz und Distribution deutscher Verben* (Leipzig: Verlag Enzyklopädie, 1973).

7. Jeffery M. Paige and Herbert A. Simon, "Cognitive processes in solving algebra word problems," in Benjamin Kleinmutz, ed., *Problem Solving: Research, Method and Theory* (New York: John Wiley & Sons, 1966).

8. Charles J. Fillmore, "The case for case," in Emmon Bach and Robert Harms, eds., *Universals in Linguistic Theory* (New York: Holt, Rinehart & Winston, 1968).

9. Stephen R. Anderson, "On the role of deep structure in semantic interpretation," *Foundations of Language* 6 (1971):197–219.

10. David Johnson, "On the role of grammatical relations in linguistic theory," in *Papers from the 10th Regional Meeting of the Chicago Linguistic Society*, 1974, pp. 269–83, and "Toward a theory of relationally based grammar," Ph.D. diss., University of Chicago, 1974; and David Perlmutter and Paul Postal, Linguistic Institute lectures on relational grammar, MS., 1974.

11. Edward Keenan and Bernard Comrie, "Noun phrase accessibility and universal grammar," MS, 1972; and Edward Keenan, "Some universals of passive in relational grammar," in *Papers from the 11th Regional Meeting of the Chicago Linguistic Society*, 1975, pp. 340–52.

12. J. Otto Jespersen, *A Modern English Grammar*, vol. III (London: Allen & Unwin, 1927), p. 230.

13. Jeffrey S. Gruber, "Studies in lexical relations," Ph.D. diss., MIT, 1965, p. 24.

14. Albert C. Baugh, *A History of the English Language* (New York: Appleton-Century-Crofts, 1957), p. 387.

15. The way of dealing with the "hierarchy" presented in these lectures differs somewhat from what I suggested in another paper written at about the same time, "The case for case reopened," to appear in Peter Cole and Jerry Sadock, eds., *Syntax and Semantics*, vol. VII (New York: Academic Press). The view I present in that paper is more or less like the "case hierarchy" I proposed in Fillmore (1968): that is, noun-phrase roles were determined by their fit into the preestablished hierarchy of role types, their relative ranking determined by the ranking provided by that hierarchy. Here, however, I am suggesting that such matters as subject-selection (of the "unmarked" kind) might be determined by an ordered set of ranking considera-

tions. I do not have good reasons for preferring one of these proposals to the other. The main advantage I see to the proposals offered in this lecture is that it eliminates the need to determine the "final, correct" list of cases.

16. Anna Wierzbicka, "Emotion," in *Semantic Primitives* (Frankfurt: Athenäum, 1972), pp. 57–70.

Semantic Domains and Componential Analysis of Meaning

Eugene A. Nida, Johannes P. Louw, and Rondal B. Smith

The preparation of a completely new Greek–English dictionary of the New Testament for translators has made necessary a completely new approach to lexicology.[1] In this new dictionary some 20,000 meanings of the New Testament vocabulary (including both words and idioms) are classified in more than 300 structurally significant domains so that the related meanings of different lexical units may be treated together.[2] As a result of this arrangement, all the glosses associated with the different meanings of a single lexical unit will be found listed together only in the Greek–English index. For example, the diverse meanings of the Greek term *pneuma*, usually glossed as 'spirit', are treated under a variety of domains: 'wind' under Physical Events, 'breath' under Physiological Events, 'spirit (of a person)' under Features of Personality, and 'evil spirit' and 'Holy Spirit' under Supernatural Beings.

Furthermore, the meanings of lexical units are given in terms of componential features,[3] rather than by means of English glosses or correspondences. Such an approach is essential if one is to determine the potentially equivalent lexical units in another language. For example, in place of glossing Greek *aphiēmi* simply as 'forgive', the meaning is discussed in terms of four basic componential features: (1) an occurrence of injustice or injury (physical or psychological) caused by A; (2) a feeling of resentment or animosity on the part of B; (3) the removal of the resentment by B, with or without some action by A; and (4) the restoration of an interpersonal relationship essentially equivalent to what existed prior to the injustice or injury. Such a definition of meaning may seem somewhat involved, but it provides an important basis for testing the adequacy of presumably equivalent expressions in other languages.

In the third place, this dictionary provides a number of suggestions as to equivalences in other languages. This is an essential help for translators who may be working in languages having quite different grammatical systems and lexical structures reflecting distinct cultural contexts. An important reason for the use of definitions based on semantic components is that they provide a basis for determining the adequacy of corresponding expressions. In one of the dialects of Enga, a language of the highlands of eastern New Guinea, the apparent closest equivalent of *forgive* is 'to no longer hang up jawbones'. This idiom derives from the custom of hanging the jawbone of a murdered relative on the doorpost of one's house as a reminder that vengeance must some day be taken on the enemy clan responsible for the murder. When one forgives another, he no longer harbors resentment and plans revenge— he "no longer hangs up jawbones."[4]

This type of dictionary, with its new approach to some of the basic problems of lexicography, is a necessary tool for translators for three reasons: (1) the tendency of persons to think merely in terms of a single corresponding lexical unit for each source-language word, (2) the importance of considering groups of related meanings rather than considering only a single apparent equivalence, and (3) the need to think in terms of lexical units (whether words or combinations of words) rather than merely in terms of single words.

The tendency for people to think that each source-language word has only one corresponding lexical equivalent in the receptor language may with some justice be called the "root of all evil" in translating. It is particularly pernicious in the translating of texts such as the Bible, in which the verbal forms of the original text are so emphasized. Students tend to learn a first (often literal) meaning of a source-language word and then almost automatically expect it to fit thereafter any and all contexts. For example, a serious error in Bible translating has been the tendency to assume that the Greek term *sarks*, glossed literally as 'flesh', could be so rendered whenever it occurs, even though in reality it must be rendered by several different English expressions if one is to reproduce accurately the variety of meanings found in this one Greek term—e.g., "body" (Galatians 4:13), "human being" (John 1:14), "earthly descent" (Romans 1:3), "race" (Romans 11:14), "human standards" (1 Corinthians 1:26), "human nature" (Romans 8:4), and [normal] "sexual desire" (John 1:13). Obviously, it is wrong simply to say that *sarks* means "flesh." One can only correctly say that one of the meanings of Greek *sarks* corresponds to one of the meanings of English *flesh*.

To linguists the lack of one-to-one correspondence in meaning is perfectly obvious, but this fact is not recognized by all people—not even, unfortunately, by professional translators, who often fall into the trap of employing routine sets of semantic correspondences. For persons who are totally unaware of the fallacies created by such a false notion of lexical equivalences, the results may be serious. For example, an important French psychiatrist once insisted that Saint Paul suffered from a serious sex complex because he was constantly talking about *la chair* ('the flesh'). It is true that the French term *chair* does have a strong connotation of sexual desire, and the psychiatrist based his opinion on the French translation of the New Testament which he used in his "analysis" of Saint Paul. That translation does quite consistently render the Greek word *sarks* as *chair*. Even the practice of most dictionaries in giving first what is regarded as the literal meaning can be misleading (as in the case of *sarks*), since the persons who are using a dictionary almost inevitably regard the first meaning as a kind of common denominator to all the other meanings. In reality, the meanings of particular words tend to form various kinds of constellations in which there are chains of shared components. It is very rare, however, to find a single set of significant components for all the meanings of a particular word.

In determining which one of several possible terms should be employed in the translation of a source-language word, it is essential to consider all the semantically related lexical units in the same domain. For example, in dealing with the meaning of *repent* in its religious sense, it is important also to consider the related meanings of such terms as *conversion* and *remorse*, since all three of these terms belong to an important domain involving bad actions followed by regret and/or a possible change of behavior. The essential components of *repent* are (1) bad behavior, (2) sorrow concerning such behavior, and (3) presumed change of behavior. For *remorse*, the behavior is likewise bad, and the intensity of the sorrow may be regarded as even greater (though usually egocentric), but there is no suggestion of change of behavior. In the case of *conversion*, there is again a prior bad behavior, followed by a change in behavior, but without reference to an emotional attitude (sorrow) concerning the bad behavior. Only by carefully determining the significant contrasts in the componential features of a related domain can one be reasonably certain that the right term in the receptor language has been chosen.

An equally important reason for incorporating a componential approach in lexicography is the need for lexical units to be described in terms of the complex relations that may exist between the semantic components. A single word such as *mediator* may involve a very complex set of semantic features and relations, e.g., (1) the existence of three parties, (2) significant differences between two of the three, (3) the role of the third party in negotiating with each of the other two separately, and then possibly jointly, and (4) the goal of reaching an accord. Even a monomorphemic term such as *heir* involves quite complex semantic elements, e.g., (1) a person, (2) who will receive (or has received) some property (tangible or intangible), (3) normally upon the death of the person bequeathing the property.

The semantic complexity of single lexical units does not, however, create as many problems as the lack of conformity between languages with respect to phrasal units. In order to translate such expressions as *begin working, stop working, complete working*, or *continue working*, some translators attempt to find verbs meaning 'begin', 'stop', 'complete', or 'continue' in the receptor language. Such verbs only express aspects of the following action (in this instance, *working*), and in a number of languages such concepts are expressed by affixes. In the classification of domain structures all such aspectual elements are treated simply as aspectual abstracts of events, for they are not events in and of themselves.

The lack of formal correspondence in phrases is clearly evident in the case of idioms, which consist of combinations of lexical items in which the meaning of the whole cannot be deduced from the sum of the meanings of the parts. Though to some extent the Koine Greek expression rendered literally as 'opened his mouth and said' can be understood as a form of speaking, it cannot be fully or correctly understood simply by adding up the meanings of the parts, for this expression refers to the beginning of a discourse that is more or less formal in character.

The Essential Features of a New Approach to Lexicography

The new approach to lexicography employed in the preparation of this Greek–English dictionary is distinctive in several respects: (1) the use of an emic, rather than etic, system of analysis, (2) the recognition of semantic structures as being structurally coordinate with syntax, (3) the treatment of meanings in terms of componential features, (4) the classification of domains on the basis of shared components, (5) the emphasis upon multidimensional relations of meaning and non-orthogonal structures, (6) the careful distinction between linguistically marked and encyclopedically known information, and (7) the difference between meaning and reference. Other dictionaries may reflect one or more of these lexicographical features, but none so far have attempted to introduce all of them to the same extent or with the same degree of emphasis as this present work.

Insofar as possible an emic approach is employed in the classification of the meanings of Greek lexical units. For example, the meaning of Greek *pur* ('fire') is classified in the domain of substances rather than as an event, since according to the views of people in classical times fire was one of the four basic substances (together with earth, air, and water). In fact, it was only after fire was recognized as a process (or event) that alchemy could become chemistry. Similarly, certain of the meanings of *katharos* ('pure') and *hagios* ('holy') are treated in terms of negative and positive taboo; that is to say, *katharos* ('pure') involves the elimination of defilement, while *hagios* ('holy') denotes the addition of a positive element of the awesome or the divine.

In attempting to maintain an emic classification of objects, it has been necessary to adopt the cosmological view of the ancient world, in which the earth is regarded as a flat object covered by an arching dome or vault (Greek *ouranos*). This corresponds to "the second heaven" in which the stars, planets, sun, moon, and clouds were thought to exist. Here also were the "windows of heaven," through which rain came down. Above this dome was "the third heaven," the abode of God, and beneath it was the expanse of the air (Greek *aer*), both of which were also spoken of as *ouranos*. Only by using a cosmological framework can one make any sense out of such phrases as "birds of the heaven" and "the third heaven" or relate these phrases to such semantically equivalent expressions as "Abraham's bosom" and "paradise."

It is also necessary to recognize certain specializations of meaning that are characteristic of New Testament usage. For example, *deēsis*, a general term for 'entreaty' and 'petition', is used in the New Testament almost exclusively for 'prayer', and *agapē* is employed in some contexts to refer to a 'fellowship meal' (similar to the Jewish Passover meal), while *kerussō* generally means the preaching of the gospel, not the heralding of some important general communication. The meaning of the Greek term *tapeinos*, which in nonbiblical Greek Koine usage referred to something low and vulgar, becomes a distinctive Christian expression for the virtue of humility. In fact, some expressions seem to be almost ideolectal, as, for example, Saint Paul's use of *en khristō* ('in Christ').

It would be wrong to imply that this type of emic approach to the meanings of terms provides a completely consistent picture of the semantic referents of all lexical units. Language is never completely consistent. But it does mean that only by approximating insofar as possible an emic approach can one hope to provide a reasonably clear and accurate picture of the semantic system in question.

In order to provide an accurate account of the semantic structures, it is essential to free them from the domination of grammatical categories. That is to say, semantics must be viewed as a structure in its own right, touching reality in terms of its referents, and not merely as an appendage to syntax. This separation of semantics from syntax does not imply a denial of the constant links between the semantic and the grammatical structures, but each structure must be treated in terms of its own inner consistency. Since, however, a lexicon is designed primarily to deal with the word level, it necessarily overlooks certain semantic features that have important relations with syntactic structures. For example, for a verb form such as Greek *lelukamen* ('we have loosed'), the perfective formation *le . . . ka* is a time-aspect abstract and is classifiable along with various other independent abstracts in the same domain. Similarly, the suffix *-men* corresponds to the independent pronoun *hēmeis*, in that both forms refer to the first person plural ('we'), but the suffix *-men* has an additional component of voice, while the occurrence of *hēmeis* marks emphasis.

In a lexicon everything that can be defined in terms of grammatical structures is left to the syntax. For example, the differences between the active and middle/passive forms of *keirō*—'to cut the hair', 'to cut one's own hair', or 'to have one's hair cut'—are not introduced into a lexicon, but all so-called deponent forms, that is, middle or passive forms that have active meanings and no corresponding active forms must be treated in a lexicon, since they are not regularly derivable by so-called syntactic rules.

But semantic analysis must go beneath the lexical level. For example, the Greek term *pseudoprophētēs* ('false prophet') is ambivalent in meaning. The preposed element *pseudo-* may indicate (1) a false role (a person who pretends to speak on behalf of God but who does not), (2) or a false content (a lie), or (3) both a false role and a false content. On the other hand, the term *pseudapostolos* ('false apostle') refers only to the falseness of role.

The classification of meanings in terms of domains inevitably results in putting together the meanings of lexical units belonging to quite different formal classes. In Greek, for example, the particle *aei*, the adjectives *aidios* and *dienēkēs*, and the substantive phrases *eis aiona* and *aiōn tōn aionōn* may all occur with the meaning of 'forever' or 'eternal', and so they are classified together. Expressions for duration of time include nouns, adjectives, verbs, and prepositions. This means that one simply cannot assume that the grammatical word classes are basic to the arrangement of semantic classes. In English the meaning of *kind to* is best classified as an event, not as an abstract. The meaning of *growth* is an object in a context such as "the growth on his leg," but it is an event in the context "the growth of a child." The first meaning belongs to the domain of *tumor, swelling, bulge,* etc., while the second belongs to the domain of *increase, augment, enlarge,* etc.

Componential analysis is most effectively employed on the level of restricted domains, that is, between meanings that have certain minimal differences. In treating the componential structure of the related meanings of *mumble, shout, scream, whisper,* and *babble* (as defined by the common components of event, noise, human, and vocal), one may describe the contrasts and similarities by means of a matrix having the following sets of distinctive features: (1) verbal, (2) voicing, (3) loudness, and (4) high pitch (Fig. 1).

	mumble	shout	scream	whisper	babble
verbal	+	+	±	+	−
voicing	+	+	+	−	+
loudness	−	+	+	−	±
high pitch	−	−	+	−	−

Fig. 1

With matrices such as this, there are always, of course, certain difficulties. The plus (+) and minus (−) symbols mark only relative, not absolute, differences. For example, the degree of loudness may differ in *shout* and *scream,* the + only indicating that in regard to this feature there is a contrast between *shout, scream,* and possibly *babble,* on the one hand, and *mumble* and *whisper,* on the other. Second, the meanings in question are those that normally occur; that is to say, they are the unmarked meanings of such lexical units. *Whisper* may, for example, involve a degree of voicing in "stage whisper," but this is a marked kind of whispering.

It is important to note that this type of analysis involves only certain meanings of forms and not all the meanings. *Babble*, for example, in the sense of the babbling of a brook is not included in such an analysis, nor should the *scream* of a siren be included in such a set of closely related meanings. In too many instances analysts do not carefully define their domains by specification of common features and thus include too wide a variety of referents. As a result the definitions of meaning are either too generic to be useful or too filled with exceptions to be clear.

The listing of distinctive features for the verbal elements in the series *mumble, shout, scream, whisper,* and *babble* can be made somewhat more distinctive. For example, one may distinguish between "verbal" (generally applicable to *shout* and *whisper*), "indistinctly verbal" (normally applicable to *mumble* and *scream*), and "pseudoverbal" (applicable to *babble*). This more specific characterization of the verbal features would result in a reduction of the necessary and sufficient components and in a greater precision of definition.

One cannot, however, overlook certain supplementary components that are connotatively relevant. *Mumble*, for example, shares certain connotative features with *grumble, mutter,* and *murmur*, while *scream* suggests fear and/or anger. *Whisper* connotes secrecy, and *babble* suggests the action of children or of psychotics.

Rather than set up semantic domains on the basis of any a priori system constructed on some framework of philosophical or logical categories, it is essential that the domains reflect the extent and types of shared components. This means, for example, that expressions of time can be best handled in terms of meanings that involve points of time, units of time, and durations of time. Most units of time are either specific (i.e., calendrical), e.g., *century, year, month, day, hour*; or relative, e.g., *yesterday, today, tomorrow*. Duration of time may be (1) relative, e.g., *brief, forever*; (2) defined by a point, e.g., *until, still, afterwards*; or (3) coterminous, e.g., *during, while*. In English the term *time* itself has two principal meanings: one indicating point, e.g., *it was the right time to go*, and the other specifying duration, e.g., *he spent time there*.

While most attempts at semantic analysis stress the systematic nature of meaningful relations, it seems much better to reckon fully with the multidimensional and nonorthogonal elements. As long as one is dealing with a relatively restricted set of meanings (e.g., consanguineal kinship terms, color terms, foods, fauna, and flora), the structures appear to be relatively neat, but an examination of a broad segment of vocabulary in any language soon reveals the fallacy of Trier's concept (1931) of a neatly arranged mosaic of meanings covering in a relatively systematic way the totality of experience. The classification of meanings inevitably involves a number of what mathematicians call "fuzzy sets," that is, units that in certain respects belong to more than one set. Furthermore, there are holes in semantic structures and numerous relations, so that one simply cannot construct neat binary outlines of superordinate and subordinate categories into which to insert the various meanings. How, for example, is one to classify such simple meanings as those of *once* and *twice*, which involve both time and number? Only a recognition of dual membership can do justice to the facts. The Greek term normally glossed as 'pain' likewise involves a classificatory complexity. Should it be classified under Sensory Experience (it is certainly felt), under Physiological Events (the result of dysfunction or damage), or under Experience of Hardships? These three domains are all important categories, and the meaning of *pain* is in some sense related to all three. The New Testament expression *to cast lots* may be classified in two quite different domains: (1) play, in the sense of gambling (the action of the soldiers casting lots for Jesus' robe); or (2) divination, i.e., determining divine will (as in the choice of an apostle to take the place of Judas). There is no way to resolve this classificatory problem, since Koine Greek has no linguistically marked contrasts between these two culturally different events. On the linguistic level there is no difference of meaning, but there is a vast difference of meaning on the cultural level.

This problem in the classification of the expression for casting lots indicates yet another special feature of this lexicographical approach, namely, the distinction between linguistically marked and encyclopedically known information. Without linguistic marking there is simply no way to establish a semantic distinction. Just as in the case of its term for casting lots, Koine Greek makes no distinction in the use of *paradidōmi* ('to hand over'). This term may refer to the handing over of a guilty person to the law courts or to the betraying of a friend to an enemy. In English there is the lexical contrast between *to turn [someone] in* and *to betray*, but in New Testament Greek there is no such formal contrast and therefore no way to set up two different meanings belonging to two linguistically marked domains. This does not mean that the events referred to by *paradidōmi* had no differences in cultural significance. They most surely did, but this fact is not reflected in the lexical structures.

Generally speaking, no attempt is made to deal with encyclopedic information, that is, with cultural meanings based on encyclopedic information and not on lexical contrasts; but in some instances it is important, especially for translators working in quite different cultural settings, to have some idea as to the meanings of cultural events. For example, in New Testament Greek 'gnashing the teeth' may indicate either anger or suffering, and 'tearing one's clothes' may indicate either grief or indignation; but in some cultures such activities would indicate a state of dementia. Clearly then the symbolic value of such events is to be understood culturally rather than linguistically.

In lexicography it is constantly necessary to distinguish between reference and meaning. In the Greek New Testament the verbs *stauroō* and *prospēgnumi* are both used to refer to crucifixion, and one might assume that they both mean 'to crucify', but in reality only *stauroō* has that meaning, while *prospēgnumi* means 'to fasten to'. It is true that this latter term is often used to refer to crucifixion, but it cannot be said to have that meaning.

In determining the meaning of a particular term within a set of contexts, one should look for the minimal contribution that it makes to the total meaning. In New Koine Greek both *peritithēmi* (literally 'to put around') and *periballō* (literally 'to throw around') can be used in reference to putting on clothing, but with *peritithēmi* there must be a specific contextual reference to clothing, while with *periballō* the meaning of 'to clothe' may occur without a term for clothing occurring in the context. That is to say, only *periballō* can be used absolutely to refer to the process of putting on clothing. Accordingly, one can only define *peritithēmi* as meaning 'to put around', while *periballō* can be described as having the meaning of 'to put on clothing'. Traditional Greek dictionaries tend to err considerably in this particular area of defining meaning, for they often define a word such as *ballō* as meaning not only 'to throw' (its most common meaning) but also 'to sow', since it may be used together with terms for seed to refer to the process of sowing. But *ballō* can also be used with terms for 'spear', 'javelin', 'stone', 'anchor', etc., and though the actions involved are somewhat different, it would certainly be wrong to set up separate meanings for each type of throwing. In reality, the meaning of *ballō* should be described in terms of physical movement (that is, employing the arms and causing an object to go through the air), for that is the minimal contribution *ballō* makes to such contexts.

Basic Processes

In following the implications of this new approach to lexicography, two principal processes have evolved: (1) grouping the meanings into domains and (2) determining the componential structures of the classified meanings. Each process depends in large measure on the other, for the domains cannot be set up without at least a preliminary analysis of the componential structures, and the resulting componential analyses reflect the domain classification. It is true that such an approach runs the risk of circular reasoning, but this danger is inherent in the analysis of any system. It is impossible to understand completely the relevance of any part to the whole until the whole has been analyzed, and yet one cannot understand the structure of the whole until its parts have been analyzed. In the processes of setting up domains and working out sets of componential features, the ultimate goal is consistency of description and simplicity of explanation. In other words, one must aim at the highest possible level of generality consistent with the often "awkward facts" of language.

In order to describe some of the significant aspects of these two processes of domain classification and componential analysis, it seems best to consider the problems of componential analysis first and then to take up some of the difficulties involved in the classification of domains.

Componential Analysis

In undertaking any componential analysis of a related set of meanings, it is necessary to recognize three structurally important types of components: common, diagnostic, and supplementary. The common components are those features that any set of meanings have in common. The diagnostic components are those that are characteristic of one or more of the meanings but not of all, and the supplementary components are those that may be connotatively but not denotatively relevant or that may be denotatively valid but not really necessary or significant for establishing a minimal set of contrasts. These types of components have, in fact, already been discussed in connection with the domain of *mumble, shout, scream, whisper,* and *babble.*

Componential analysis also requires the recognition of several other structurally significant ways of cross-classifying the common, diagnostic, and supplementary components: (1) implicational vs. focal, (2) graded vs. nongraded, (3) redundant vs. essential, (4) ordered vs. unordered, (5) dominant vs. nondominant, and (6) psychologically relevant vs. structurally relevant.

Implicational components are of two types: (a) presuppositional and (b) inferential, and these contrast with focal components. In the case of the three components of the English word *repent* in its religious significance, the fact of prior bad behavior is presuppositional and is not affected by negation. In the two expressions *he repented* and *he did not repent*, for example, the implication remains that the person in question did something bad. The component of significant change of behavior is for many speakers of English simply an inferential component, for one can say *he repented, but kept on sinning*. Repentance is expected to lead to a change in behavior, but not necessarily so. This means that for *repent* in English the focal component is contrition. However, in the corresponding Greek term, *metanoeō*, change of behavior is the focal component, and hence this term is often equivalent to the English term *conversion*.

Some componential features can only be described in terms of degrees. For example, in the series *tall, big, huge*, and *colossal* one may employ the components of height and breath, as in Fig. 2.

	tall	big	huge	colossal
height	+	+	$+^2$	$+^3$
breadth	−	+	$+^2$	$+^3$

Fig. 2

One could, of course, also set up matrices in such a way as to indicate that any item to the right represents a higher degree of the same feature, but regardless of the system employed it is essential to recognize the fact of degrees of difference in the exponency of certain components.

In any complete series of components of the meaning of a term the upper hierarchical components are often completely redundant. For example, one may define the term *beer* as consisting of the following components: (1) object, (2) mass, (3) liquid, (4) beverage, (5) alcohol, (6) made from grain (as well as certain other ingredients), and (7) without distillation. But components (1)–(3) are completely redundant to component (4), since any beverage is an object, a mass, and liquid. In the actual discussions of the meanings of lexical units one normally does not list all the redundant components, but these are very useful in setting up the semantic domains. They also come into play in collocational restrictions and in some contexts may actually carry the contrastive load.

In many instances the semantic components of a lexical unit are structurally unordered. For example, the componential features of sex, generation, and lineality in the analysis of consanguineal kinship terms in English are completely unordered with respect to one another. But in many instances there is an ordering of components, either temporally or logically. For the components of *repent* the ordering is temporal, but for the components of *beer* the ordering is logical: objects may be divided into masses and nonmasses, masses into liquids and solids, beverages into alcoholic and nonalcoholic, alcoholic beverages into those made from grain and those made from other plant products, and finally alcoholic beverages made from grain may be distilled or nondistilled.

In some instances the apparent differences in meaning between two terms may involve merely factors of dominance. In contrast with the meaning of *all* in a context such as *all the boys*, the terms *every* (in *every boy*) and *each* (in *each boy*) involve not only totality (which *every* and *each* share with *all*), but also distribution. That is to say, *every* and *each* specify that all the members of a particular class are involved, but that they are specified distributively, not collectively. In the case of *each*, moreover, the component of distribution seems to be more dominant in the case of *every*. One may say, therefore, that for *each* the order of dominance in the components is (1) distribution and (2) totality, while for *every* the order is (1) totality and (2) distribution.

The contrast between psychological and structural relevance of components is crucial, for it affects in significant ways the types of classifications and analyses. The basic problem can be illustrated by analyzing the distinctive components of *run* and *walk* in their meanings of physical motion in space by an animate being. Undoubtedly the most psychologically relevant distinction between the meanings of these two terms is speed, for running is normally faster than walking. Nevertheless, some persons can walk faster than others can run. Hence, speed cannot be one of the "necessary and sufficient" diagnostic features. If English-speaking persons are asked to name the action of animate beings engaged in various types of bipedal motion, they consistently make a distinction between running and walking based on whether or not one foot (or two feet in the case of four-footed animals) is always in touch with the surface of the ground. Differences in speed are important supplementary features of the meanings of *run* and *walk*, but speed is not a diagnostic feature, in that it is not crucial in determining the usage of *run* and *walk* in actual contexts.

Different Meanings of the Same Lexical Units and of Morphologically Related Units

Though the componential analysis of meaning is based primarily on sets of related meanings of formally distinct lexical units, e.g., sets such as *mumble, shout, scream, whisper, babble*; *run, walk, hop, skip, crawl*;

repent, remorse, convert; etc., it is also necessary to recognize the existence of relevant differences of meaning for the same lexical unit or for related forms of the same lexical base. The lexical term *water* in the two contexts *he drank the water* and *he will water the lawn* obviously involves two related sets of meanings that may be conveniently described as derivative. The semantic event in *water (the lawn)* may be derived from the semantic object *water* by the addition of a component meaning 'to employ water in a particular activity', since all the components of the object *water* are incorporated in the related event. A similar relation exists between *build* and *builder*, but in the latter the component of actor (an object) is added to the underlying event of the former, for a *builder* is simply "one who builds." There may, however, be no morphological marker for such a semantic addition, e.g., *he will cook the meal* and *he is a cook*. We know, however, that the noun *cook* is semantically complex, for it includes not only an underlying event but also an actor. In the expression *he is a good cook*, the qualifier *good* refers specifically to the activity of cooking and is not a comment about the person's moral character, unless, of course, specifically marked by content, e.g., *most cooks steal food, but George is a good cook*. Some lexical units may be semantically complex in that they imply two or more different underlying semantic classes without there being any formally distinct base to which the distinctive classes may be related. For example, in *he is a good carpenter* the adjective *good* modifies the limited activity, but there is no underlying event expression such as *to carpent.

Figurative meanings differ from derivative ones in that the related meanings belong to quite different semantic domains, and the semantic relation is established either through some supplementary feature, as when a person is spoken of as a *pig*, or through a completely reinterpreted set of diagnostic features, as when one speaks of a wife *running* her husband.

For a lexicographer analyzing any written corpus in a foreign language, one of the greatest difficulties involves distinguishing between conventional figurative meanings and instances of figurative usage. For example, in the New Testament passage that speaks of trying to remove a *speck* from another person's eye while overlooking the *beam* in one's own eye, it is necessary to decide whether *beam* and *speck* represent conventional meanings, e.g., "trivial fault" vs. "serious failure or sin," or whether they are simply instances of figurative usage, that is, fresh metaphorical expressions that represent no widespread usage. In the Parable of the Talents the meaning of *talent* is quite clearly a large sum of money, but since the story as a whole has a higher level of significance, the figurative meaning of *talent* eventually largely replaced the earlier meaning of a large sum of money. Thus the analysis of poetic texts of "dead languages" poses constant difficulties in determining the status of figurative expressions.

Even more difficult to analyze than the derivative and figurative relations between meanings are the constellations of closely related meanings of single lexical units. Such clusters of meanings are often spoken of as central and peripheral, but in many instances there may be no single central meaning, but rather a constellation that may have a relatively well-defined structure, as in the circular constellation of *code* analyzed by Joos (1958). More frequently, however, the constellations of meanings are irregular in their structure. Compare, for example, the following instances of *run*, each of which involves physical movement:

1. The man ran
2. The water ran
3. The bus runs between New York and Boston
4. The motor runs well
5. His heart is running

The four meanings: (1) physical movement in space involving the use of lower limbs, (2) movement of a liquid, (3) scheduled movement of a vehicle, and (4) internal movement of a machine or organ, cannot be arranged neatly into any well-defined, symmetrical constellation. The lack of such a structure should not be disturbing, however, for the actual defining of these meanings must be undertaken by relating them to the specific domains to which they belong. Meaning (1) is analyzable in terms of contrasts in the domain of *run, walk, hop, skip, jump, crawl*, etc. Meaning (2) is analyzed in terms of the domain of *pour, drip, flow*, etc. Meaning (3) may be described in terms of contrasts with the meanings of *journey, trip, depart/arrive*, etc.; and meanings (4) and (5) may be handled together with certain meanings of *function, operate, work*, etc.

There is a tendency for lexicographers to depend largely on historical developments in deciding whether or not different meanings of a lexical unit are related, that is to say, whether they represent homophony or polysemy. One could, for example, point out how the following uses of *bar* are historically related:

> a bar against the door
> no bar to his success
> he is a member of the bar
> he entered the bar
> the stocking bar
> candy bar

But in the mind of the average speaker of English the various meanings share few if any components. For the person who knows something about the history of these uses of *bar*, there are, of course, certain semantic links, at least on the level of supplementary components, but for most speakers there are no lexical structures in which possible ambiguities of meaning would point to significantly related meanings.

The ultimate test for distinctiveness in meaning rests on sets of potentially or really ambiguous expressions. In the phrase *poor worker* the two meanings of *poor* become evident, since the meaning of poverty refers to the actor component in *worker* and the meaning of incompetence refers to the activity component. In the phrase *poor fellow* there is likewise an ambiguity involving the meanings of poverty and of unfortunate state. By setting up series of such ambiguous contexts it is possible to work out the major distinctions in meaning, which can then be assigned to their respective domains and further defined with greater precision on the basis of minimal contrasts within closely related sets of meanings.

The extent to which distinct meanings may be determined by sets of ambiguous contexts can be illustrated by the types of contrasts occurring in Fig. 3, which indicates the nature of certain primary contrasts in the meaning of *good*.

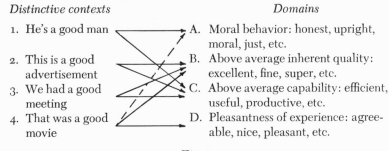

Distinctive contexts

1. He's a good man
2. This is a good advertisement
3. We had a good meeting
4. That was a good movie

Domains

A. Moral behavior: honest, upright, moral, just, etc.
B. Above average inherent quality: excellent, fine, super, etc.
C. Above average capability: efficient, useful, productive, etc.
D. Pleasantness of experience: agreeable, nice, pleasant, etc.

Fig. 3

In the statement *he is a good man* the reference may be either to the person's moral character or to his efficiency or capability. The statement about *a good advertisement* may refer to the quality of the layout or to the usefulness of the publicity. In the phrase *a good meeting* the reference may be to the quality of the arrangements, the usefulness of the results, or the pleasantness of the experience. The phrase *a good movie* may refer to the agreeable nature of the experience, the fine quality of the production, or even to the moral aspects of the character portrayal.

Of course, Fig. 3 does not include all the meanings of *good*. For example, good behavior consists of two types: (1) moral, honest, upright, etc. and (2) well behaved, obedient, etc. The first meaning is normally implied in *good man*, but the second in *good child*. The phrase *good boy*, however, is ambiguous, since the reference may be to either moral or obedient behavior. In these instances the meanings of *good* are to some extent conditioned by the behavioral expectancies for the classes of the headwords, e.g., *man, boy, child, baby* (in the last instance the reference is primarily to lack of crying).

The Size of Lexical Units

A complete analysis of the semantic structure of any language would require a componential analysis of each lexical unit (from morpheme to idiom) and the description of each meaningful relation between elements (from morpheme to discourse). The first type of analysis involves the semantics of basic units (the normal province of lexicographical studies), and the second involves the semantics of grammatical constructions. But lexicons normally include only clitics, words, and semantically exocentric combinations of words, i.e., those phrases whose meanings cannot be determined on the basis of adding up the meanings of their constituent parts. There are relatively few difficulties involved in determining the meanings of clitics and word units, but the task of deciding whether a phrase constitutes a lexical unit is often complex, for there are so many diverse types of phrases. In general phrases may be most satisfactorily classified on the basis of the semantic class of their respective heads: events, objects, and abstracts.

Lexical units with events as head words are of two major classes: (1) those with semantic goals, normally consisting of objects, e.g., *kick the bucket*, *give him a hand*, and *skinny as a rail*; and (2) those with relational qualifiers, e.g., *give in* (*to his father*), *turn out* (*an article*), (*the milk*) *gave out*, (*he*) *turned in* (*for the night*), and *they ran up* (*a bill*).

For idioms such as *out of the frying pan into the fire* and *bats in the belfry*, the relation of the literal meaning to the figurative meaning is relatively clear, but in many instances most speakers are not aware of the backgrounds of particular idioms, e.g., *kick the bucket*, which they nevertheless may use quite correctly. There is, however, always the tendency to reinterpret idioms to fit more well-known expressions. For example, most English speakers regard the idiom *between the devil and the deep blue sea* as having something to do with Satan, while in reality *devil* in this context is a reference to the chine plank built along the water line of wooden ships. Similarly, many English speakers think that *skinny as a rail* must be a reference to fence rails or the rails of a railroad, rather than to the bird so named.

Most idioms with event heads and semantic goals have quite specific single meanings, but a few may be ambiguous. For example, *to give a hand* may refer to applauding or to lending assistance.

Lexical units consisting of events plus relationals are far more numerous in most languages, and their classification and analysis involve many more difficulties. Note, for example, the occurrences of *in*, *out*, and *up* with *give*, *turn*, and *set*:

> He *gave in* for the sake of his job
> The milk *gave out*
> They *gave up* the fight
> He *turned in* a good paper
> The play *turned out* well
> He *turned up* at eight
> The rain *set in*
> He *set up* the conference

Special attention must be given to the distinction between endocentric and exocentric meanings of such phrasal units. In the expressions *he ran down the road* and *the water ran down the gutter*, the meanings are clearly endocentric, but in the sentence *they ran the thief down*, no literal running may be involved; the reference is to overtaking and apprehending. However, in the sentence *in his speech, he ran down the mayor*, the meaning is unquestionably exocentric, since the reference is to verbal abuse. Likewise, in the sentence *they ran down the quotation*, the reference is to the discovery of a verbal source.

Exocentric units with objects as semantic heads are of three types: (1) those in which the attributive belongs to one semantic class when occurring in semantically exocentric constructions but to another class in endocentric constructions, (2) those to which the semantic head belongs to one semantic class when occurring in semantically exocentric constructions but to another class in endocentric constructions, and (3) those in which both attributive and head exhibit these diversities in semantic class membership. Lexical units such as *white oak*, *goldfish*, *sweet pea*, *red bugs*, and *darkroom* are all illustrative of the first type. *White oak* belongs to the class of oaks, but the qualifier *white* serves to denote a number of features of white oaks that have only a definitely restricted relation to the normal endocentric meaning of *white* as a color.

It is true that *red bugs* are red, but *red* serves to identify a specific class of bugs, namely, chiggers, rather than any bug that is red.

The phrase *White House* is often cited as illustrative of this first type of phrasal unit, with an attributive that belongs to a class other than when occurring in normal endocentric usage. But the lexical unit *White House* has two quite different references: (1) the particular building occupied by the President in Washington, D.C. (in which case the meaning does belong to this class with semantically exocentric meaning of the attributive); and (2) the executive branch of government, which is a figurative meaning of the unit based on metonymy.

Exocentric phrasal units in which the head word belongs to one class in semantically exocentric constructions and to another class in endocentric constructions may be illustrated by such lexical units as *yellowtail* (the name of a fish), *redhead* (a person), *blackcap* (a type of berry), and *doubletree* (a wagon hitch). In such biblical phrases as *son of peace* and *son of consolation*, the semantic head *son* does not belong to the class of biological offspring but to the class of "person having the quality of."

For many exocentric phrasal units referring to objects, both constituent elements belong to semantic classes other than those that they normally belong to in endocentric constructions, e.g., *pineapple*, *blackeyed Susan* (the name of a flower), *custard apple* (another name for cherimoya).

Exocentric phrasal units that function semantically as abstracts may refer to almost any abstract quality or quantity, e.g., time (*by fits and starts, in the long run, time and again*), movement (*hither and yon, to and fro*), extent (*all in all*), degree (*as good as, good and* [as in *good and dead*]), and speed (*by leaps and bounds*). Their formal structures are also quite varied.

It is essential to distinguish phrases that are truly exocentric from certain other types of phrases that appear to be single lexical units but that are more satisfactorily analyzed in other ways. English verbs such as *do, make, give, receive, get,* and *show* exhibit a number of rather specialized distributions, e.g., *do the sweeping, do the work, do the cooking, make a speech, make an offer, make a deal, make a proposition, give a speech, give a talk, give a performance, give a lesson, receive a beating, receive blame, receive punishment, get a beating, get the blame, get a whipping, show grace, show mercy, show kindness,* etc. In all of these phrases, the principal semantic element is the postponed nominal, and the verbs *do, make, give, receive, get,* and *show* function primarily as expressions of tense or of voice (marking the agent, as in *make a speech*, or the experiencer, as in *get the blame*). In combination with postposed nominals these highly generic verbs make possible the particularization of an event (a type of aspect) and thus provide a base for quantification, e.g., *give a speech, give ten speeches*.

Semantic Domains

The primary semantic domains, classified in terms of the types of components and the internal relations of components to one another, are objects, events, and abstracts. The primary semantic classes of objects consist of animate beings (groups as well as individuals, both natural and supernatural), plants, artifacts (including constructions of all types), masses (both natural and manufactured), and geographical and celestial objects. In dealing with the various subdomains within these primary classes, the procedure is to treat first the more highly generic lexical units, e.g., *object, thing, matter, mass*, etc., and then the substitutes, i.e., the pronouns, since their meanings are defined in terms of class membership. Theoretically, proper names do not have meaning, since they refer to unique objects and are supposed to have only reference. In reality, however, some proper names do carry certain types of meanings, e.g., distinctions of sex (men's vs. women's names) and animate vs. inanimate (persons vs. places). Titles constitute a further problem in that the reference is unique within any context, but the meanings may be highly generic, e.g., *Lord, rabbi, Holy Spirit*. These titles are, of course, best treated under the domain that includes other similar referents.

The principal classes of events[5] seem to be best treated in terms of physical events (e.g., *rain, thunder, snow*); movement (e.g., *come, go, fly*); impact (e.g., *break, hit, press*); interactional (e.g., *associate, lead, rule, help*); complex activities that are not role-related (e.g., *mix, bind, wrap, take hold of*); complex activities that are role-related (in the sense of being rather highly specialized and often requiring professional training, e.g., *agriculture, herding, domestic, commercial, building, metallurgy, ritual, legal, military*); physiological processes (e.g., *live, die, eat, digest, sleep*); and psychological activities: sensory (e.g., *hear, smell, taste, touch, see*), emotive (e.g., *desire, love, hate, fear, grieve*), intellectual (e.g., *think, understand, learn, believe*), and communicative (e.g., *speak, converse, argue, declare*). For events there are also a number of highly generic expressions, e.g., *happen, take place, come about, exist*, and *do*, that frequently serve as a kind of verbal substitute. For example, *do* may substitute for *mow, sweep,* and *wash,* respectively, in *do the lawn, do the floor,* and *do the dishes.*

The principal distinction in classes of abstracts is between (1) those that qualify objects and (2) those that qualify events, but considerable overlapping occurs. The abstracts of objects involve primarily number (e.g., *few, many, one, two*), quantity (e.g., *little, much, big, small*), spatial relations (e.g., *in, out, far, near, through, around*), status (e.g., *slave, free, noble, commoner*), esthetics (e.g., *beautiful, elegant, ugly*), and state (normally implying the result of some event, e.g., *sick, well, lame, blind*). The abstracts associated with events involve primarily time (e.g., *occasion, year, day, while*), aspect (e.g., *begin, continue, complete, stop*), mode (e.g., *possible, probably, may, can*), voice/case: e.g., agent (*do, make*), experiencer (*get, receive*), instrument (*use, employ*); speed (e.g., *fast, slow*), direction (e.g., *in, out, through, around*), logical relations (e.g., *because, but, if, though*), negation (e.g., *not*), degree (e.g., *very, intensely*), and ethical/moral (e.g., *good, bad, kind, holy, sinful*).[6]

In the above distinction between abstracts of objects and those of events, there is a considerable degree of overlapping. Lexical units such as *much* and *little* can be qualifiers of both objects, e.g., *much bread* and *little chair,* and events, e.g., *work much* and *slide a little.* The spatial relations such as *in, out, far, near, above, below, through, around* can readily qualify both objects, i.e., the relative position of objects, and the location of events with respect to objects or space.

When lexical units involve only a single major semantic category, the classificatory problems are not great, but there are many lexical units that involve two or more major domains.[7] Combinations of object and event components are quite frequent, e.g., *dancer, heir, musician, gift, payment,* and *growth* (as in *the growth on his leg*). In many instances the relation between event and object is one of agent, e.g., *dancer,* but often the object is the result of an event, e.g., *gift* (i.e., that which is given).

Other complex combinations involving objects include the following types of associated components: states/conditions (e.g., *paralytic, leper*), qualities (e.g., *the poor, the humble*), quantities (e.g., *many, none*), spatial relations (e.g., *those, these*), events plus relations (e.g., *mediator, reconciler, go-between*), and events plus abstracts (e.g., *sanctifier, purifier*). Since these object classes involve primarily only an object component added to another semantic base, the meanings are treated at the same place in the lexicon as the base, and the semantic development is indicated as derivative.

Event expressions may also be complex. *To sicken* and *to enslave* involve the combination of event and state (i.e., a change of state, with focus on the final condition). The combination of event and change of state (or condition) is essentially a process, and it may be either highly generic (e.g., *change, alter, restore*) or quite specific (e.g., *widen, enlarge, archaize*).

Types of Domain Structures

In addition to the classification of domains in terms of their major semantic components, it is advisable to determine the structural types of domains, since the relations between the components within any series are important for the clearest presentation of the meanings. Domains are primarily of two structural types: taxonomic and associative. The taxonomic domains are hierarchical, but may involve a certain amount of overlapping and a number of lacunae. Taxonomic series are well illustrated by classifications of terms for fauna and flora in typical degree diagrams. Series such as *animal, mammal, dog, poodle* and *animal, reptile, snake, cobra* are typical of the lines in such hierarchical series.

Associative domains are also of two types: part–whole and series. Part–whole sets may be illustrated by body parts or parts of a building. Frequently, however, lexical units in a part–whole domain can also be classified in other domains. For example, the meaning of *window* can be determined by contrast with a domain including *aperture, hole, opening, door*, etc., and *roof* can be analyzed in terms of contrasts with the meanings of *cover, top, lid*, etc.

Series may be either open, e.g., numbers (either cardinal or ordinal), or closed. And closed series may be either nonrecursive, e.g., lineal (e.g., *a, b, c, d, e*, etc.) or ranking (e.g., *general, colonel, major, captain, lieutenant*, etc.—such ranking series exist in commercial, academic, religious, and other types of institutions), and recursive (or cyclical), e.g., days of the week, months, seasons.

One of the major problems of traditional taxonomic classifications has been the tendency to relate only individual lexical units in series of specific superordinate or subordinate relations, that is, in typical tree structures. For many domains this is quite impossible, for the hierarchical relations exist between domains and not between specific lexical units. For example, under the highly generic meaning of *move* (in the sense of movement in space) the immediately subordinate meanings are *come* and *go*, to which directional components have been added. Immediately subordinate to *come* and *go* is the series *return, leave, arrive,* etc., in which a component of spatial orientation has been added. A further subordination of two classes occurs: one involving vehicular movement, e.g., *drive, fly, ride,* etc., and another involving nonvehicular movement, e.g., *walk, run, hop,* etc. A domain including *accompany, lead,* and *follow* is subordinate to both vehicular and nonvehicular movement, but involves animate accompaniment, while the set *carry, fetch,* and *lug* is also subordinate to the same two sets, but the objects associated with such events are normally nonanimate, and for *fetch* there is a double directional component. The meanings of the lexical units *haul* and *transport* are subordinate to vehicular movement, and the series *saunter, stroll, stride* is subordinate to *walk,* with such added components as slow rate of movement, vigor of action, and indefiniteness of direction. These relations may be diagrammatically indicated as in Fig. 4.

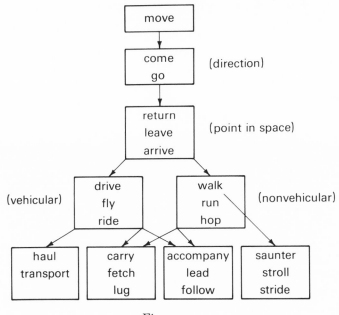

Fig. 4

Semantic Relations within Nuclear Domains

The classification of meanings into various large domains is important for an orderly and revealing explanation of meanings, but for determining the distinctive features of meanings of particular lexical units it is important to set up those nuclear domains that indicate most readily the significant contrasts. Nuclear domains often consist of no more than five or six close meanings that exhibit those nominal differences of meaning necessary for incisive definitions of the diagnostic components.

The semantic relations between the meanings within such nuclear domains (or sets) are of four types: contiguous, included, overlapping, and complementary. The contiguous sets, e.g., *walk, run, hop, skip, crawl* or *yodel, hum, chant, croon,* are the most important in setting up diagnostic components, since in such sets each meaning is separated from each other meaning by at least one diagnostic component (matters already noted in the discussion of the set *mumble, shout, scream, whisper, babble*).

Included sets (based on taxonomic hierarchies of meaning) are likewise important, since each included meaning contains at least one more distinctive component than the immediately superordinate meaning. In the series *move, walk, stride* one may define *stride* as a kind of *walking* and *walk* as a form of *moving*.

Overlapping sets, e.g., *give/bestow/donate* and *answer/reply/respond/talk back/argue,* are significant, for they mark crucial areas of synonymity, thus requiring statements as to those contexts in which substitution may or may not occur.

Complementary sets are of three types: (1) opposites, e.g., *good/bad, many/few, go/come, this/that*; (2) reversives, e.g., *tie/untie, build/dismantle, alienate/reconcile, marry/divorce*; and (3) conversives, e.g., *buy/sell, lend/borrow* (in which the role relations are reversed).

Basic Problems of Classification

In attempting to classify meanings in terms of domains, one inevitably encounters a number of problems, one of the most serious of which involves grouping the meanings into sets. Actually there is no satisfactory solution to this problem. When very many meanings represent multidimensional relations, one cannot by means of lists or outlines do justice to the variety and intricacy of the relations. Even a gigantic matrix would not be adequate, since not only are there multiple relations between meanings but also the degree of semantic "cohesion" differs significantly. Even a multidimensional matrix of six or seven dimensions would scarcely be adequate; and even though it might be possible to construct such a matrix, it would probably be too complex to be very useful. Such a relatively simple problem as the classification of the central meaning of *kill* illustrates some of the difficulties. One can readily justify the classification of *kill* under events of impact, but it is also interactional in the sense of normally resulting from conflict. *Killing* can also be described in terms of physiological processes, that is to say, causing physiological activity to cease.

The classification and analysis of complex role-related activities also provide a serious problem. Such domestic activities as *cooking, washing, cleaning,* etc., are highly complex in that they involve many specialized movements and related objects. Quite obviously one cannot specify the meanings of such terms by describing all the activities involved, for such information would be encyclopedic, not semantic. One can only define meanings negatively, in the sense that the meaning of *cooking,* for example, must be clearly distinguished from all other terms within the same domain. Semantic analysis does not describe all the referents of a term; it only defines the limits of meaning by specifying the distinctive features of a particular semantic area.

Semantic analysis would be so much easier if all semantic domains were essentially systematic in their structures, but this is not the case. The biblical phrase *heaven and earth* would seem to include all possible space and related objects, but in reality the sky is not specifically included in the meaning of English *heaven,* nor would the underworld (i.e., the abode of evil spirits) be included in *earth.* The Greek series in Acts 14:15, *ouranos* ('heaven'), *gē* ('earth'), and *thalassa* ('sea'), likewise appears to be all-inclusive, but for Saint Luke there seems to be a clear distinction between *thalassa* ('sea') and *limnē,* a relatively small body of water surrounded by land. One can, of course, argue from Acts 14:15 that for Saint Luke *limnē* was simply a kind of *thalassa,* in which case *thalassa* would have two different meanings, each on a different hierarchical level. One can only say that the series *ouranos, gē, thalassa* is conceived of as being all-inclusive, and that therefore the meaning of the combination is best regarded as greater than the meaning of the sum of its parts.

The problems of negation and semantic privatives are particularly difficult. In English, for example, one cannot assume that *unkind* is merely a negation of *kind.* In reality, *unkind* does not mean "lacking in kindness" but "acting in a harsh, unfriendly manner." *To be unkind* is therefore somewhat different from *not to be kind.* On the other hand, the privative *impossible* is equivalent to *not possible.* (However, the prefix *un-* may also be reversive, rather than privative, e.g., *untie* and *undo.*)

This unsystematic nature of language should in no way be regarded as a liability. In fact, if it were not for the unsystematic nature of language, as reflected in the various competing analogies of meaning and multidimensional semantic relations, languages would be so semantically stable as to prevent or seriously impede growth, innovation, and creativity. Without the multidimensional nature of semantic relations many of the subtler aspects of poetry would be impossible.

This rather new approach to some of the basic problems of lexicography has certain important theoretical implications that should perhaps be made explicit. As already indicated, semantics is here regarded as a structure in its own right. It cannot be made subordinate to syntax if one is to arrive at the most consistent and generalized explanation of semantic functioning. Conversely, syntax should not be swallowed up in semantics. All significant relations are semantic, but some are lexical (the meaning of units), some are syntactic (the meanings of combinations of units), and a few are phonological (symbolic because of their sounds).

No existing model or theory of language appears to be completely adequate to reveal all the facts of language structure and function. Each model is essentially a metaphor,[8] and it certainly should not become a Procrustean bed. A model should be a window to let in the light that comes from a particular structural perspective. The lexicalist position is important in emphasizing the significance of the lexical level in language, but it fails in the extent to which it refuses to explicate the sublexical semantic structures, which in so many respects parallel some of the syntactic structures.

In treating the semantics of sublexical structures, due recognition must be given to the generative-semanticist position; but all semantic structures cannot be reduced to features of propositional logic. Stratificational analyses (Makkai, 1972) and the neo-Firthian approach of Halliday (1968, 1970) are also extremely important for semantic analysis, although they do not serve to explicate the entirety of either competence or performance in language. All of these models of language are important, but only within the limitations of their distinctive perspectives. Unfortunately, there are too many claims that a particular model can and must explain everything about languages. To make such a claim for any model is the surest way to guarantee its early obsolescence.

NOTES

1. This Greek-English dictionary to the vocabulary of the New Testament is sponsored by the United Bible Societies and will be a major tool for the

use of the translators who are presently engaged in the translation of the Bible, in whole or in part, into more than 900 languages. In addition to supplying a detailed analysis of the meanings of the Greek terms, the dictionary will contain extended statements concerning a wide variety of ways in which the closest natural equivalents of these terms may be found in other languages. The dictionary will have two extensive indexes: from Greek to English and from English to Greek. The authors of this paper constitute the editorial committee for the undertaking. It is expected that the work will be completed and ready for publication about 1979.

2. Though certain of the concepts involved in the determination of semantic domains derive from the work of Trier (1931), the basic theory is more closely related to that of Voegelin (1948), Voegelin and Voegelin (1957), and Lehrer (1974). A number of the problems of domains have also been treated by Nida (1964, 1975a).

3. For the basic theory and practice of componential analysis of meaning see Lounsbury (1955, 1956), Goodenough (1956), Conklin (1962), Lehrer (1974), Nida and Taber (1969), and Nida (1975a).

4. There are, of course, some definite limitations in the semantic analyses being undertaken in connection with this Greek–English dictionary. The corpus is relatively limited, consisting of some 500 pages of text and some 5,000 different words. Also, the subject matter is relatively specialized. A very serious handicap is the obvious impossibility of consulting native speakers of Koine Greek, and the extant Koine papyri, though relatively abundant, supplement the lexicographical data in a very restricted manner. In addition, the Greek vocabulary of the New Testament is greatly influenced by the meaning of corresponding Hebrew terms. In fact, some scholars have contended that the New Testament is merely a Hebrew document in Greek words. For example, the term *logos* (John 1:1) must be understood as reflecting the Old Testament concept of the wisdom of God, and not simply as a neoplatonic demiurge. Likewise the phrase *Son of God* must be related to such Hebrew expressions as "son of peace," "son of consolation," and "sons of thunder," and not to typically Greek concepts that suggest biological relations more than similarities of attitude and personality.

Despite its limitations, however, this Greek–English dictionary is a rather unusual project in that it involves the largest and most diverse body of data yet submitted to componential and domain analysis. Also it involves a thesaurus based on shared componential features rather than on philosophical categories, and it will provide an abundance of cross-cultural data that are encountered in quite diverse semantic structures.

5. The domain classifications for both events and abstracts are still tentative. The nuclear domains are relatively certain, but some of the larger domains may be regrouped on the basis of further sorting of relevant components. This problem of indeterminacy in the classification of domains points to one of the serious difficulties in semantic analysis, namely, the lack of an adequate metalanguage to deal with class structures.

6. The classification of ethical/moral as being primarily related to events may seem strange, since one so frequently employs phrases such as *good man, bad boy, kind woman*. But qualifiers such as *good, bad,* and *kind* actually refer to the behavior of such persons and not to the person as an object, as in the case of *tall man, short boy,* and *ugly woman*.

7. For a more detailed systematic treatment of semantically complex classes of lexical units see *Componential Analysis of Meaning* (Nida, 1975a).

8. This equation of models with metaphors is very effectively described in Turbayne's volume, *The Myth of Metaphor* (1962).

REFERENCES

Conklin, Harold C. 1962. Lexicographical treatment of folk taxonomies. In Fred W. Householder and Sol Saporta, eds., Problems in lexicography. *IJAL* 28(2):119–41. Indiana University Research Center in Anthropology, Folklore, and Linguistics, Publication 21.

Goodenough, Ward H. 1956. Componential analysis and the study of meaning. *Language* 32:195–216.

Halliday, M. A. K. 1961. Categories of the theory of grammar. *Word* 17: 241–92.

———. 1968. Notes on transitivity and theme in English, part 3. *Journal of Linguistics* 4:179–215.

———. 1970. Functional diversity in language as seen from the consideration of modality and mood in English. *Foundations of Language* 6:322–61.

Joos, Martin. 1958. Semology: a linguistic theory of meaning. *Studies in Linguistics* 13:53–70.

Lehrer, Adrienne. 1974. *Semantic Fields and Lexical Structure.* Amsterdam: North-Holland Publishing Company.

Lounsbury, Floyd G. 1955. *The Varieties of Meaning,* pp. 158–64. Washington, D.C.: Georgetown University, Institute of Language and Linguistics, Monographic Series no. 8.

———. 1956. A semantic analysis of the Pawnee kinship usage. *Language* 32:158–94.

Lyons, John. 1968. *Introduction to Theoretical Linguistics.* Cambridge: Cambridge University Press.

Makkai, Adam. 1972. *Idiom Structure in English.* The Hague: Mouton.

Nida, Eugene A. 1964. *Toward a Science of Translating.* Leiden: E. J. Brill.

———. 1975a. *Componential Analysis of Meaning.* The Hague: Mouton.

———. 1975b. *Exploring Semantic Structures.* Munich: Fink Verlag.

Nida, Eugene A., and Taber, Charles R. 1969. *The Theory and Practice of Translation.* Leiden: E. J. Brill.

Trier, Jost. 1931. *Der deutsche Wortschatz im Sinnbezirk des Verstandes: die Geschichte eines sprachlichen Feldes.* Heidelberg: C. Winter.

Turbayne, Colin Murray. 1962. *The Myth of Metaphor*. New Haven: Yale University Press.

Voegelin, C. F. 1948. Distinctive features and meaning equivalence. *Language* 24:132–35.

Voegelin, C. F., and Voegelin, Florence M. 1957. Hopi domains, a lexical approach to the problem of selection. *IJAL* Memoir no. 14.

Zgusta, Ladislav. 1971. *Manual of Lexicography*. The Hague: Mouton.

Intentions, Assumptions, and Contradictions in Historical Linguistics

Henry M. Hoenigswald

The relationship between linguistics in general and the historical-comparative tradition within it is quite extraordinary. The story has often been told how historical and 'comparative' linguistics—at one time the dominant, almost exclusive, activity in the discipline—was overtaken by the new synchronistic wave a few decades ago. Yet it is strange that historical linguistics, even after its alleged dethronement, hardly suffered damage worse than novel competition for attention and support, and occasional outbursts of ill-informed temper. On the whole the diachronic study of language, now presumably visible in its true context rather than in the earlier, absolute fashion, was judged to have come through the fire of relativization unscathed. Though its generalizations had often been questioned from within—a matter to which we shall return below—it continued to be admired for its achievements, and especially those who had found other interests would profess admiration from afar and would spread a feeling that here was a tradition that should not be touched because it could not easily be improved upon and that, in fact, deserved a pedestal.

In one sense the eulogists were right; in another, their attitude spelled mischief. Pragmatically, comparative and historical study had been a success; its procedures and results were coherent and, being testable in principle, had stood the test wherever it could be applied. They were even discovered to be more general than had been thought, and not at all limited to particular languages in particular historical conditions. Yet the same practitioners who had brought about this state of affairs and whose erudition and sagacity was so plain when they were seen dealing with their data could also be found discussing their concepts and their methods in the abstract—not to mention even more ambitious forays into philosophy. Experience tells us how brittle such activities can be when contemporary, and what additional scrutiny they demand and how easily we misunderstand them when we confront them in retrospect, with altered presuppositions and different expectations, though, alas, frequently still armed with a deceptively unchanged vocabulary. We must in any case remember that tacit assumptions have a way of being at least as powerful as assumptions openly proclaimed, and that the price for missing the relationship between the two can be heavy. In this vein we shall examine certain tenets of historical and comparative linguistics; and we shall do so in a spirit of deep respect for our distinguished predecessors' record, but also with the wariness that is called for when we discuss their own descriptions and evaluations, no matter how often repeated and how well established, of that very record.

In introducing a field of knowledge it is customary, at least as a matter of style, to begin by proclaiming some self-evident axiom. In the case of historical linguistics the traditional opener is to the effect that 'all languages change'. It is quite clear what the original target of the statement was: it was rightly directed against the idea that languages existing in a fixed literary form and deliberately cultivated in this form (like Latin or classical Arabic) should be representative of language as a general human activity. In actual fact, Latin and Arabic have of course changed from the form on which the literary variety was once based, and live on in their 'descendants'. But aside from this, let us have a look at the axiom and its claim to self-evidence. To begin with, let us consider some of the obvious analogies. To say that a language changes seems not unlike saying that an object or a substance (say, a rock) changes properties—color, temperature, consistency—or that an individual changes (a caterpillar into a chrysalis, and a chrysalis into a butterfly; or a sick child into a healthy adult), or that a city or a political institution changes in history; and even if this kind of thing should not be intended, the reader is still bound to understand it so. What is more, it may occur to him that the same ubiquitousness of change that is being claimed for languages may exist for some of the analogs: he may believe that all living beings change or that all cities change. In no event, however, is he in any doubt about the perseverance of the object or substance to which changeability or change is attributed. He is convinced—naively, perhaps—that a changing rock, caterpillar, child, or city is the same rock, insect, human individual, or city both before and after the change; that the substance remains identifiable as such and that only some of its accidental traits have become different. His natural inference must then be that a language, even as it is affected by change, also remains identifiable.

At this point, to be sure, certain terminological matters are explained to him, and he is told that our customary labeling may be misleading and that, along one *line of descent*, a language may change the name by which it happens to be known: 'Anglo-Saxon' (if the term is used instead of 'Old English') 'becomes' Middle English; Latin (or something like it) 'becomes' French or Rumanian; and so on. Still, the purpose of this warning is only to insist that while the label does not matter, there is reality to what is being labeled, namely, the line of descent. It is implied that the business of recognizing Old English (Anglo-Saxon) and Latin as 'ancestors' or 'earlier stages' of Middle English and of French, respectively, is either not a problem at all, or one that can be separated from another problem, namely, that of describing the changes along the line. On the preliminary plane on which we are at present moving there has been very little discussion of just what the criteria for establishing an ancestry-and-descent relation might be other than, perhaps, 'inspection'. At best there is agreement that certain particular conceivable factors are no more dependable than labeling: habitat (American English is not the descendant of any pre-Columbian language), physical descent of the speakers (it does not matter what languages a person's ancestors spoke at specified times in the past), explicit folklore rife among speakers or observers, and the like.

The fact is that the expert has at this point nothing to say to his reader. The pronouncement that all languages change, however meaningful he feels it is and whatever meaning we may be able to give to it, is not in the nature of a coherent report of some indubitable experience so long as we cannot say what it is that change is ascribed to. The quasi-truism we need, at least rhetorically, at the outset, must be less specific. It can only be to the modest effect that *no two forms of speech, found in different places and at different times, are the same*. In this formulation, the expression 'different places' should not be pressed,[1] and 'form of speech' means what is usually called a language (or dialect) at a given time—that is, the kind of object that historians find or construct.

Let us also assume that 'sameness' can somehow be defined, and let us agree, as perhaps we may, that the pronouncement just made is acceptable in an empirical sense.

Our subject matter, then, is forms of speech or language states, each one unique, with their coordinates of time and space, but so far without lines of a meaningful sort connecting them. Nor do we ask at this juncture how we have come by our data: whether from direct observation, from written records, or through inference.

The next step is to identify those forms of speech among which historical relations of some sort exist ('descent', 'relatedness', but also 'contact'). In order to do this, we must for a moment digress and anticipate, and we hope that we can do so once again by staying close to empirical matter on which we may agree without much hesitation. We may begin by observing that while we do not yet know how to determine a line of descent, we do know something about certain effects of the lapse of time on speech communities and on the speaking individuals making up speech communities. We may for instance notice that while words like *sick* and *miss* contrast with *thick* and *myth* in normal English, *thick* may become homophonous with *sick*, and *myth* with *miss*[2] both (1) when 'borrowed' into the speech of certain German-speaking immigrants, and (2) when occurring in their English. We have little difficulty in understanding this bit of phonemic substitution; in fact we expect it, given the sound systems of the two languages in contact,[3] and we expect it to occur with 'regularity', that is, in all the words that are either (1) borrowed or (2) learned by those speakers at that time. If we now choose to match the original shapes with the (1) borrowed or (2) imperfectly learned shapes that only came into existence with the contact situation, we conclude that a contact situation may result in a phonemic *merger*. What is more, if we knew nothing about the chronology of the two language states, the very fact that there is one kind of English (ordinary English) in which the two pairs of words are different, and another (the English spoken by our special group) in which they are identical would inform us that the latter had *innovated*.

Now let us suppose that history partly repeats itself and that another contact situation arises, this time involving speakers of a language similar to Japanese, (1) borrowing *right* and *light* from ordinary English into their language, or (2) learning to say those two words in speaking English; and let us suppose that the contrast disappears in the process. By virtue of the logic employed above, a matching of ordinary English with the special English of this group will lead to the judgment that the latter has innovated in merging the original *r* with the original *l*, while ordinary English has *retained* the contrast. And, to take the next step: if our quasi-Japanese English is directly matched with our German English, both may be seen to contain one innovation each. The matching procedure has of course become well known as the 'comparative' method (in the narrow sense of the word) with which to reconstruct a common 'ancestor' even in cases where it is not available in uninnovated shape. If we imagine for a moment that ordinary English has died out and only our two special varieties have survived (and if we assume, for the sake of the argument, that 'quasi-Japanese' English somehow[4] preserves the distinction between words with *s* and words with *th* [θ]), we have the situation shown in Fig. 1. From Fig. 1 we reconstruct ordinary English, as shown in Fig. 2.

Fig. 1

Before we stop to consider the meaning of the connecting lines, a disclaimer is in order. The preceding remarks are offered only to illustrate the fact that there are known sociolinguistic situations (for instance, language contact) that result in merger, and to lay the groundwork for the thesis that when historians speak of lines of descent they have processes in mind that share fundamental properties with those particular situations. No one should think for a moment that these are exactly and literally the very ones that we have here constructed for our oversimplified skeleton cases. In particular, the languages involved in this substratum[5] model need not be widely different and mutually unintelligible; it has, in fact, long been pointed out that gross effects of this sort frequently fail to survive, because gradual

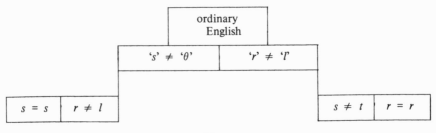

Fig. 2

assimilation of imperfectly learned forms of speech to a persistent standard tends to eliminate long-range effects even if such imperfect versions arise and exist during a limited period. The real breeding ground for the development in which we are interested must be a much subtler and much more pervasive condition, in which the contact is one among dialect varieties, styles, and other entities of the sort that add up to produce ranges of *variation* within a speech community and with regard to which the speaking individuals possess richly diversified degrees of control. Only to the extent that the crude models in Figs. 1 and 2 have their counterpart in this infinitely more finely graded context, are those models applicable. Yet, as the record of comparative linguistics shows, it is reasonable to believe that indeed there are such counterparts and that it makes sense to look upon phonemic mergers as the prototypes of linguistic innovation.

We may now return from our digression. Historical relations among forms of speech are, in part, revealed by a degree of 'regularity' or absence of phonemic randomness as we translate from one language into another. Tentatively, and subject to further interpretation, we suggest that two forms of speech that are linked by such ties are so linked in one of two ways: either in such a way that one form of speech has all the innovations, or in such a way that each has at least one innovation. In the former case we have a line of descent from the retaining ancestor (or older stage) to the innovating descendant (or later stage). In the latter case we have a collateral relationship with two lines of descent emanating from a third form of speech: the common ancestor, which may be either known or reconstructed, but which in any event *can* be reconstructed as possessing none of the innovations.

The lines drawn in Figs. 1 and 2 represent, of course, such lines of descent in our primitive model, where the descendant languages were not typical forms of speech such as historians and comparatists usually encounter, but special languages resulting from known or essentially familiar contact situations, equated *ex hypothesi* with ordinary descendant languages. Yet there is no doubt that the principle carries over, since actual controversies such as the question of whether or not the Romance languages really come from (literally) Latin are actually argued in this fashion. Those who maintain that Latin is not the source but a collateral must show that there is at least one innovation in Latin that is not in the Romance languages. To illustrate the formal factors that enter into such decisions, let us imagine three forms of speech, A, B, and C, occurring, in this order, at three successive times and found 'linked' to one another in the sense alluded to above (Fig. 3).

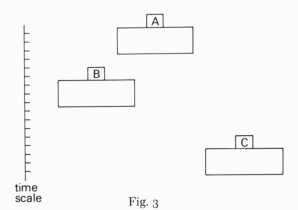

time
scale   Fig. 3

In particular let there be three kinds of contrasting pairs in A: (1) such that the contrast is answered, as the words are translated, by a homophone in both B and C, (2) such that it is answered by a contrast in B and by a homophone in C, and (3) such that it is answered by a contrast in both B and C, such as that shown in Fig. 4. Clearly, A contains

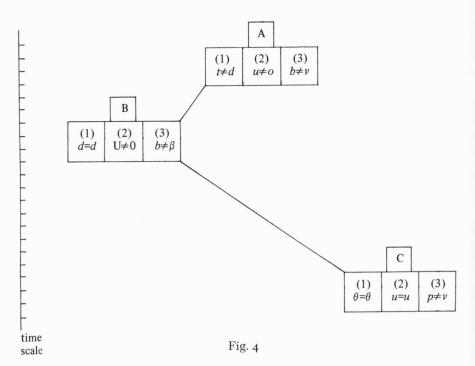

time
scale   Fig. 4

no innovations with respect to either B or C, nor does B carry any innovations with respect to C, so that A is an older stage of B and of C, and B an older stage of C.[6]

If, on the other hand, we let C be so constituted (C′) that the first class of contrasting pairs in A is answered by (1) a homophone in B and by a contrast in C′ (with the other two classes, (2) and (3) as before), we obtain the diagram in Fig. 5, where A is separately ancestral to B

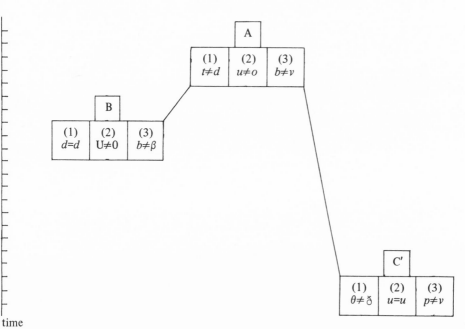

time
scale

Fig. 5

and to C′. It should be noted that the relative location of B on the time scale with regard to C is predictable from the properties of B and C in Fig. 4, but that the same is not true (except with recourse to glottochronological assumptions that do not enter here) with regard to B and C′ in Fig. 5. A, of course, must antedate B, C, and C′. What is perhaps most remarkable about the line of descent is that although it is a natural and, to us, entirely familiar construct, it is not a primitive. The notion of descent is built on the notion of relationship, not vice versa.

It is perfectly true that all innovations (that is all phenomena to which we would reasonably give that name) are not phonemic mergers. If, however, we choose our lines of descent on a phonemic basis, we are frequently rewarded by the discovery that a good many innovations of different kinds—semantic, syntactic, and, generally, morphemic—occur along the same lines of descent. There are two principal reasons for relying initially on phonemic merger: first, as pointed out earlier, that we can relate it to phonemic substitution in fairly well understood sociolinguistic settings, and, secondly and most prominently, insofar as the history of the discipline is concerned, phonemic merger is the phenomenon that may be recognized as an innovation in the 'comparative' matching process itself. In the other areas the criteria are less clear-cut and depend more on universals (e.g., such universals of semantic change as may be generally accepted), on internal reconstruction, and on extraneous information. It is no accident that comparative linguistics, even when it continues to carry the ancient label of comparative 'grammar', is to such an overwhelming extent in fact comparative phonology.

Even so, we are not yet rid of all of our unspoken assumptions. In particular, the recognition of merger is not a simple matter, because what observation typically yields are conflicting regularities. Assuming, for the sake of the argument, some direct knowledge of a form of speech known as proto Indo-Iranian (it is actually only obtained through reconstruction), we find that in a certain chronologically later form of speech, Old Persian (the language of the royal Achaemenian inscriptions), certain proto Indo-Iranian contrasts are matched by homophones: both d and dh by d, for example. But the case of words with pI-I $\acute{g}$ and $\acute{g}h$ is not so clear: in some words g and gh are both matched by OP z, whereas in others, OP has the same d that also corresponds to pI-I d dh. One suspects that the two classes of words reflect two historical situations, or two diverse *channels of transmission*. It is customary in such cases to assign primacy to one of these channels and declare it the true line of descent, and let the other channel (or channels) represent a body or bodies of loanwords. In this specific instance the merger of g gh with d dh is considered genuine and a *sound change*, while the z-words are classified as borrowings from the language or dialect of the Medes.

There are material reasons for this assignment, but they are a matter of external and accidental knowledge. It is doubtful whether the true line could be distinguished from the effects of borrowing in a formal way. Sheer numbers are no guide, since a language may be 'swamped with loanwords', and there is increasing skepticism concerning any a priori argument of the kind that says that syntactic or semantic structure, presumably immune to replacement by borrowed matter, will reveal the true ancestry. The study of loan translations and our growing acquaintance with the mechanisms that impart common traits to languages forming an areal complex have cast a fundamental doubt over all such notions. One may wish to rely on the criterion of the basic vocabulary to decide which is borrowing and which change along a primary line, on the plea that individuals and populations continuing to speak their language will borrow basic vocabulary last, whereas to acquire a new language would seem to mean to acquire the basic vocabulary first of all. In any event, as we have seen, since the same phonemic substitution plays its role both in assimilating loanwords and in shifting to another language, there will be phonemic regularity on both sides. Apart from the matter of the basic vocabulary, there is, in other words, no easy formal criterion to decide whether the z-words are loanwords in a d-dialect or vice versa.

In one sense, this does not matter much. It turns out that we are free to treat the two strains in the vocabulary, even though we find them combined in the same form of speech and in the same texts, quite as if they represented two different descendant languages appearing in separate bodies of text. This recourse to the assumption of dialect borrowing is not, as is sometimes suggested, a shamefaced and arbitrary way out of embarrassing contradictions that cannot be handled by supposedly ordinary means, and thus an admission of methodological bankruptcy. On the contrary, it is a normal and constant necessity, and in no way destructive to the classical assumptions. It does not, for example, invalidate the comparative method for a moment. The two components of the Old Persian vocabulary are simply made to function as two separate witnesses in the task of reconstructing proto Iranian and proto Indo-Iranian. There is, to be sure, the technical problem of deciding between (rightly) recognizing the same proto entity coming through along two channels of transmission and (wrongly) setting up only one channel of transmission but contrasting entities in the reconstructed proto languages, one to account for the words in which z in most other Iranian languages is matched by an Old Persian z and another for those in which it is matched by a d. There are technical remedies, based on doublets (that is, one and the same morph passing through both channels [-*zana*/-*dana* ('race') comes close][7]), or based on the occasional association of more than one competing regularity in different segments of one and the same morph.[8]

Likewise, we need not choose—although, on the basis of partly extraneous yet decisive considerations, we in fact do choose—between classifying Middle English as a descendant of Old English and classifying it as a descendant of Old French, since nothing is lost by using the 'Anglo-Saxon' vocabulary of Middle English as a Germanic language and the French-based vocabulary of Middle English as a Romance language, along with the other Germanic and Romance languages, in the reconstruction of Germanic, and of (Vulgar) Latin, respectively. Things like this are done: the otherwise imperfectly known Latin of Illyria has left loanwords in Albanian, and these loanwords, complete with the phonemic substitutions attendant upon their transfer into Albanian, simply take their places alongside the rest of the evidence, presumably direct-line, for Vulgar Latin.

Looking back, the following points seem worth stressing. Rather than claim to be able to recognize, by inspection, two forms of speech as successive stages of one language and then be caught in difficulties and contradictions, we have found it more consistent and more congenial to the observable practices of historical linguistics (though not always to its professed tenets) to define descent as a relationship between two 'related' forms of speech such that only one of them shows innovations. This presupposes an ability to recognize innovation: encouraged by the observation of certain sociolinguistic situations (contact, variation, code switching, dialect learning and unlearning, etc.), we feel that we can interpret correspondences between a phonemic contrast in one form of speech and a homophone in another as the effect of merger in the latter. Thus we use merger as the innovation *par excellence*—not because there are no others (there are, and they are, once recognized, at least as important) but because phonemic merger is identifiable *ipso facto*. As the ancestry-and-descent relationship is sharpened by relativizing it in terms that are slightly more primitive, we also realize that it does not immediately link entire forms of speech but only, as it were, their constituent strands. Limiting ourselves, once again and perforce, to words and their phonemic shapes, we are more directly sure of the descent of each of the two components of the English vocabulary than we are of the descent of English as a whole or, for that matter, of what it means to assign a unique and exclusive ancestry to a form of speech as such. Even without the customary appeal to pidgins and creoles, the concept of the mixed language cannot simply be shrugged off; if it has real weaknesses they must surely be more hidden than that.

The preceding remarks are a plea for asking how two languages must be constituted for us to declare one of them, with a reasonable choice of metaphor, to be 'descended' from the other. This seems preferable to asking, given that one language is descended from another, what properties two such languages turn out to possess. The differences between the two styles is neither great nor unfamiliar, and our preference is simply a tribute to the definitional nature of the whole question, designed to keep us from getting bogged down in a pseudo-question. This advantage is even clearer as we take a closer look at the process of *sound change*, to which we have already attached such special importance, and which, in turn, appears as a facet of language descent: as Italian is descended from Vulgar Latin so are Italian sounds specifically descended from Vulgar Latin sounds. The concepts that come into play are, again, best handled as truly definitional (as indeed they have long been handled in the course of substantive work) and not in the pseudo-factual form in which they have encumbered much of the general debate. Not unlike the pronouncement that 'all languages change', the pronouncement that 'sound change is regular' has been presented as a finding, though, in this case, not as a self-evident one. The implication is that sound change might just as well have been expected to be 'irregular', but was discovered to be regular instead. Those who deny the finding still agree on the factual nature of the expectation that they merely claim has not been borne out. This framework leaves room for three processes: (1) regular sound change, (2) irregular sound change, and (3) change other than sound change, that is, absence of sound change.

But how is sound change defined? Surely not as 'change in sound', since every linguistic change must be that, and since the ability to distinguish sound changes from other linguistic changes is nevertheless rightly praised as a fruitful achievement. The replacement of *gluff* by *glove*, of *cweðan* (cp. *quoth*) by *say*, of *holpen* by *helped*, of *ey* by *egg*, all constitute alterations in sound, but they are precisely not classified as sound changes within the meaning of the pronouncement on regularity. On the other hand, the replacement of *hring* (and, much later *wring*) by *ring* is said to be a sound change in the technical sense. Why?

Before answering this question, it may be necessary to justify the use of the term 'replacement' as an equivalent of, or perhaps even an improvement on, 'change'. We have already encountered the difficulty inherent in the term 'change' when applied to forms of speech in toto: it is the difficulty of identifying the quasi-genetic substance to which the accident of change is attributed. For this reason we prefer the notion of *correspondence*: as we translate—and surely this *is* a question of translation, presupposing the existence of a theory of translation of some sort—from, say, English into Dutch, we observe that *thumb* and *dumb* 'go to' words with *d-* in Dutch; and as we follow, specifically, what we called a line of descent, we may note that *hring* and *wring* 'go to' or 'become'—these words now taking on the familiar chronological sense in the special context of translation from stage to stage—*ring*. So did *gluff* 'go to' *glove*, *cweðan* to *say*, *holpen* to *helped*, and *ey* to *egg*. Only, this way of putting things is not equally familiar in all cases. It is quite customary to say that *hring* becomes *ring*, and even that *gluff* and *holpen* become *glove* and *helped* (though it is probably more natural to say that 'the singular of *gloves*' goes from *gluff* to *glove*, and 'the past participle of *help*' from *holpen* to *helped*). What we traditionally do in these cases is (I) keep the meaning constant and record how the morphs, one from each stage, are paired in replacement.[9] The same may of course be done for *cweðan* : *say* and for *ey* : *egg*, and it is done when we say that a certain meaning used to be expressed by *cweðan* but is now expressed by *say*, or that an ovum was once denoted by *ey* and later by *egg*. It is, however, more common in these instances to switch to a different principle of classification (II) and keep the morphs constant,[10] following them through their denotations and their altering pattern of co-occurrence. We will say, for instance, that *cweðan* became obsolete (except in *be-queath* and, in a sense, in *quoth*); that *secgan-say* changed its meaning, in part by losing certain nuances ('relate', 'speak [truth, lies, etc.]') and in part by taking on new ones (like the simple quotative 'he said'); or, finally, that *ey* became obsolete, and that *egg* is a loanword from Scandinavian.

If, however, we adopt style I for all these examples, we may proceed to classify them according to certain special relationships that may or may not exist among the paired (that is, the replaced and the replacing) morphs. Clearly, a special relationship of a simple sort (1) exists for *glove* and *helped*: in each of these histories one allomorph has replaced another, inside the morpheme as it were, so that *glove-* now occurs outside the plural *glove-s*, to which it was once limited, and so that *-ed*, instead of *-en*, is found after one more verb than was the case before.[11] A special relationship of a different kind (2) exists for both *ring* and, again, *glove*, as we should have discovered if all the material had been in: the difference in the morphemic shape of the paired morphs recurs. *Hring-ring* is matched by *hrēow-rue*, *hrefn-raven*, etc.; the (incidentally, more recent) replacement *gluff-glove* is matched by *staff-stave*.[12] No special relationship is present in *cweðan-say* and in the context as constructed in *ey-egg*, and certainly in a case like *ēam* (the old word for 'uncle')-*uncle*.

It is well known how this classification is interpreted. *Ring* is called a sound change. *Glove* and *holpen* are classified as analogic changes; *say* is a semantic change; and *egg* and *uncle* are loanwords. The reason why *glove* is not also called a sound change is that the replacement of *f* by *v* occurs in instances where *f* alternates with *v*, but not in all such cases (*wife*), let alone in cases where there is no alternation.[13] In short, the reason why *hr* > *r* is considered a sound change is that it is a residual case:[14] it is not built on an alternation nor is there a conflicting regularity that would call for the setting up of a separate channel of transmission (in other words, *hr-* always goes to *r-*). It is considered a sound change because it is 'regular'. We already know how to interpret competing regularities. We are free to consider the replacement of *g gh d dh* by *d*, as well as the replacement of *g gh* and of *d dh* by *z* and *d*, respectively, either as examples of 'sound change' along two lines of descent ('true Persian' and 'Median') or as an example of dialect borrowing interfering with the true line of descent for Old Persian. If this is how we reason, there is no occasion for surprise in Leskien's formula that sound change occurs without exception, since it is a tautology; and of the three processes envisaged above only two would be properly defined, namely, (1) regular sound change, and (3) change other than 'sound' change. How, then, has it been possible again and again to raise the question of the regularity of sound change with the thought that not only is it a matter of observable fact (rather than of definition) but also that sound change can be irregular and that Leskien was wrong?

This is not the place to study in detail the arguments with which Chen and Wang wish to prove that the neogrammarians (and, presumably, scholars like Meillet and others after them) "underestimated the extent of exceptions to the so-called 'exceptionless' sound laws."[15] But 'extent' is the last thing that matters; the literature is full of cases in which the truly 'regular' development is reported buried deeply under the surface. In any event, Chen and Wang themselves are champions of 'lexical diffusion'. Their principle of explanation is that processes that in retrospect are judged to be regular sound changes, or that may be predicted to end up as such processes, do not affect all morphs at "one and the same time" or, shall we say, at the same pace, but rather spread from morph to morph 'until' they become regular. Some of their material may be open to criticism, but much of it is greatly to the point. Only, it is a mistake to believe that, however misleading Leskien's wording may have proved to his readers, lexical diffusion is incompatible with neogrammarian principles as practiced.

In Glarus German, 'ew' and 'iw' have almost merged by sound law (the formulation is that of Leonard Bloomfield, a defender of the regularity principle) into *y:*, but for the words for 'deep' and for the name of the local knoll known as the 'Kneeridge', both of which have *œj* (the word for 'knee' itself has *y:*).[16] This shows "that the *y:* for old 'ew' is really an importation"—the 'real' Glarus form is the 'exceptional' *œj*.

(The surrounding areas have *y:* throughout.) Of course, once these two items, too, are borrowed with *y:*, the dialect borrowing will have become a sound change. The traditional argument can only be which is which: have the Glarus speakers shifted to the surrounding dialect so that the two exceptional words are loanwords from old Glarus German (as, on a gross level, French—namely the Latin of Gaul—contains Gaulish loan words), or do we decide, as Bloomfield would like to do but for the precarious material, that all the other words are borrowings so long as at least one item with *œj* is left in the speech of the locality? It should be obvious that the quarrel is not about the events in dialect history, which remain the same, in all their presumable complexity, in both descriptions. Rather, the issue is the wording. To be sure, there remains, if one wishes, the criterion of the basic vocabulary: the survival of the local place-name, Kneeridge, in its ancient form, may be taken as justification to view the process as borrowing (the most familiar terms stay to the last) rather than as language shift or learning (the most familiar words are changed first). But this merely opens up the depths of possible disagreement on the notion of basicality itself.

Advocates of 'sporadic' sound change (that is, of the separate validity of class 2, above) will have their claim neither proved nor faulted until they can specify the circumstances under which competing regularities are to be interpreted neither as (a) 'analogic' play among allomorphs the morphophonemic nature of which creates phonemic recurrences, nor as (b) representing different channels of transmission, including the one dubbed the main channel, but instead as (ç) sporadic 'sound' change. If this is only a case of labeling, in all sobriety, regularities of nonanalogical origin for which we cannot name or care to construct a reasonable historical background (the Medes or the Scandinavians), 'sporadic' means no more than 'somehow competing' and is noncommittal. It is, however, sometimes said that such processes tend to have special phonetic properties; reportedly, they are distant dissimilations and assimilations, metatheses, haplologies, and the like. In actual fact, however, these so-called minor sound changes seem to offer no more difficulty to interpretation than the major ones such as, say, ordinary and 'regular' contact assimilations. The often-cited Greek and Latin haplologies of the type *hēmimédimnon* > *hēmédimnon* ('half-medimnos [a measure]'), *nūtrītrīcem* > *nūtrīcem* ('nurse [acc.]') are apparently like other sound changes in being typologically constrained (they may be said, if one so wishes, to help maintain a favored syllable structure for words), as well as in having transparent analogical re-formations for exceptions (*hēmi-médimnos* ['remade'] also occurs). As a matter of fact, the 'exceptions' to the more ordinary sound laws are often far richer than what we have here. This, however, is not even the issue. It seems that sporadic sound change is either a contradiction in terms or merely a traditional and not particularly well chosen collective designation for other than main-channel material.

It is odd that Leonard Bloomfield, who did so much to reinterpret nineteenth-century principles in clearer and more consistent language, should have thought the minor sound changes so "very different from those covered by the assumption of [regular] sound change"; odd, also, that he may have continued to regard this 'assumption' as material rather than definitional.[17] Part of the explanation is that the tradition on this point was both exceptionally powerful and at the same time encumbered with another, extraneous problem: that of graduality. In classical nineteenth-century linguistics the sounds of language were, after all, frequently thought of as forming a substance (liable to alteration in time) to which speakers only give utterance, almost as if they were performers reciting some preexistent text. Consequently, the question usually asked was not what it is that speakers do, in the exercise of 'normal speech activity',[18] that looks in retrospect like sound change, but rather how speakers cope with alteration when they discover it. Graduality, that is, continuous change in imperceptibly small steps or something of the sort, was postulated to explain why speakers will accept the merging of precisely those phonemic contrasts the observance of which seems to be the essence of 'normal speech activity' as long as that observance lasts (it goes against the grain to imagine that speakers will begin to make *click* and *lick* alike, and yet this is what happened to *hl-/l-*, and later to *kn-/n-*): if the speakers had been aware of the aberration they would have corrected it, and it was graduality that prevented awareness. This speculative notion of *necessary* physical graduality has had remarkable staying power. To what extent sound changes move in *fact* through small or infinitesimal stages—in the sense that individual speakers go through the paces as they live through the change—is an empirical question so far as measurements of variation in 'apparent time' are concerned; but there is nothing empirical about proclaiming that all sound changes must be physically gradual as some phenomena disappear and are replaced along what the historian selects as his line of descent.[19] Moreover, it is entirely characteristic of classical historical linguistics that for many of its contexts the issue of graduality does not matter. The formulation of sound changes and the validity of the resulting alteration in question could or could not have been gradual.

One reason for this lies in the familiar truth that a distinction may be made between phonemic and (merely) phonetic changes and that the distinction is fruitful. Subphonemic change, we often say, may for certain purposes be disregarded. It is perhaps not relevant to the phenomenon studied here. Subphonemic change is, in a sense, without shape so that its incidence or absence cannot be clearly ascertained in a given case; and although it may have direction (and is often reported as having direction), it is, for instance, capable, in theory, of having its direction reversed. All this leaves us without a clear-cut criterion to decide whether or not innovation has occurred, except in some statistical sense—a sense that is clearly uncongenial to the fundamental historical-comparative practices, whatever standing and potential it might otherwise have. The traditional reliance on phonemic changes is surely not just an accident of scholarly history, though we must also remember that many of the virtues of our familiar methods were born of a necessity: recorded material from the past yields little subphonemic detail, and our procedures for reconstruction have naturally been judged first and foremost by their ability to give us the kind of information for unrecorded speech forms that written records give us for known ones.

A phonemic merger, as we have seen, is a different matter. Not only do we claim that we know whether or not the absence of a contrast is a fact for a given form of speech, as compared with another (cognate) form of speech, but also we think of the merging of a contrast along a line of descent as irreversible, because its reversal, further down the line of descent, would be a split, and, so we say, we neither know nor can construct a mechanism for phonemic split *per se*. This is, to be sure, a circularity. Lines of ancestry and descent were defined on the basis of merger in the first place, and it is only in deference to that definition that wherever we find a (possibly subsequent) form of speech with a contrast where another (possibly earlier) form of speech has no contrast, we posit a collateral rather than a directly ancestral relationship for the two. We had of course arrived at the definition because of our interest in the workings of phoneme substitution and because of our desire to find the irreversible process we need for purposes of reconstruction. Hence we must assign what would otherwise qualify as a case of spontaneous split to a relationship other than descent. We say, for example, that a population A may acquire the contrasts of a form of speech B[20]—that is, that it may learn a new language or dialect 'perfectly' (rather than 'imperfectly'). True to our framework, we record neither 'change' (i.e., a conflicting regularity) affecting B-words borrowed into A, nor 'sound change' occurring in a descendant of B,[21] nor even sound change occurring in a descendant language of A such that this language has come about by 'total borrowing' from B. Instead, we only say that B has not undergone sound change even as it has spread to new speakers. If the acquisition of B by A-speakers is less than perfect with regard to some *other* contrast, and there is a substitutive merger, this will then constitute a sound change affecting B (and not A).

Roughly and schematically, these are some of the rules of what is by no means an empty game even if the rules are by way of definitions. There is a conviction that this way of determining ancestry is not inappropriate to social, political, and demographic history and that the trees that result are not too far removed from the pedigrees and tables of descent with which students of history have traditionally animated their chronicles.

The elaborate phonologies that are the glory of historical and comparative linguistics do of course contain many instances of phonemic split or conditioned sound change. But these follow Polivanov's Law; they are, in other words, not independent, spontaneous split processes *per se*, but consequences, or, better, aspects of mergers. The specific nature of the relation between a split and the merger with which it belongs must in part be viewed as a matter of notation. Accepting the more usual notational conventions, one distinguishes two types. The first (1) is characterized by the circumstance that the splitting-off allophone is the very one that does the merging (with an outside phone), as when (1a) *d* before -*er* goes to *ð* in early modern English, with the result that *weather* (with an old *d*) and (*bell*)*wether* (with an old *þ*) become homonyms; *d* in other environments (= other allophones of *d*) appears in modern English as *d*, occurring in environments in which *ð* (from old *þ*) also exists: *load, loathe.* It is clear that the split of *d* (*load,* but *weather*) depends on the effective merger of *weather* with *wether*, etc., to attain phonemic standing, since until this merger is a fact, the (presumably) special allophone of *d* before -*er* is still just a positional variant of /*d*/. Just so, (1b) Indo-European **t* splits, in early Germanic, into **þ* and **t*—the latter (for instance) after **s*, where **t* merges with **d*. But this old **d* goes to **t* generally (that is, not only after **s*; =[z]), so that we have, in one of the Germanic

(1a)

_ _ _ _ = 'bef. -*er*'

(1b)

_ _ _ = 'after *s*-'

Fig. 6

descendants, Gothic, *ast-* ('branch'; from *-*d*) and *ist* ('is'; from *-*t*), and, on the other hand, *þah-* ('be silent'; from **t-*), but *tah-* ('tear apart'; from **d-*). See Fig. 6. The difference between (1a) and (1b) is only that in (1a) the splitting phoneme of the earlier stage and the merged phoneme of the later stage occupy merely adjoining places in the kind of phonological framework that one might be tempted to set up as descriptively common to both stages. In (1b), on the other hand, they are the 'same'.

Polivanov's Law covers a second kind of split (2), which is on the surface different from the first: here it is a merger in the conditioning *environment* that makes former allophones contrast with one another (*Phonologisierung*), without necessarily or essentially involving any physical alteration in the segments that are thus changing their status. In Indo-Iranian the older (proto Indo-European) sequences *pe *po **k^we* **k^wo* have turned into *pa pa ča ka*, respectively; **k^w* has split into *č* and *k*. It is customary and, indeed, natural to stress the compensatory function of this variety of phonemic split, on which we tend to look as separate from, if connected with, the merger. We say, in fact, that the vowels *e and *o have merged (as it happens, into *a*) and have, in the process, produced one homonymous *pa*, while the earlier **k^we* (> *ča*) has remained different from **k^wo* (>*ka*). That the difference is regarded as having shifted from the vowel to the consonant is a tribute both to the circumstance that the 'same' *e's and *o's have resulted in homonymy elsewhere (e.g., after *p), and to the phonetic facts. But these are not guaranteed to be clear-cut. If, as is only plausible, the 'allophone' of *a* after *č* was different (in 'onset', degree of fronting . . .) from that occurring after *k*, the matter takes on an indeterminate aspect such that only a further appeal to the *č*'s and *k*'s in still other environments could furnish some vague guidance. Apart from this, it is notationally possible to retain the vowel phone as the seat of distinctiveness while making the preceding consonant dependent on the vowel; in other words, it is possible to decree that it is the lowering and centralization, to the extent that it took place, of both *e and *o that was subphonemic. True, such a notational choice is not pleasing even in this instance and would be quite absurd in others; but the fact that it can be entertained at all gives us some understanding of how the two kinds of split process are related. For if the first (1) may be represented by Fig. 7, the second (2) might be represented by Fig. 8, where, at the later stage, ^+a is a vowel with distinctive fronted on-glide, and *k* is = [č] before ^+a and = [k] before *a*.

We may say in conclusion that as some of the generalizations from

earlier *d*	earlier *ð* ("*þ*")	
lād > load	*lāþian* > loathe	later *d*
weder > weather	*weþer* > (bell)wether	later *ð*

Fig. 7

e	*o*	
k^we > $k+a$		$+a$
	k^wo > ka	
pe > *pa*	*po* > *pa*	*a*

Fig. 8

historical and comparative work were stated they were bound to offend common sense and provoke attacks on common-sense grounds. We asked ourselves earlier how it was that these attacks never really succeeded in shaking the edifice that had been erected in laborious trial-and-error fashion. The answer lies partly in the fact that the generalizations were problematic as such: the language in which they were couched necessarily had a history of its own, replete with traditional motifs (descent, speakers' awareness, language as a physical object or substance, the naturalness of alphabetlike segmentation, etc.) not to mention traditional reticences; and while it must have been intuitively clear, at the time of formulation, just how they fitted the data, they became vulnerable as they were misunderstood later. The edifice itself has, by and large, survived and developed further on its own immense merits, which are chiefly those of internal consistency and historical concreteness. It does not stand and fall with the generalizations of the past since it was never put up in the first place by simply carrying out prescriptions. But this is not to say that generalizations are useless and that existing ones should not be reexamined. We have pointed to a few concerns in such a reexamination. The most pressing ones seem to be of two kinds: there are definitional tautologies—of a wholesome sort—to be recognized both in the business of identifying a line of descent and in separating so-called sound changes from other changes; and there are subtle relationships to be interpreted between the phenomena of variation and of replacement at the crucial point where the synchronic study of speech communities and the domain of the historian abut.

Although long known as 'comparative grammar', historical and comparative linguistics became more and more preoccupied with phonology as time went on. We have tried to show that this was not an accident

and that it was instead connected with the fact that some sound changes
are mergers and that mergers, under certain implicit or explicit assumptions, may be seen as 'irreversible'. We might also say that sound
changes, unlike some other change processes, produce effects that are
ipso facto recognizable as innovations, and that it is on this powerful
property that the so-called comparative method[22] of reconstruction—
that is, of reconstructing the phonemic shape of morphs and of certain
morph sequences—rests. The *de facto* adoption of this principle (however formulated) is the best illustration of the process of formalization
that linguistics underwent, so early in its history and "against the pre-
disposition and expectation of the discoverers."[23] Precisely because it
was not expected, it caused intellectual discomfort, and there was a
good deal of discussion of the chances for comparative reconstruction
of entities other than morph shapes. There is much to be said, and even
more yet to be found out on this subject.

One of the forms the discussion took is worth looking at. This is the
search for 'semantic laws', to which Stephen Ullmann devotes a sub-
chapter in his work on *The Principles of Semantics*.[24] This search, he
says, is "as old as semantics itself" in a general sense; but it had a
special meaning for the neogrammarian and post-neogrammarian linguists because of the "existence of sound laws." That language has two
dimensions, 'sound' and 'meaning', must be a very general belief, existing
on many levels from folklore to technical sophistication, though no doubt
suggesting very different things to different individuals. In the general
folklore and in what passes for ordinary common sense the idea that the
two factors are somehow symmetrical is perhaps not so pronounced;
rather, there is a familiar feeling that words (1) *consist* of such-and-
such sounds (as a rock has such-and-such a composition, or such-and-
such measurements), and (2) *possess* the property of meaning (or naming, or referring to) something (as a rock may have the property of
whiteness, or beauty, or usefulness). The scientific profundity of this
feeling is not the issue, but its all-pervasiveness is; and linguists, in the
act of speculating, have often appealed to all-pervasive common sense
as a source of self-evidence. On the other hand, historical linguists had
developed the distinction between sound change and changes other
than sound change, including change of meaning, as an important
principle, and this did suggest a degree of symmetry. Since sound change
proceeded by (neogrammarian) sound laws, the quest for semantic laws
to match sound laws was natural enough. Ullmann reports that scholars
were largely discouraged because they found a lack of symmetry in this

respect. No semantic laws, of a kind to match sound laws, could be discovered. He reproduces Nyrop's famous statement to the effect that

La science phonétique a . . . acquis une telle sûreté, que dans beaucoup de cas il est possible de prédire le développement que subira tel mot, vu qu'il n'y a pour un groupe de phonèmes qu'un nombre assez restreint de changements possibles. Il en est autrement de l'évolution sémantique; ici les conditions qui déterminent les changements sont tellement multiples et tellement complexes, que les résultats défient constamment toute prévision et offrent les plus grandes surprises.[25]

This is, as Ullmann implies, rather surprising in itself. Nyrop claims that there are universal, 'panchronistic' laws of a sort that allow us to predict sound changes; to predict, in other words, what are (and what were in Nyrop's day) called 'sound laws'—namely, the specific, presumably 'exceptionless' replacements observable at given times and places or, as we said above, characteristic of given channels of transmission. He then declares that no such laws are available to predict changes of meaning.

We need not pursue the matter of panchronistic laws since the claim for the existence of such laws in the realm of phonology in the form here made is fantastic, and since the compelling question was in any event quite different, aiming, as it did, at the semantic analogs for the specific time-bound and space-bound sound laws. Gustaf Stern, who was aware of the problem, offered a famous example, as follows:

English adverbs which have acquired the sense 'rapidly' before 1300, always develop the sense 'immediately'. . . . Exceptions are due to the influence of special factors. But when the sense 'rapidly' is acquired later than 1300, no such development takes place. There is no exception to this rule.[26]

The formulation is meant to recall the form in which sound laws (that is, statements of sound changes) are written or should be written; in particular, it contains the requisite references to time and place. It does indeed parallel the kind of statement that is sometimes found in the more perceptive and interpretive historical phonologies, if the data will allow it. Without going into the technical detail, it is enough to remember descriptions of how sound changes will repeat themselves for a time: in pre-proto Greek, an Indo-European intervocalic *s* becomes first *h* and then zero; later, in the special Greek dialect of Sparta, *s*'s which have again arisen between vowels from other sound changes) are again changed to *h* (and, to round out the parallel to Stern's formula, it is not known that the 'same' change has occurred again in the modern descendant—if indeed it is the 'true' descendant—of this dialect, Tsakonian). Stern's observation was fruitful and to the point, and it illustrates an interesting case. But questions remain. The history of s-like sounds in Greece is not statable as a simple, single sound law, but rather as a typological concatenation of sound laws involving judgments on what constitutes 'sameness' from stage to stage (in what sense are the Indo-European s and the Spartan s the same?). The constituent individual sound laws do not have this form, but, then, they cover more: in fact, ever since August Schleicher, total accountability has been the professed or implied requirement for a valid historical phonology. Is it only the much-invoked greater number and complexity of semantic units or of morphemes, as contrasting with phonological units, that makes us despair of any hope of writing a full semantic history for a given language in terms of exhaustive Sternian laws?

One might well hesitate to go further, on the ground that the analogy between phonological and grammatical processes has led to trouble before. But some concepts are after all legitimate both in phonological and in grammatical analysis—such as the notion of contrast. Besides, there remains the fact that the question was posed, rightly or wrongly, by serious scholars of the past and present: if it leads into difficulties, it might be helpful to learn something about these difficulties.[27]

Let us recall the two styles of statement for morphemic change in general, including semantic change: we have a choice between saying (II) that *say* changed its meaning from the older reference to formal announcement, etc., to the more general meaning of today, which used to be expressed by *cweðan*, on the one hand, and, on the other, (I) that *cweðan* was replaced. It so happens that the former style is the one commonly used in description of semantic changes; semantic change is something attributed to a given morph, in this case, *secgan-say*. It is also a fact that it is the latter style that parallels the customary form of the sound law: as s is replaced by, or 'goes to', h in Greek, so *cweðan* is replaced by—one does not ordinarily say 'goes to'—*say*. But if this is taken seriously, we end up with a semantic law of a disappointing sort, inasmuch as it tells us something that we do not usually question. Just as $s > h$ is a sound law because we formulate it in such a way that *all* instances of s are replaced by h, just so it is a regular law that *cweðan* goes to *secgan-say*. It happens in *all* sentences and discourses in which *cweðan* occurs; and to the extent that it does not—in *quoth*, and certainly after the *be-* of *bequeath*—we may, and do, speak of conditioned replacement, and hence of conditioned semantic change. No doubt it is worthwhile to go on looking for patterns in semantic history. But the analogy with sound change holds no promise. We have had that all along, and it is empty.

NOTES

1. There is no implication here that a speech community in a 'given' place is uniform.

2. Presumably with [s] for both.

3. There is, of course, a problem in predicting which is the 'nearest' phonemic entity; studies dealing with the phonology of loanwords are full of surprises. Suppose a source language has *st* as a word-initial cluster while the importing language does not: what general principles are available to predict that the replacement of *ste* . . . will be *este* . . . rather than *te* . . . *sete* . . . or what not (assuming that all these sequences exist in the borrowing language)? The real interest lies in turning the question around: it is the observed substitution that tells us which entity is 'nearest.'

4. Perhaps as '*s*' and '*t*.' Real Japanese speakers are said by Lehmann (1962:77) to replace English *th* with *s*.

5. Something like this is operative in Garde's principle (1961) that a non-contrast dialect area will increase at the expense of a contrast area, other things being equal; but see note 20 below.

6. The alternative would have to be that A exists side by side with B and C (and B with C) in unchanged fashion, in violation of the truism above.

7. Brandenstein and Mayrhofer (1964:157).

8. As in *vispa-zana* 'containing all races,' instead of °*visa-dana*, where -*sp*- is also Median (ibid., 12).

9. Special provision of a formally difficult kind has to be made in cases where there is both sound change and semantic change in the same etymon.

10. That is, hold on to the phonemically identical item.

11. The morphs referred to are of course -*ed* and -*en*. The vowel alternation in the stem (*help/holp*) should be disregarded.

12. Disregard the word *staff*. We are here only concerned with *stave*.

13. Again, this is complicated by the fact that morphophonemes may occasionally spread. The past tense *dove* is more recent than *dived*.

14. The relation of bulk to residue is of course reversible. If one believes that sound changes can be identified by inspection the non-sound change examples may be treated as residues (Bloomfield, 1933:352).

15. Chen and Wang (1975:260).

16. Bloomfield (1933:339).

17. In Bloomfield (1933:391) and Hockett (1970:247), we have Bloomfield's memorable review of Hermann's *Lautgesetz und Analogie*: "we formulate this type of change . . . by saying that *phonemes change* [B.'s emphasis]. This is an assumption." But then B. goes on to allude to a good many factors

in the situation ("our assumption fits the fact that . . .") and to conclude that "all this of course, is what Leskien meant by his 'laws without exception'." This sounds as if B. had in mind something close to a definitional interpretation of this particular assumption. On the minor sound changes see Szemerényi (1970), who reaffirms their special status but does not explain how an irregular sound change can be classified as a 'sound' change without contradiction. Latin intensives like *cantitare* are in no way different from *hēmimédimnos* and thus from innumerable analogical restorations not involving 'minor' but 'ordinary' sound changes. Reduplications do indeed furnish cvcv sequences "in great numbers," but precisely *not* in the word-interior positions where such sequences, or some such sequences are haplology-producing; when they do come to stand in word-interior position (*repepulī* > *reppulī*) through prefixation, they are in large part syncopated, with the result that haplology does not apply. The point, supported by Posner (1961: 209), is that in this respect as in others the so-called minor sound changes are not essentially different from the major ones; and where they seem different at first, the exception could prove the rule. It could be, for instance, that distant conditioning (of assimilations, etc.) produces the appearance of sporadicity by leaving so much more scope for morpheme boundaries to intervene and hence for analogic change to operate (Hoenigswald, 1964:213). Compare Bloomfield (1933:391) to the effect that "it is possible that they [the minor sound changes] are akin rather to . . . analogic change and borrowing." See also Malkiel (1968:33–45).

18. Hermann Paul's key concept (1898:29, etc.).

19. There are other uses of the term 'graduality': there may be a gradual increase in the amount of vocabulary affected, in the number of speakers, localities, dialects, etc., participating, or a gradual widening of the phonological conditioning in which a change is 'regular.' There is room for a study of another traditional motif, namely the distinction between internally caused ('evolutive') and externally caused ('adaptive') sound changes (see, for instance, Andersen, 1972; Vachek, 1975). The *prima facie* reasonability of this distinction depends to some extent on the *prima facie* acceptance of the line of descent, and of the homogeneous speech community. But this does not begin to describe the problem fully, nor should anybody deny the existence of restrictive universals, typologies, and directionalities as 'internal' factors.

20. That this happens should need no emphasis, but it does of course raise questions with regard to Garde's principle, note 5 above. In Low German, West Germanic þ and d are not distinct from each other (both are d); in Standard German, WGc þ is d, and WGc d is t, and yet Standard German is spreading, though perhaps by some process not intended to be covered by Garde. The example is trivial; the question is to find the limits of the principle.

21. Based on an A-substratum.

22. In the narrow, technical sense of the word.
23. Bloomfield, in Hockett (1970:425).
24. Ullmann (1957).
25. Ibid., p. 251.
26. Quoted after Ullmann (ibid., p. 254).
27. Bazell (1965:95) is quite right in saying that "the comparison with phonological change remains superficial and sterile," and the reason, so far as I can see, is the faulty identification of homologues in the analogy. The earlier generations of scholars who may have gone astray in this respect were not the linguists who were primarily concerned with the discovery of sound laws and who hammered out Indo-European comparative phonology (and whom it is absurd to accuse of failing to see or refusing to acknowledge 'exceptions' in the raw material—see note 15 above), but rather those who speculated on what laws of semantic change would be like if there were any. It is entirely pertinent to analyze their efforts.

REFERENCES

Andersen, H. 1972. Dipthongization. *Language* 48:11–50.

Bazell, C. E. 1965. Review of J. H. Greenberg, ed., *Universals of Language*. *Journal of Linguistics* 1:94–95.

Bloomfield, L. 1933. *Language*. New York: Henry Holt and Company.

Brandenstein, W., and Mayrhofer, M. 1964. *Handbuch des Altpersischen*. Wiesbaden: Verlag Otto Harrassowitz.

Chen, Matthew Y., and Wang, W. S-Y. 1975. Sound change: actuation and implementation. *Language* 51:255–81.

Garde, P. 1961. Réflexions sur les différences phonétiques entre les langues slaves. *Word* 17:34–62.

Hockett, C. F., ed. 1970. *A Leonard Bloomfield Anthology*. Bloomington: Indiana University Press.

Hoenigswald, H. M. 1964. Graduality, sporadicity, and the minor sound change processes. *Phonetica* 11:202–15.

Lehmann, W. P. 1962. *Exercises to Accompany Historical Linguistics: An Introduction*. New York: Holt, Rinehart and Winston.

Malkiel, Y. 1968. *Essays on Linguistic Themes*. Berkeley: University of California Press.

Paul, H. 1898. *Prinzipien der Sprachgeschichte*, 3ᵉ Aufl. Tübingen: Max Niemeyer Verlag.

Posner, R. 1961. *Consonantal Dissimilation in the Romance Languages*. Oxford: Blackwell Scientific Publications.

Stern, G. 1931. *Meaning and the Change of Meaning in English*. Reprint 1964, Bloomington: Indiana University Press.

Szemerényi, O. 1970. Review of Cardona, *On Haplology in Indo-European*. *Language* 46:140–46.

Ullmann, Stephen. 1957. *The Principles of Semantics*, 2d ed. Reprinted 1967, New York: Barnes and Noble.

Vachek, J. 1975. Zum Zusammenspiel von internen und externen Faktoren bei der Sprachentwickelung. In D. Cherubim, ed., *Sprachwandel*. Berlin: De Gruyter.

Metonymy and Misunderstanding: An Aspect of Language Change

Rulon S. Wells

The theory that follows is more easily illustrated with examples than formulated in general terms. The difficulty with general formulations is that, for want of a precise quantification, vague phrases like *much* and *a great deal* have to be resorted to, and the result sounds banal. The interest will lie, then, in showing, by way of examples—of samples— that a proposition admitting only of a banal general formulation can have applications that are fresh and important.

It proves convenient to enter into the subject via a discussion of metaphor and metonymy.

Metaphor and metonymy are familiar concepts in diachronic semantics. In particular, Roman Jakobson has given them renewed prominence by taking up the thought of the Kazan School (Baudouin de Courtenay and Kruszewski, especially the latter) that metaphor and metonymy are the two basic steps in semantical change. For them, and for him, the thesis is deduced from the psychological theses that (a) the basic psychological process is association and (b) the two varieties of association are association by similarity and association by contiguity.

Of course one might adopt the linguistic thesis without intending any commitment to the psychological thesis that gives it a pedigree, and that is what I do here. Not that I reject the psychological thesis, but in order to make my linguistic points I do not need to take any stand on it. Neither am I committed to treating the class of metaphors and the class of metonymies as constituting a strict dichotomy, i.e., as two mutually exclusive and jointly exhaustive species of the genus-class semantical changes. All that I need for my present purpose is that (a) both classes are very large—in other words, that there are many occurrences of metaphor and many of metonymy—and (b) the classes are mutually exclusive—in other words, that no occurrence of metonymy is also an occurrence of metaphor. Joint exhaustiveness is not necessary for my purpose; there may be semantical changes that are neither metaphorical nor metonymic.

It will turn out that many occurrences of metaphor and of metonymy are hypothetical; not that they could not be observed, but that (relative to the body of data with which we are working) they have not been observed.

One last preliminary remark. Jakobson uses 'metaphor' and 'metonymy' in a sense considerably wider than what is usual. With 'metonymy' this does not matter very much, since the term has no currency outside of linguistics and is not much used even there. With 'metaphor' it is quite different. 'Metaphor' has both a well-established ordinary or popular sense and a well-established sense among literary critics; Jakobson's sense is different from both of these. Here I need do no more than call attention to the fact that there is a difference.

Between metaphor and metonymy (taking these terms in the broad sense given them by Jakobson) there is a difference of great importance to the diachronic linguist: metonymy much more than metaphor is bound to an extralinguistic situation. Most metaphors can be understood fairly well without knowing anything about the circumstances, i.e., the extralinguistic situations in which the process of metaphor occurs, whereas with metonyms a knowledge of the circumstances is much more often required.

There are exceptions on both sides; I speak only of prevailing tendencies. A few examples will show what I mean.

Waiter. In the literal or etymological sense, anyone whose profession or occupation or habitual practice it is to wait is a waiter. (This involves one of the two meanings of the English suffix *-er*; the other meaning, inanimate, applies to instruments; as it happens, English uses this meaning too in forming a derivative from *wait*. Because *-er$_1$* and *-er$_2$* are homonyms, we would correspondingly treat *waiter$_1$* [in a restaurant] and *waiter$_2$* [occurring only in 'dumb-waiter'] as homonyms.) In actual usage, *waiter* is used in a narrower sense. This is because, in actual fact, in recent Western culture, the only people who waited as a matter of occupation or of habitual practice were (with the exception of those who waited under other circumstances, but who were not called waiters because they were called by other names, such as *valet*) people who waited 'at table', i.e., who waited around while other people ate. The narrowing from literal to actual meaning would count as metaphor in Jakobson's sense, though not in the popular sense or in that of literary critics. The reason is that narrowings of sense just as much as widenings are founded on similarity. Waiters on table would be found in the houses of the wealthy. In private clubs, public restaurants, and the like, the ratio of guests or patrons to waiters would be higher, perhaps so high that the patrons would wait for the waiter as much as the waiter would wait on the patrons. Nevertheless, there is a striking similarity—namely, a similarity of function—between the waiter (flunky, garçon) in a great house and the employee in a public restaurant who carries in food and carries off empty plates; and the sense that will be found current in the United States in the 1970s and the literal sense, whenever and wherever it was first employed, are related as wider and narrower, respectively. It follows that the step from the original literal meaning of $waiter_1$ to the narrower meaning 'waiter at table in a great house' as well as the step from this to the wider meaning now current in the United States both count as metaphor.

The foregoing account has, at every turn, mentioned circumstances, i.e., extralinguistic situations. The point I have wished to make is not that no reference to the extralinguistic situation is needed when the linguist is describing metaphor; it is, rather, that appropriate situations are readily imagined, so that special Wörter-und-Sachen research is not needed.

There are hard instances of metaphor and easy instances of metonymy, as a few examples will show. Bloomfield (1933:400 §22.6) quotes *Othello* III, 3, in which Desdemona is compared with a hawk. A reader today is completely baffled by the passage because he does not know (a) anything about falconry or (b) the technical terms used by Shakespeare. If his second-mentioned ignorance were corrected, his first ignorance would still prevent him from making sense of Shakespeare's metaphor. Similarly a person must understand a game (petteia, a board game, and astragalos, a dice game, for the ancient Greeks; baseball for present-day Americans) to understand metaphors based on that game.

On the side of metonymy, the polysemy by which one and the same word signifies (i) the act of doing something that is relatively transient, perhaps momentary, and (ii) the result, relatively enduring, perhaps even permanent, of the act—the polysemy that Ogden and Richards (*The Meaning of Meaning*, 1930:134) eccentrically style the Utraquistic

Subterfuge—is easy to understand, because the situations that give rise to it are so ubiquitous; the ease of understanding results from everybody's familiarity with the extralinguistic situation.

Many euphemisms are based on metonymy, e.g., *loins* for genitals and *bathroom* for the room used not only for bathing and washing but also for eliminating. Insofar as euphemism is a response to a verbal taboo and insofar as a verbal taboo is widespread (cross-cultural), the extralinguistic situation will be self-explanatory.

Here are some examples of things that in universal experience go together: (1) 'Right and skillful'; 'right and straight'. The etymology of Latin *dexter*, etc., reveals the former and that of English *right*, etc., reveals the latter metonymy. The basis in universal experience is that in all societies a heavy majority of the population are right-handed. (2) Latin *vertex* is manifestly derived from *vertere* ('turn'). In the sense of 'top of the head' and 'peak of a hill or mountain'—even more clearly with the latter—it is obvious that this sense is metonymically connected with the literal sense 'turning point': If you are passing across a hill, the turning point is where you stop climbing up and start climbing down. Even if (Nida, 1951:197) the people of Yucatan are unacquainted with hills, they are acquainted with pyramids and with gravity, and so with the experiences that underlie the metonymic step from 'turning point' to 'summit'.

In all these situations, a semantical change can be understood by one who correctly supposes the situation and not by anyone else, and correct supposition may be caused by direct experience of similar situations, or by a vivid imagination (including empathy), or by a lucky guess, or no doubt in other ways. It is an empirical fact that, broadly speaking, more metaphors than metonymies are intelligible (*durchsichtbar*, as German felicitously says) without special instruction; the explanation must be that (speaking again in broad terms) the felt similarities on which metaphors are based are fairly universal, in marked contrast to the contiguities on which metonymies are based. Some contiguities are more universally, others more restrictedly experienced, and—here is the salient point—a meaning-change based on a more restricted contiguity is nearly as likely to win eventual currency as one based on a more nearly universal one.

We can be more specific. To understand a semantical change, say the change of expression e_1 from having sense s_1 to having sense s_2, one must understand both s_1 and s_2. One circumstance in which we would say that so-and-so did not understand $e(s_1)$ is that in which he was simply unacquainted with the referent; another is that in which he was acquainted with the referent but did not know that it was the referent of $e(s_1)$. (It sounds self-contradictory to say that he was acquainted with the referent of $e(s_1)$ but not with the fact that it was the referent of $e(s_1)$; to make it clear that it is not a self-contradiction, the medievals would have employed the concept of 'insofar as' (Latin *qua* or *inquantum*), and said that he was acquainted with the referent of $e(s_1)$ but not qua referent of $e(s_1)$. Present-day philosophers, notably W. V. Quine, would put the same point in terms of the failure of substitutivity in the case of 'opaque' reference.) An example: Most Americans today do not know that Homer's word *knemis*, and the now obsolete English word *greave*, have approximately the same sense as current American English *shin guard* (and also as the word *puttee*, which was used in World War I). This is the situation obtaining when a hearer does not understand a foreign language (or a foreign dialect) whose grammar is the same as that of his own language or dialect. For in that case the differences in question are purely lexical. All normal speakers/ hearers of English have experienced *children*, but relatively few know that in German the word to express that experience is *Kind*. In the example from *Othello*, the obstacles are partly linguistic and partly nonlinguistic. They are more linguistic than nonlinguistic, as is shown by the fact that if Shakespeare's words were translated, or paraphrased, even roughly, into modern English, an average speaker/hearer—who in this day and age would not have any direct experience of hawks and falcons, except perhaps from watching educational television, but would have direct experience of various other birds (pigeons and sparrows in Central Park)—would be enabled thereby to have a pretty good grasp of the purport of Othello's extended metaphor.

It may already be plain from these few examples that there is a continuous gamut from utterly commonplace and familiar experiences to extremely unusual ones. One would expect this gamut to be reflected in a gamut of degrees of ease with which a student of semantical change can guess (surmise, conjecture, hypothesize) the situation in which a given change took place. And my proposition that by and large the circumstances of metaphors are comparatively easy to guess, those of metonymies comparatively hard, would seem to introduce a dichotomy, a gulf, a difference of kind where the general considerations given above would lead us to expect a continuum, a difference of degree.

If there should be any clash I would withdraw the proposition and stick with the general considerations. The proposition has no basis but low-level induction; it reports an impression gained from study of cases, but will not be insisted upon. But one of the points I hope to make is that experience, effort, and attention can increase a student's ability to make good guesses, such as he can make about metaphors, even without these three inputs. However, even with metaphor, experience, effort, and attention make him able to do better than he would without them. Let me give an example or two.

I will define two types of problem. Suppose that there is a general theory of semantical change such that every problem, of whichever type, is the problem of finding one or more explanations that explain in terms of this theory; in other words, one or more explanations that *apply* this theory.

In both problem types, it is a datum that a certain word or expression, e_1, has senses s_1 *and* s_2, and in both types the problem is to find one or more explanations, applying the general theory, that explain the datum. (It may be as well to caution the reader that the word *datum* does not signify that the proposition so called is true, but only that it is functioning as a premise in reasoning.) The types differ in that in Type I, the datum includes a proposition relating the two *s*'s chronologically, i.e., a proposition telling us that the word has the first-mentioned sense before, after, or at the same time as it has the second-mentioned sense. In Type II, by definition, the datum does not include information of relative chronology.

It is obvious that solutions of Type II problems are easier, and (for the same reason) riskier, i.e., more likely to be refuted, than solutions of Type I problems. Type I has all the data of Type II, and more; so Type I imposes an added constraint in advance of explanation, and Type II offers more possibilities of constraint *after* explanation, some of which will be incompatible with the explanation.

In terms of these two types, I can describe some differences between metaphor and metonymy. Each type can be divided in various ways; consider subclass I-P, defined as the subclass of I subject to the condition (=constraint) that the explanation is explanation by metaphor, and subclass I-N subject to the condition that the explanation is by metonymy. (The acronymous letters P and N appended by hyphens to the Roman numeral I are meant mnemonically, to recall the words metaPhor and metoNymy respectively; the ordinary English pattern of forming acronyms would yield the same acronym, M, for both.) Correspondingly there are subclasses II-P and II-N. One more refinement—we want to be able to compare problems in pairs, of this sort: The two members of each pair are the same, except that the second member includes some extralinguistic data. Using E as an acronym for extralinguistic, we may describe each such pair of problems of Type I as consisting of a member of Type I-P and a member of I-P-E, and similarly for the other three types. These expressions as I am introducing them here are loose, not rigorous; e.g., the expression I-P, in the absence of any mention of E, is intended to signify that the datum does not include any extralinguistic propositions, but it would take a very elaborately constructed formalization to make a plausible version of such a supposition available; in lieu of that, I will simply explain that I mean not 'absolutely nothing extralinguistic' but 'no special extralinguistic propositions'.

Now I can state in these terms what I want to say. Given a pair I-P, I-P-E, the problem I-P-E is not appreciably easier to solve than the problem of I-P, whereas given a pair I-N, I-N-E, it often *is* appreciably easier. Extralinguistic data aid the solution when the sought connection is metonymical more than when it is metaphorical.

My formulations above, though loose in some respects, are meticulous about not assuming that the data are true. The requirements of the formulations are as well satisfied by false data as by true ones. Then we can treat truth as a simply added condition. According to standard philosophy of science, an explanation is (provisionally) regarded as true insofar as (1) it is able to explain data that are themselves (provisionally) true and (2) it is not in rivalry with another explanation that satisfies requirement (1). The question of what to say of explanations failing condition (2) need not concern us here.

The question was before us whether the proposition that metaphors are easier to see through than metonymies without extralinguistic help could be reconciled with the uninterrupted continuum from universal to extremely unusual experiences. In answering yes, I lean on the fact that similarity (likeness, resemblance), which underlies metaphor, is divisible into levels, such that a person who does not himself feel a similarity between A and B may yet in certain cases by understanding higher-level similarities conjecture that someone else may feel A and B to be similar; and I lean also on the fact that there is far greater agreement, among all humans who have experienced both A and B, as to how similar A is to B, than there is as to whether A occurs together with B. The philosopher's distinction between a priori and a posteriori knowledge is involved here: similarities between experienced things are not themselves merely experienced, as contingent, but are known a priori, as necessities; whereas contiguities, in time or in space, between objects of experience are themselves merely experienced, i.e., are learned by experience.

An interesting example of an opaque metonymy is offered by the phrase *kick the bucket*. The explanation given in the *New English Dic-*

tionary, s.v. bucket (substantive, 2) tells us that in Norfolk the beam from which pigs are suspended by their heels for slaughtering is called a bucket; reasoning from this lexicographical, linguistic datum we might readily go on to the hypothesis that the animals in their death throes literally kick the bucket (in this to us new sense of bucket) to which they are tied, and that the contiguity of the events of struggling in this way and of dying is the extralinguistic basis of the metonymic step from the literal meaning of *kick the bucket* (i.e., 'kick the slaughtering-beam') to the meaning of dying. There is still much remaining to be told: how and when, in Norfolk or wherever, *kick the bucket* subsequently came to be transferred, this time by metaphor, from the dying of pigs in the slaughterhouse to the dying of any animal, including human beings, under any circumstances; how long the transfer took (years? decades? centuries?); whether, at any stage in the transfer, there was emotive meaning involved—such as a feeling that human beings are in this regard no different from brute animals: they both go to their death unwillingly. All this remains to be told, and the hypothesis-forming linguist is no better able to supply the details for a metaphor than for a metonymy.

But there is room for some skepticism as to whether the *NED* account is linguistically adequate. Assuming that (apart from questions about the adequacy of the way in which linguistic facts are distinguished from extralinguistic ones) the account is correct in its facts, one can still detect, just from reading that account, the amateur's mistake of failing to distinguish the intension of a word, which governs its range of possible uses, from the set of properties characterizing that specific situation, just one of its possible uses, which gives rise to the discussion. We are not told whether, at the time and place in question, *bucket* was applied to a beam whether or not it was used for slaughtering. If *bucket* was simply the Norfolk dialect word for *beam*, then learning this lexicographical fact would not help one to pass from the meaning 'kick the beam' to the meaning 'die'; the metonymy would be, as I said, opaque. And if in that dialect it meant specifically 'beam used for slaughtering', so that the lexicographical fact itself supplies the linguist with the basis for metonymy, then the linguist would want to press back to the anterior metonymy that is obviously presupposed.

I will now define another problem type, illustrating it with the word *fine*. In present-day English it is not obvious whether $fine_1$, as in 'before signing the agreement, be sure to read the fine print' and in 'a fine-tooth comb', is connected with $fine_2$ as in 'it's a fine day', whatever we mean by 'connect'. The diachronic problem is, then, whether to hypothesize for every stage of English (prior to the present) in which *fine*$_1$ and *fine*$_2$ occurred that they were mere homonyms—the same in sound, but unconnected—or whether, the other chief possibility, to hypothesize that at some stage they expressed different but connected senses of one word. To put the point less formally, were they always unconnected or were they once connected?

(The entire discussion of the problem will be relative to a theory. I am not saying that there is no occasion for discussing theories—the present lectures are just such an occasion—but only that by a fiction or idealization I will assume that in the problem types as I set them up, the general theory remains constant, and the only question is, what data to apply it to.)

In problems of Type III, which I am now introducing, the datum includes less in one way and more in another way than in Type I; also, less and more than Type II. Types I and II dealt with one later sense coming from one earlier sense. Type III deals with two later senses and one earlier sense. In it, the problem is: Given two contemporaneous senses of what is either one word or two distinct but homonymous words, is there an earlier sense with which each of the two senses later than it but contemporaneous with each other can be connected by the theory?

Type III, like Types I and II, is defined in terms of single-step connections. Naturally, complex types have to be acknowledged; for example, the semantical change culminating in the present-day phrase *kick the bucket* is, according to the account adapted from the *NED* and given above, a complex of at least three component simpler steps: (1) metonymy from 'kick the beam' (while tied to it and being slaughtered) to 'die' (when tied to the beam and slaughtered); (2) metaphor from 'die by slaughter in a slaughtering-house' to 'die'; and (3) misunderstanding of *bucket* ('beam' in Norfolk dialect) as *bucket* ('pail' by speakers of standard English). The present lectures do not attempt to work out a list of either the possible or the useful complex types.

Offhand there seem to be in present-day English two adjectives *fine*, with no synchronic connection detectable: *fine*$_1$, as in 'fine print', 'fine-tooth comb'; and *fine*$_2$ as in 'fine day'. Historically (diachronically) considered, either they were always mere homonyms or else there was a time when one of them arose from the other, or both arose from some third word. To restate slightly, either there was never a time or else there was once a time when they had a common source (either one of themselves or a third thing).

The two alternatives involve a point of logic and a point of scientific method. The first alternative is a universal, the second a particular (=existential) proposition. A universal proposition is inherently incapable of decisive, conclusive verification by induction, whereas an existential proposition *is* capable. This consideration dictates the heuristic order that, as between the two alternatives, we try first to verify, i.e., either to confirm or to disconfirm, the existential proposition, and, if we fail in this, turn by default to the universal proposition. The decision when to conclude that our effort to confirm the existential proposition has gone on long enough, and that the time has come to give up, does not admit of being subjected to any rule. And it itself is equivalent to a universal proposition, because equivalent to 'If I were to search further for a confirming instance, I wouldn't find one', which is in turn equivalent to 'None of the instances not yet examined by me is a confirming instance'.

Suppose in our investigation of *fine* we have reached the point of posing our problem thus: Can *fine*$_1$ and *fine*$_2$ be connected by metonymy? To answer affirmatively is to hypothesize, generically, that there is a connection, and, specifically, that the connection is metonymic. It is not often that the linguist has at his disposal evidence sufficiently detailed to let him confirm such a hypothesis conclusively. But often he can confirm it with less or with more probability. The first point I particularly want to emphasize here is that if there is a substantial collection of pretty well confirmed hypotheses, all applying the same general theory, then these confirmations strengthen one another and confer probability of confirmation on the general theory itself. My second point of emphasis is that experience with a collection of pretty well confirmed hypotheses that hypothesize metonymy has heuristic value for the linguist in teaching or cultivating the knack of guessing where, if at all, situations appropriate for metonymy would be found.

With the word *fine*, here is such a situation. Cloth that is fine in the first sense ('fine-grained', 'made of fine threads') is also fine in the second. For most purposes, cloth of finer grain, i.e., with more threads to the inch, woven of finespun thread, is more desired than cloth of coarser grain, i.e., with fewer threads to the inch. It is also more expensive, partly because the labor cost in its production is greater. Here, then, are three properties associated by contiguity: (1) fine-grained; (2) desired, prized; (3) expensive. I say no more about (3) because it has not affected the diachronic semantics of the word *fine*. Property (1) underlies the sense of *fine*$_1$, and property (2) of *fine*$_2$. If *fine*$_1$ and *fine*$_2$ are connected historically through this contiguity, their connection is metonymic.

We find here a typical situation in which metonymy occurs. It may not be the only situation, but still the situations (all taken together) in which (1) and (2) are both present make only a very small subset of the situations, however we may enumerate them, in which human beings find themselves. The task confronting the diachronic semanticist, when he is trying to verify the hypothesis that *fine*₁ and *fine*₂ are connected in one step by metonymy, is to find situations belonging to that subset, however small it may be. He can say a priori, before searching, that *if* there was metonymy there must have been such a situation.

Metonymy, however, is not a process. We may loosely call it a step, but if we examine what we mean we will find it more appropriate to explain that we mean the result of a process rather than a process.

The theory proposed in the present lectures is that metonymy is a result of a process of misunderstanding. It involves acts of communication in which S (the speaker) intends his utterance U in one way and H (the hearer), *hearing* U correctly, *takes* it incorrectly: mis-takes it, misinterprets it, misunderstands it. In conformity with prevailing theories about speech and language, I assume further that a change in the language is some sort of result or effect of a large number of individual changes. In the simplest possible case, only one S and one H would be involved; S would speak of fine cloth, intending (=signifying), as was customary up until then, cloth with a high thread count (by the way, note that even today, spooled thread is identified as to thickness by the number of threads it takes, laid side by side, to make a width of one inch; thus, Number 12 is a coarse thread, suitable, say, for sewing on overcoat buttons; Number 50 is very fine, suitable for mending a tear as invisibly as possible); H would hear S, would be with him in the extralinguistic situation of examining cloth—S is, perhaps, a salesclerk, and H a prospective buyer; would be unfamiliar with the word *fine*; would judge from S's gestures, expression, and manner that S admired the cloth and expected that H would admire it, and would (silently, to himself) advance it as his first hypothesis about the word *fine* that S (1) was using the word in the way standard with those who were familiar with it and (2) intended to signify by it that the thing called 'fine' was desirable and desired.

Here are two ways of describing what happened. (i) For S, the property (1) fine-grained is central, (2) desired is marginal; H takes (2) to be central, and takes (1) as marginal if he considers it at all. (ii) For S, (1) is figure, (2) is background; for H, (2) is figure, and (1) is in the background, if present at all. Description (i) is the way that Bloomfield (1933:149 §9.8; 430–31 §24.4; 440 §24.7) adopts from

Hermann Paul; description (ii) is cast in terms of Gestalt theory. I believe that the reason why (i) and (ii) are so close is that (i) was gotten by Paul from the proto-Gestaltist Wilhelm Wundt, whereas (ii) comes from full-fledged (Koffka; Köhler) Gestalt theory. There is, however, beneath the surface, another difference. For Bloomfield, the difference between central and marginal is quantitative: the more frequent (for a given individual) is central for him, the less frequent is marginal; Bloomfield, in the behavioristic manner, views centrality and marginality summistically, in marked contrast to the gestaltist view.

As I will soon explain more fully, my own theory, if it has to choose between a more summistic and a more gestaltist theory, will choose the latter, because it assumes that in a single act of communication a misunderstanding can take place that eventually leads to metonymy. However, my theory does not accept either of the two descriptions presented above, but rather a third one. Before I give it, let me elucidate my imaginary account of how *fine* might have acquired the meaning 'desirable'. H, I said, would silently and to himself advance a certain hypothesis. Experience has shown that such a statement regularly draws certain objections that I wish to forestall. There are those who will say that H does not advance a hypothesis, or ratiocinate, or infer, or anything like that; H just goes ahead and takes *fine* in a certain way. For such people, it is part of the meaning of such expressions as 'infer' and 'advance a hypothesis' (='hypothesize') that the acts they apply to are deliberate, or, at the very least conscious, so that such a phrase as Helmholtz's 'unconscious inference' is a contradiction in terms. There is a way of neutralizing such people without going into the controversy. It is to insert the modifier *virtually*, or its synonym *in effect*. The result of virtually doing x is the same as the result of actually doing x; and here it is only the result that I care about, not the means. The inferential steps I hypothesize are virtual steps; as long as the result is the same, it does not matter whether it is a native user of the language who—as it were—goes through them almost instantaneously, or someone learning the language as a second language who goes through them laboriously, or a scientist (linguist) studying the language who goes through them analytically, or whoever.

This account has considered a single episode of communication. We have reason to think that it is very rare that a single episode effects a change in a language. With the word *fine*, the likelihood would be that a large number of episodes was involved. We may use the concepts 'microscopic' and 'macroscopic' to describe the relation. A change in a language is a macroscopic event, being an aggregate of microscopic events. We only have occasion to invoke the microscopic–macroscopic contrast when the number of aggregated events is quite large. (In language phenomena the number is much smaller than in physical phenomena.) In some fields, one has been able to determine macroscopic minima; for instance, in perception, there are just-noticeable differences. Linguistics has not as yet established minima of macroscopic semantical change; the present lectures neither attempt to determine such a minimum nor assume that there are any. Most work in diachronic semantics—indeed, most work in all of diachronic linguistics—is simply observational, not experimental; each macroscopic change is a brute given, not subject to direct experimental modification. It is true that, starting, say, from the data in the *NED*, we may propose an explanation that hypothesizes certain intermediate stages, and then, looking further, we may find new documents—previously unpublished diaries, say—that confirm or disconfirm our hypotheses; but although these new documents shorten the time interval, they will never or hardly ever be so close together but that still shorter directly observable intervals must have existed. The sparsity of data in his sample is a basic fact confronting the diachronic linguist, which his methodology must take due account of.

Much remains to be done with the linguistic theory of reducing macroscopic to microscopic events, but even with presently prevailing theory we may say what I have said already, that with very few exceptions, a macroscopic linguistic change is not caused by a single microscopic change, or even by a small number. In the present example there must have been a number of episodes, numerically distinct but qualitatively alike, and thus a number of hearers who misunderstood the intention of their respective speakers as regards the word *fine*. Let us consider further whether it is plausible that there should have been a number of such episodes.

If *fine* was a common word, how would there have been a number of such hearers? If we suppose that they were children, this commits us to supposing that a children's misunderstanding became current; Jespersen (1922, Book II) has urged this commitment, but he leans heavily on rather general arguments, with little hard support. If it was adults who misunderstood, is it that they were simply unfamiliar with the word? There is another possibility: In each episode of the set that caused the semantical change, H heard the word *fine* and was familiar with it in the sense 'fine-grained', but he inferred that S, using the word *fine*, must be intending it in some other sense. S intends 'fine-grained', H is familiar with 'fine-grained', and yet H thinks that S does not intend 'fine-grained'. My next task is to make this comedy of errors plausible.

Consider a customer looking at bolts of cloth or articles of clothing. One bolt, or one jacket, is made of coarse-grained, the other of fine-grained, cloth. The clerk or salesperson first shows the customer the coarse-grained cloth, then shows him the fine-grained cloth and says: 'Now here is a very fine cloth'. The clerk means more than he says ('pregnant meaning'). All he says is that the cloth is fine, but he means both this and, additionally, that it is also desirable and good. The customer, H, hearing the clerk, S, say this, and supposing (=inferring; here is where the misunderstanding enters) that S is saying all that he is meaning, is obliged (in order to back up his supposition) to infer further that *fine* has a different meaning for S than it has for H himself. He does not need to be told that the cloth is fine-grained; he can see that for himself. If, then, S takes the trouble to mention it, it must be that S is telling H something that S could not see for himself. H's inference here is not wholly wrong, but it is partly wrong.

It may be that H made a linguistic mistake as well as a nonlinguistic one. It is not universally true that what is fine-grained is good. In some cases it is, in some cases it is not. We would not consider a fine-toothed comb or a fine file either better or worse, speaking absolutely, than a coarse-toothed comb or a coarse file; it is better for some purposes, worse for others, and indifferent for others. Sugar and salt can be ground coarse or fine (sugar finer than salt); for most culinary purposes it does not matter, within a certain range, whether the grain of one's salt and pepper is coarse or fine. With nails, pins, and needles, the situation is different: it generally *does* matter whether they are coarse or fine. And as for cloth, if the customer H did not already know that with fabrics fine is considered better than coarse, then naturally the *sous-entendu* of the clerk would escape him; and so, mistakenly failing to infer that there is a *sous-entendu*, and confronted with an utterance that (if *fine* be assigned the meaning familiar to H) would seem incomplete, H virtually considers assigning it a sense that would make the utterance complete.

The utterance would seem incomplete in the respect that something more would need to be said to give it point. By itself, as it stands, it seems pointless. The ordinary-language phrases *by itself* and *as it stands* are analyzed in linguistics with the help of the concept of the discourse. The discourse is the next unit above the sentence. Morphemes compose words, words compose phrases, phrases compose sentences, sentences compose discourses. The possibility exists that a discourse will consist of a single sentence, a sentence of a single phrase, and so on. In an episode of the sort I am now imagining, 'Now here is a very fine cloth' occurs as a one-sentence discourse. If H takes this sentence in the way that would first occur to him, he will find it pointless because it tells him what he can see for himself, and he will be surprised that S does not follow it (or precede it) by one or more other sentences, in the same discourse, that would make clear what its point was. And, surprised, he will virtually infer that the way in which it first occurred to him to take the sentence is not the way S intended it.

Now H might be making the nonlinguistic mistake of not knowing that fine cloth is generally considered to be desirable and good cloth. (If anyone objects to calling simple ignorance a mistake, let him find some other ordinary and convenient label for it.) But he might know this and yet misunderstand S. For even if he knew this, he might suppose S to be saying all that he meant; and this supposition, this hypothesis, this inference, would be a mistake, and of a kind that we can fairly call a linguistic mistake. The nonlinguistic mistake makes the linguistic mistake more likely, but is not a *sine qua non*. H might think it was pointless for S to tell H something that H could see for himself, and yet not think it was pointless for S to tell H something—viz., that the cloth in front of both of them was desirable and good—that would follow deductively from something (that cloth is fine-grained) that H could see for himself when conjoined with something (fine-grained cloth is desirable and good) known to H to be the general opinion. In that case, the misunderstanding on H's part can be described as follows: S treated the connection between fine grain and desirability as going without saying, and H did not realize that S was treating it that way. Note that it is irrelevant to H's misunderstanding whether or not he would treat the connection as going without saying; what is in question is not whether H *agrees* with what S is doing, but whether he *is aware of* what S is doing.

A last point about *fine*. The linguistic mistake—overlooking S's *sous-entendu*, i.e., supposing that S said all he meant—entails a second linguistic mistake on H's part, viz., ascribing to *fine* a new sense. Conceptually, this second linguistic mistake is a distinct step from the first; and we must take note of it, because we will then go on to hypothesize that H, equipped now with a new sense of the word *fine* will on future occasions when functioning not as hearer but as speaker use this word *fine* (='desirable'), and sooner or later will use this new word (or this old word in a new sense, whichever it is for him) in a situation, such as when speaking about the weather, where it would never occur to him to use the old word. When that happens, the new word is launched. Whether the newly launched word floats or sinks is another matter.

Using the example *fine*, I have sketched a theory of processes causing metonymy. The example can be used to illustrate both why and how metonymy differs from metaphor as regards intelligibility. To guess successfully the metonymic connection between $fine_1$ and $fine_2$, it is not enough to know the signification (=connotation) and the denotation of $fine_1$ (i.e., what it means and what things it would be predicated of) and the signification and the denotation of $fine_2$; one must know where the two denotations overlap. Of course with perfect knowledge of the denotations one would know their overlap, but one might have a fair, ordinary knowledge of their denotations and yet a poor knowledge of their overlap. It is part of the training of the diachronic semanticist to become skilled at finding, for any two given words with *possibly* overlapping denotations, whether there is any *probable* overlap.

We may now resume the discussion of the microscopic–macroscopic relation. So far I have shown (not with high probability but with initial plausibility) some conditions under which metonymy could take place. But this does not suffice to show that it would and did take place. Supposing that the circumstances for *fine* were more or less as I imagined them, it remains to be shown that these repeated misunderstandings of $fine_1$ (used with a *sous-entendu*) as $fine_2$ (used straightforwardly) would become current in the language. The standards for adequate confirmation are not as high in linguistics as in the physical sciences, but still there is a difference between a merely possible and an adequately verified hypothesis. In the present lectures I do not address myself to that part of a hypothesis that is concerned with thorough testing, but only to that prior part in which the hypothesis is put forward and is given a first, preliminary testing to see that it has enough plausibility and promise to be worth testing further.

One of the uses of the English noun *will* is its legal use, as in 'This is my last will and testament'. In connecting this with the use as in 'It is my will that my property be given to my church' we may well make reference to Charles Peirce's distinction between a Type and a Token. The relation between $will_1$ (as in 'It is my will that. . .') and $will_2$ (as in 'This is my last will. . .') is not that between type and token, but is derived from it. When we speak of the Bible, we sometimes mean the type and sometimes a token. If someone wants to take a solemn oath and says 'Bring me a Bible to swear on', he means a token, as also in the colloquial 'I wouldn't believe him if he swore to it on a stack of Bibles'. If he says 'I want to take a solemn oath; bring me the Bible', he may mean a token, for example he might be referring to the large Bible kept on the parlor table, which is not the only copy but is the largest copy in the speaker's household, or he might mean the type, without caring to stipulate any particular specimen (any particular token) of that type.

The only way to bring a type to a person is to bring a token of it to him, but if the requester means the type and not a token, then any token of it would do.

The type–token relation is a general pattern, freely extendible. Therefore we cannot ask which came first, the type or the token, as we can ask which came first, $fine_1$ or $fine_2$. Every word that signifies a type signifies a token and vice versa, and if a sentence containing such a word is unambiguous, it is because of the other words in it that determine whether, as used in that sentence, the word is intended to signify a type or a token. For some words, it will have happened that the first speaker to use that word will have intended a token by it; for others, the type; but these are merely new instances of the pattern that yields for every type a token (more precisely, a word signifying a token) and for every token a type. The origin of the pattern does not concern us here; the pattern is found in ancient Greek, and may have diffused to the speakers of English or may have arisen independently among them.

Besides types and tokens, there is a third mode, in the mind, otherwise described as in the memory (the tablets of the heart, Proverbs 3:3, 7:3; Jeremiah 17:1; 2 Corinthians 3:3), where Jews and Christians carry the Ten Commandments and Christians the Lord's Prayer. Any recitation, silently to oneself or aloud, is a token, but the ability (disposition) to produce a token at will is the third mode of existence.

Now thanks to this pattern, one may say 'I read in the Bible that . . .' or 'I read in the Bible I carry around with me that. . .'; these are not quite the same, because the latter suggests the possibility of discrepancy between one copy of the Bible and another, but otherwise they are the same. With *will*, the facts are appreciably different. One's will in the legal sense is not any token of a type; it is a certain singular document, standing in an asymmetrical relation to copies of it. Speaking of copies of it, we would say of any of them that it is a copy of the will but not, vice versa, that the will is a copy of it, nor that it and the will are copies of the same thing. The status of a will is rather like that of a holograph or of an autograph manuscript in that it is epistemically unique, with the further feature that because of its unique epistemic status it is also given unique legal status. The status of the Magna Carta and of the Declaration of Independence is similar.

There is, nevertheless, a type determined by any legal will whose tokens are (i) that will itself and (ii) all copies of it. The question I am considering here is whether there is a connection between *will* in the legal sense and *will* in some other sense. I answer with the hypothesis that there is a connection, that (given a certain understanding of 'metonymy') it is metonymic, and that the process causing this metonymy involves certain ambiguities.

Whether the connection between $will_1$ as in 'It is my will that. . .' and $will_2$, as in 'This is my last will and testament. . .', is metonymic depends on whether a thought and a document expressing that thought are contiguous. Most discussions of contiguity are vague on this point. They make it clear that it makes sense to say, whether truthfully or falsely, that two physical things are contiguous in space or in time, that two processes (whether physical or mental) are contiguous in space or in time, and that a physical thing is contiguous in space or in time with a process. But as to whether it makes sense to say that a mental thing is contiguous with a physical thing, they are silent. Without giving an elaborate discussion of the question, I think we may reasonably agree to call a thought, or other state of mind, contiguous in time and in space with any physical manifestation of it. Under that agreement, $will_1$ and $will_2$ are metonymically connected.

I had two reasons for introducing $will$ as an example. One was that it raises a question about the meaning of contiguity, and so of metonymy. The other is that the process causing metonymy involves language in a way I have not hitherto mentioned.

I hypothesize as with *fine* an extralinguistic situation where an utterance is intended in one way by its speaker and is taken in another way by its hearer. But with *fine*, the hearer's mistake consists of ignoring a *sous-entendu*. With *will* it must be of a different sort. What utterances could have been taken as referring either to $will_1$ or to $will_2$? Such utterances as 'Who are the witnesses to his will?', 'Can you prove that that was his will?', 'He changed his will twice'. There are many other utterances that one would expect that could not be taken either way, at least not with equal readiness, and in attempting to carry my hypothesis beyond the stage of formulation (which is all that I do here) to the stage of testing it, one would tackle the question of whether utterances of the sort that could be taken either way would probably have caused $will_2$ to become current in the standard language. In leaving the example, I will hazard two suggestions. One is that a legal will will commonly have at the head of it, and/or on the outside back or cover of it, the simple word WILL, which has just the ambiguity that we are looking for. The other is that no matter when the semantical change took place, even if it was in the Middle Ages, there was never a time when copies of documents were not made, so that at all times of English history when there was any literacy at all, there must have been a distinction between documents of which there was only one official copy—royal proclamations, letters patent, letters of identification, licenses, etc.—and other documents; and wills belonged to the former class. For all such documents, the contiguity between state of mind and manifestation of it—and therefore the possible metonymy between a word signifying that state of mind and the same word signifying a manifestation of it—would have been simple and straightforward, because it would have been one-to-one: within the class of documents that I am now speaking of, each state of mind would have at most one manifestation of it. The effect of this fact would be to make it unnecessary to speak of an instance or a specimen or a token of the manifestation, or even to speak of a manifestation at all.

We speak of the barometer as rising and falling. Many of us will admit that strictly speaking it is not the entire barometer but the mercury column englassed in it that rises and falls. But the fact is that we do not speak strictly. Let us consider the hypothesis that once people spoke only strictly about the barometer, and that the current loose speaking may be viewed as a semantical change.

The most important part of a barometer is the glass tube containing mercury. It is the most expensive part, the most fragile, and the hardest to repair. Moreover, it is the most indispensable part of the entire instrument. This fact is commonly expressed by various metaphors: it would be called the heart, the core, or the essence of the instrument. Most people who use barometers have only a superficial acquaintance with how they work and why they are designed as they are. The word *barometer* is Greek to them; if required to define it, they would say something like 'a thing for telling what the weather will be'.

All this being so, a hearer H may be very familar with the word *barometer* and yet very shaky in his grasp of it. Familiar, in that he has heard it a hundred times, and yet shaky, in that these hundred times have left him with a wide latitude of interpretation. In an extreme case, all hundred occurrences might have been merely in so many different tokens of the one sentence type, 'Look at the barometer'. A case as extreme as this is unlikely, but if the hundred occurrences were all in one or another of the following sentence types: (1) 'The barometer is rising/falling', (2) 'Is the barometer rising/falling?', (3) 'Look at the barometer', (4) 'What does the barometer say?', (5) 'The barometer says. . .', the case would be not at all improbable, and yet the hearer H with only these hundred occurrences of the word at his disposal would find himself presented with a considerable latitude of interpretations any one of which would fit his data. Whether we think of him as inferring, or supposing, or guessing, our explanation should reckon with the possibility, and should estimate the likelihood, that the interpretation he settles on is not the interpretation the speaker intended; in that case it will be a *mis*intepretation, or misunderstanding. The misunderstanding will not come to light as long as H uses the word only in the sentence types he has heard, or in certain others, but only when he uses it in sentence types such that the word as intended by the previous speakers would not have been used in those sentence types. (It would have been meaningless there, or meaningful but somehow wrong.) The same will be true, for example, for sentences such as 'The barometer has a gauge next to it', where under older usage the proper thing to say would be 'The barometer includes a gauge next to its mercury-filled tube', or the like.

Examples could be multiplied.

REFERENCES

Bloomfield, Leonard. 1933. *Language.* New York: Holt, Rinehart & Winston.
Jespersen, Otto. 1922. *Language: Its Nature, Development, and Origin.* London: Allen and Unwin.
Nida, Eugene. 1951. A system for the description of semantic elements. *Word* 7:117–99.
Ogden, Charles K., and Richards, I. A. 1930. *The Meaning of Meaning.* 5th ed. New York: Harcourt, Brace and World.

The Recall and Verbalization
of Past Experience

Wallace L. Chafe

It happens very often that we see, hear, and otherwise experience things happening around us, that we later remember these things, and that for one reason or another we are motivated to use language to communicate what we remember to other people. In other words, we often talk about recalled experience. In so doing we convert into verbal form something that may have been partially or even wholly nonverbal to begin with. How do we do this? How are we able to take nonverbal experience, store it away for a while, and subsequently recall it and turn it into words that convey to other people something of what the experience was like? If I pretended to have an answer to this question, I would be pretending to know the solution to problems that have plagued investigators of the human mind for thousands of years. My intention is much more modest: to try to make it clear that the question is an important one for linguists to consider, and that we really cannot expect to understand much more about language without committing ourselves wholeheartedly to an attack on the vexing problems that the question raises.

It is necessary to have some kind of model, however imperfect, on which our discussion can be based. Fig. 1, which ignores a number of factors I will not bring up here, is intended as such a simplified model. On the left in this diagram is a box labeled 'stimulus', which is meant to represent the physical input to our sense organs when we first experi-

215

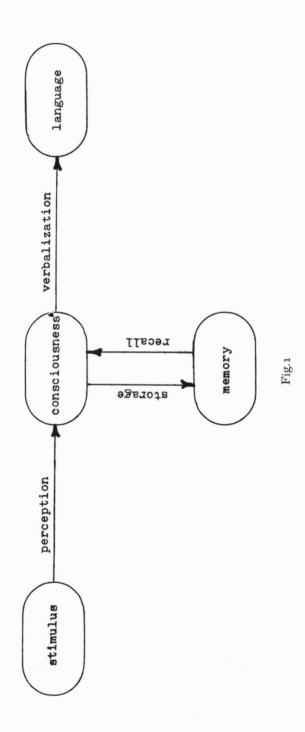

Fig.1

enced the incident we later tell about. There is an arrow leading from this box to the one labeled 'consciousness'. This second box is meant to represent our phenomenological awareness of the experience in question, or, if you prefer, the presence of some information related to the experience in our short-term memory. The arrow is labeled 'perception', and my intention with this label is to emphasize that what enters consciousness is not a faithful replica of the stimulus (whatever that might be), but rather an *interpretation* of it. To take a simple and familiar example, when we look at something like Fig. 2 we are likely

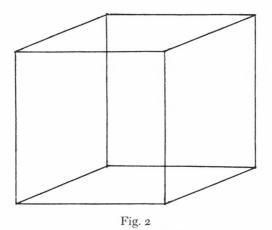

Fig. 2

to see, not a collection of horizontal, vertical, and diagonal lines—which in a sense is closer to what the physical stimulus contains—but a transparent cube. With some effort, too, we can interpret the cube in two different perspectives, with either the face in the lower left or that in the upper right being closest to us. These are different interpretations our conscious minds are able to give to one and the same physical stimulus. What is in consciousness constitutes a kind of belief about what is in the outside world. This belief may be derived from what is presented to the senses, but it is heavily influenced by contextual expectations as well as cultural and individual predispositions. All these things combine to produce in our minds some kind of interpretation of what is going on outside. The key notion for us here will be that *perception is interpretive*. (See Hochberg, 1964, for a useful introductory survey.)

Consciousness evidently has a very limited capacity (cf. Miller, 1956, for a suggestion of how much we can hold in consciousness at one time). At any given moment we can be aware of only a narrow range of phenomena. But at least some of what has been in consciousness can pass by way of the arrow labeled 'storage' in Fig. 1 into the box labeled 'memory'. Using different boxes to represent consciousness and memory may be misleading, since it is likely to suggest that two different areas of the brain are involved. But undoubtedly it is preferable to regard these as two different *states* in which information or knowledge can be at different times. I like to think of what is in consciousness as being knowledge that is activated or 'lit up' at any particular time, while what is in memory as inactive or not lit up at the moment, but still 'present' in some fashion in the mind.

Another arrow leads back from memory to consciousness to show that information can be 'recalled', or reactivated. There are thus two inputs into consciousness: one through perception and one through recall. When an incident is first experienced, we are of course conscious of it through perception. But when we talk about the experience later it enters our consciousness through recall. Although occasionally we may talk about something at the same time we are perceiving it, such discourse is relatively unusual; most of the time we talk about things retrieved from memory. Most experience is recounted in the past tense, which is used for information that has traversed the 'recall' arrow in Fig. 1.

As linguists we are presumably most interested in the arrow in Fig. 1 labeled 'verbalization', which is meant to include all those processes by which nonverbal information is turned into words. Some readers may question the fact that this verbalization arrow is pictured as leading out of consciousness, suggesting that while we speak we are conscious of nonverbal material. There are evidently individual differences here. Many people, as they talk about recalled experience, are conscious of mental imagery related to the experience. For them the placement of the verbalization arrow in Fig. 1 should seem correct. Others claim to be conscious only of language itself. In that case it might seem that memory contains only material that is already verbalized, and that recall consists of bringing this already formed verbalization into consciousness. Later in this chapter I will return to some considerations that may be relevant to this issue. In the first half of the chapter, however, I want to discuss what I think are some of the processes involved in verbalization.

In a gross way, verbalization processes may be assignable to three major types. First, there are processes having to do with the organization of content. Verbalization requires a speaker to structure the recalled experience itself in certain ways. Second, there are processes having to do with the speaker's assessment of the addressee's current state of mind and processing capacities within the particular context of the discourse. Elsewhere (Chafe, 1975) I have lumped together these processes under the term 'packaging', with the idea that the speaker has to 'wrap up' his content in an effective way to enable the addressee to assimilate it easily. Packaging includes such considerations as distinguishing given from new information, deciding whether a noun should be treated as definite or indefinite, deciding what to make the subject or the topic, and so on. Third, every language imposes various more or less arbitrary syntactic processes that also have to be applied during verbalization. For example, one language might require that a verb agree with its subject with respect to person, number, and gender, while another language might have no such requirement.

I believe that this three-way distinction between content-related processes, packaging processes, and syntactic processes captures some real differences among the kinds of things that happen during verbalization, but in what follows I will focus only on content-related processes. These can in turn be usefully divided into three major subtypes, each of which I will discuss in some detail below. In brief they are the following. First, it is necessary for a speaker to break down larger chunks of content into smaller ones. This kind of process I will call by the somewhat unattractive name 'subchunking'. Second, when a chunk of an optimal size has been arrived at, it is necessary for the speaker to decide on a propositional structure that will assign various roles to the objects involved in the chunk. I will speak of 'propositionalizing'. Third, appropriate words or phrases must be found to communicate the ideas of both objects and events. Here it is useful to speak in terms of 'categorizing'.

Having discussed subchunking, propositionalizing, and categorizing in turn, I will try to make a point that is perhaps best appreciated with reference again to Fig. 1. I mentioned initially that perceptual processes are interpretive, that what enters consciousness, and later memory, by way of perception is not a replica of the original stimulus but an interpretation of it. I believe there is strong evidence that verbalization is interpretive also. The linguistic output of verbalization processes is not a replica of the input to those processes, nor is it algorithmically determined by the input. Rather, as people speak they are constantly making choices about the best way to express what they are thinking of. The conclusion must be that what we remember is of such a nature that

further interpretive processes can be applied to it. Not all interpretation takes place during perception; there is much that takes place while
we are talking as well. That this is so will first become evident, I think,
during the discussion of categorization below. I will then try to show
that subchunking and propositionalizing may also be interpretive: that
they are not always determined by what is in memory but may be
decided on during the course of verbalization, and decided on differently by the same speaker on different occasions.

At several points I will make reference to a source of data that I
will call 'the film'. This is a five-minute film dealing with some activities
of a young boy in a rural setting, which was shown to several groups
of college students in 1972. After seeing the film they were asked to
write descriptions of what was in it, and some of them were asked to
do so again eight weeks later. Thus, some idea was obtained of how
people verbalized their recall of an (admittedly vicarious) experience
shortly after seeing it, and again after it had remained in memory for
some time.

Subchunking

Our memories appear to contain representations of discrete chunks of
experience that may be 'large' or 'small' with respect to the spatio-
temporal extent of the experience as well as the amount of detail that can
be recalled within it. Thus, at a very large level I can recall things
that I might label 'my childhood' or 'World War II'. At some intermediate level might be chunks from memory like 'my trip to Boston last
year' or 'the attempt to assassinate George Wallace'. But I can also recall
quite small events like 'breaking a shoelace this morning' or a momentary
facial expression of some political figure during a televised news conference. I am not referring to the importance or triviality of these events,
but to their 'size', possibly measurable in terms of the number of subevents into which a speaker might conceivably analyze them.

Since we are talking now in terms of a person who has recalled something from memory and is about to verbalize, it is probably best to use
an example in which the initial chunk is something resembling the size
of 'my accident last month' or 'my visit to Boston'. For more reasons
than one, it is less often that I would begin a segment of conversation by
saying 'let me tell you about World War II' or even 'about my childhood'.
Probably there are characteristic sizes of chunks that are typically introduced into discourse for various purposes, but we know very little about

that at the moment. In any case, it is often possible to verbalize this initial, global chunk by labeling it 'my accident', 'my visit to Boston', or 'what I heard from Joe yesterday'. Such labels communicate to the hearer some very general idea of what the chunk contains, and presumably set up some framework of expectations in the hearer's mind. But ordinarily they are promises of more to come, whereby the speaker will try to communicate some of the detail he is able to recall within this initial chunk.

Thus, an important aspect of verbalization is the process whereby larger chunks of recalled experience are broken down into smaller chunks, the verbalization of which will provide the hearer with a level of detail not available if it is only the largest chunk that is verbalized. To a considerable extent this process of 'subchunking' is a hierarchical one. The initial, global chunk is first broken down into chunks that are still fairly large, these into somewhat smaller chunks, and so on, until some stopping point is reached. Thus, in telling you about my trip to Boston I might start with a breakdown into (1) getting there, (2) what happened while I was there, and (3) returning home. (I am not suggesting that this is the only way or even the most common way to organize the account of such a trip, but it seems a possible way.) I might then break down 'getting there' into (1) going to the airport, (2) the plane trip, and (3) being met at the other end, or something of the sort. The plane trip might be broken down into (1) getting settled on the plane, (2) reading something, (3) eating, (4) watching a bad movie, (5) more reading, or whatever.

There may, of course, be digressions from the hierarchical structure. Any particular chunk, or some element within a chunk, may cause the speaker to think of a chunk that lies outside the main hierarchy, but that he nevertheless decides to verbalize at this point. For example, in describing one episode that he remembered from the film about the boy mentioned above, one person wrote:

> He walked down some paths and arrived at an old, chipped, red slide. I liked this scene because it had the multicolored slide, the red fire truck, and the water tower, with a backdrop of the countryside. At any rate, the boy is at the slide. . . .

The writer's comments on liking this scene lie outside the main hierarchy of the events he was describing. They constitute a parenthetical chunk that cannot be accommodated neatly within a coherent hierarchical tree. (It is interesting to note the use of the phrase 'at any rate' as a means of returning to the main hierarchy.) Digressions like that are common.

In fact, there are probably significant individual differences to be found in the extent to which speakers follow a consistent hierarchy of subchunking, as opposed to piling digression upon digression. But even the 'best organized' verbalizers are likely from time to time to insert digressions.

When we break down a larger chunk into smaller ones, we do not do so in an arbitrary fashion, but rather we are influenced by the prior existence in our minds of certain stereotyped patterns. One particular larger chunk of experience, for example, I might interpret as an instance of a plane trip. Since I have been on a number of plane trips before, this one is not a unique experience to me. In fact, interpreting it as a plane trip means that I already have a pattern in mind: a pattern that includes some kind of breakdown into subchunks (and relations between them). I will call such a pattern a 'schema', making use of a term used in approximately the same way by Bartlett (1932). (Terms like 'frame' [Goffman, 1974; Minsky, 1974] or 'script' [Schank and Abelson, 1975] have also been used in similar ways recently.)

A schema, then, is a stereotyped pattern by which experience is organized, and more specifically a pattern that dictates the way in which a particular larger chunk will be broken down into smaller chunks. I think it likely that most experience is interpreted with reference to schemas. That is, there is little that happens to us that we do not interpret in terms of patterns already existent in our minds. These schemas determine how we will conceptually organize the experience, what attitudes we will have toward it, what expectations we will have concerning it, and also how we will talk about it. Since this last is our most immediate concern, it will be well to look more closely at some evidence for schemas that is provided by the use of language.

What follows is excerpted from a story told to me by Sadie Bedoka Weller of Anadarko, Oklahoma, originally in the Caddo language. Here is a translation of the first part:

> It is said that once, long ago, Mr. Wildcat was digging roots in order to make a garden. Presently he heard someone talking. Mr. Turkey was standing there. Mr. Turkey said, "Well, well. You are busy. What are you doing?" "I'm digging roots to make a garden. What are you doing?" "Nothing. I'm just hanging around." "You'll be in my way," said Mr. Wildcat, and he caught him, plucked him, and said, "Go over to my house where my wife is. Tell her to cook you so I can eat you for lunch." Mr. Turkey went off and came to where Mrs. Wildcat was. She was pushing a cradle and singing. Mr. Turkey said, "Your husband over there sent me to tell you that you should make some parched corn for

me. After you've made it I'll go along." She made the corn quickly and he left.

(Sad to say, in spite of his cleverness, the turkey is eventually eaten by the wildcat, but that is another part of the story.)

At a certain level of subchunking we can say that such a story is composed of 'scenes', each scene being something that took place at a coherent place and a coherent time, much like a scene in a play. Between scenes there is either a jump to a new location or a jump to a new segment of time, usually both. The selection above exhibits an organization into two scenes, one at the field and the other at the wildcats' house.

Each scene appears to be organized according to the same schema. It may be noted that at the beginning of each scene (when the curtain rises) there is someone on stage doing something. In the first one it is Mr. Wildcat digging roots, in the second it is Mrs. Wildcat pushing the cradle and singing. Then there is the arrival of a visitor, in both cases the turkey, followed by a conversation between the visitor and the person already there, whom I will call the host. Then the host does something to or for the visitor, in the first scene plucking him and in the second providing him with the requested parched corn. Finally, the visitor leaves. This schema, then, consists of the following general kinds of chunks:

> Background activity
> Arrival of visitor
> Conversation between visitor and host
> Action by host directed at visitor
> Departure of visitor

This same schema seems to be manifested in a number of Caddo stories, where of course the specific events involved are quite diverse. It may even constitute the organizing principle for chunking at a higher level—that is, for the story as a whole rather than for individual scenes within it. For example, there is a story in which some ducks are engaged at the beginning in a game that involves throwing their eyes into a stream, diving in after them, and coming up on the opposite shore with their eyes back in place. Although this chunk is appropriate in 'size' (the amount of verbal elaboration) for a whole scene, it corresponds to the *background activity* that forms the opening segment of each of the two scenes illustrated above. Coyote then *arrives*, and there follows a *conversation* between him and the ducks. Eventually Coyote plays the game himself, but the ducks steal his eyes under the water and replace them with a yellow fruit called bone-nettle. This constitutes the *action by the host directed at the visitor.* Coyote then *departs*, having been blinded. Thus, the schema that formed the basis of several scenes in the earlier story here forms the basis for the entire tale.

Schemas are not just ways of organizing discourse; they are also ways of interpreting experience of the world around us and of organizing behavior. The Caddo, like other American Indian groups, have traditionally spent a great deal of their time visiting. The visit is a stereotyped pattern of behavior that plays an important role in everyday life. It can be seen that the schema illustrated in the folktales mentioned above is in fact the schema of a visit. While the host is doing something, the visitor arrives, there follows a conversation, and then there is an action directed at the visitor, normally the provision of food, after which the visitor departs. Thus, this schema underlies one of the commonest occurrences in Caddo life and determines the expectations associated with such an occurrence.

Propositionalizing

The process of breaking down larger chunks into smaller ones does not go on indefinitely, nor does it, by itself, lead directly to a linguistic output. The speaker begins with some large, inclusive chunk recalled from memory, and through subchunking arrives at various smaller, less-inclusive chunks. But these smaller chunks are no different in kind from the larger ones; all of them are memories of situations and events. They are still not language, but 'ideas'. Several other kinds of processes must be applied before language is finally achieved.

The next step toward language is one that I will call 'propositionalizing'. It is distinguished from the subchunking process in the fact that it leads to an output that is different in kind from the input. In order to appreciate this point, one needs to differentiate between (ideas of) events and situations, on the one hand, and (ideas of) objects on the other. The difference can be specified in terms of space, time, and particularity. An event (such as might be verbalized as 'The dog knocked over the chair'), or a situation ('The dog is under the chair') is particular with respect to both space and time. It is restricted to a single, unique, limited portion of space, and to a single, unique, limited segment of time. (I am omitting from consideration here generic ideas, such as might be verbalized as 'The dog is black', which require a discussion of their own that would lead us too far afield.) An object, on the other hand, appears to be particular in space but not in time. The particular dog, the particular chair that might have been referred to in the examples above, has a continuing existence through time that the particular event or situation does not. For that reason the same object can usually take part in a large and unlimited collection of different events. This particular knocking over of the chair is presumably only one of a large number of events in which this particular dog was involved. Each event occupies a relatively small segment of particular time. The dog extends through them all, and in fact is conceived of as having a continuous existence through time during those many temporal intervals when we are unaware of what he is doing—of the particular events in which he is involved.

Many qualifications have to be added to what I have just said. For example, a particular dog or chair does occupy a particular segment of time in the sense that it comes into existence at some time and goes out of existence at another. There are few objects that do not have a particular 'lifetime' in this sense. But such segments of time are, for the most part, related to human experience in quite a different way than are the segments of time occupied by events. Roughly, but I think significantly, the span of time occupied by a typical event falls within the span of conscious attention. Perhaps most of the events that we deal with are possible to comprehend in their entirety within what I have elsewhere called 'surface memory' (Chafe, 1973), where the entire segment of time from beginning to end can be held in consciousness without being relegated to deeper levels of memory. Although this is clearly not true of all events, I believe it is usually true of events at the stage of sub-chunking we are now discussing, the stage at which propositionalizing takes place. And probably it has a lot to do with our idea of what an event is, in a prototypical sense. My suggestion is that the typical lifetime of an object is of a different order of magnitude from that of the typical segment of time occupied by an event, and that we conceive of the two as being different sorts of things for that reason. An insect whose lifetime is only a fraction of a second may in immediate conceptual terms be more like an event than an object. If we conceive of this insect as an object, that is only by analogy to the typical form of animal life whose span of existence is significantly longer.

All this discussion has been preparatory to the statement that propositionalizing consists, in part, of the factoring out from an event (or situation) of the objects involved in it. Suppose, for example, that I have a particular event in mind. One way I might verbalize my knowledge of that event would be to say 'Then I ate a sandwich', having chosen to verbalize it in terms of two objects, me and the sandwich. Given the same event as a starting point, I might alternatively have verbalized it as 'Then I ate', with only one subject, me, factored out, or perhaps as 'Then I ate some salami in a sandwich', with the salami included as a third object. There are usually various ways in which objects can be factored from an event, and this constitutes one aspect of a speaker's interpretation of the event.

To a degree the process here is analogous to that by which larger chunks are broken down into smaller subchunks, but there are two differences. First, the objects factored out from the event are things of a different kind from that of the event itself. Second, the event is not itself lost in the process. In the final verbalization, the event is typically represented by a verb—for example, by the word *ate* in the sentences given as examples above. Thus, if one thinks in terms of replacing one thing with another, in subchunking a larger chunk is replaced by a constellation of smaller ones, but in propositionalizing a chunk is replaced by a different kind of entity: a structure consisting of an event (or situation) plus, as separate elements, the objects the speaker has chosen to verbalize as participants in the event. Such a structure approximates what has traditionally been called a proposition, and we might think of representing it as, for example, 'ate (I, sandwich)', or in other notationally equivalent ways.

But that is not all there is to such a structure. It is important to recognize that each of the objects factored out for separate verbalization plays its own specific role in the event or situation. The major contribution of so-called case grammar has been to recognize the existence and importance of these roles. Thus, in 'Then I ate a sandwich' there has been not only a factoring out from the holistic event of the ideas of me and the sandwich but also a decision to treat me as the 'agent' of the event and the sandwich as 'patient'. The names we give to these roles are not at issue here; the only point is that the objects associated with an event do participate in it in different ways. The standard notation for propositions is deficient in not providing a fixed way of specifying these roles. I will not say more here about what specific roles there are, or what the best notation for them might be. I believe that a new way of sorting out case roles is needed. But of the fact that they exist and are important to verbalization there can be no doubt.

In summary, when subchunking has led to a chunk of optimum size for verbalization, the speaker must interpret it in propositional terms. Propositionalizing includes (1) the factoring out of objects from the event or situation that the chunk embraces, and (2) the assignment of roles to these objects within the event or situation. But we still have not arrived at language.

Categorization

It may be possible to have a certain propositional format in mind without having decided on what specific words to use to convey either the idea of the event or the ideas of the objects that have been interpreted as participants in the event. For example, imagine that the speaker has interpreted some event as an instance of a 'transfer'; that is, as an event in which possession of a particular object changes from one particular individual to another. At this point he need not have decided whether to convey his idea of this event with the verb 'give' or the verb 'hand' or perhaps some other verb like 'pass'. Furthermore, he need not have decided whether to convey his idea of the earlier possessor by calling him 'Doug', 'the tall boy', 'your son', 'the boy on the left', or whatever else might be appropriate. Thus the ultimate sentence might be 'Doug gave the other boy a book', 'The tall boy handed a dictionary to Steve', or a number of other possibilities, none of which would necessarily have been determined by the decision as to how to propositionalize the event. We can imagine any number of sentences with the same propositional structure—benefactive verb, agent, patient, beneficiary —with different words or phrases used to convey the idea of each of these elements.

Some particulars have their own names—proper names, as we call them. This is likely to be true of certain kinds of objects, especially persons and places with which we are familiar and which we are likely to have occasion to talk about repeatedly. But let us focus our attention on what happens when a speaker has in mind a particular object or event that does not have its own name. The important point on which the following discussion will be based is that in order to communicate such an idea, the speaker has to 'categorize' it. He must decide to interpret the object or event as an instance of some category, which in the favorable case will then provide him with a word that will more or less satisfactorily convey what he has in mind. Thus, categorizing a particular object as an instance of category X will enable me to call it 'a dish' or 'the dish'. Categorizing a particular event as an instance of category Y will enable me to communicate it as 'eat', 'ate', and so on.

Perhaps the best way to approach the subject of categorization is by looking briefly at color naming, something that has been studied more thoroughly than any other kind of categorization. It is well known that the color spectrum, at least in physical, pre-interpreted terms, exhibits continuous variation along several dimensions. Most studies of color naming have concentrated on the dimensions of hue and brightness. Given a color chart in the form of a rectangle, where hue varies continuously from left to right and brightness varies in the vertical dimension, there are a few points in the chart that people are able to name very easily. It has been said that these particular colors are 'highly codable' (Brown and Lenneberg, 1954). For our purposes it is interesting to note that ease of naming shows up in four different ways. (Brown and Lenneberg mentioned a fifth: number of syllables in the word used.) First, there will be general agreement among different people as to what the color is called; everyone will call it 'red', or 'orange', or 'blue'. Second, there will be consistency in naming; the same person will agree with himself on different occasions. Having called it 'red' at one time, he will call it 'red' another time. Third, he is likely to name it with a single word, like 'red', rather than with a longer phrase like 'dark reddish brown'. Fourth, if he is talking rather than writing, he is likely to utter the name immediately without hesitation.

Suppose we call the points within the spectrum where there is highest codability the 'foci' of the various color categories. Thus, a certain point can be regarded as the focus of the category that enables a speaker to call any instance of this same color 'red'. As we move away from these foci, codability decreases and much of the spectrum is inhabited by colors whose codability is relatively low. For colors, at least, there is no clear boundary between one category and another, but only a gradual fading away from the focus of one category or a gradual approach to the focus of another. The symptoms of low codability are of course the converse of those listed above: (1) there will be less agreement between different persons as to what the color is called, (2) the same person is more likely to call it something different on different occasions, (3) it is more likely that a phrase rather than a single word will be used, and (4) a speaker is more likely to hesitate before verbalizing. These symptoms increase with the distance from the focus of any category.

This same focal property is evidently present in categories other than colors (Rosch, 1973), and it seems clear that relative codability is a quite general phenomenon. Mention was made earlier of an event in which a boy slid down a slide. We can say that the memory of the object he slid down was highly codable, as evidenced by the fact that 99 percent of the people who verbalized this piece of knowledge used the word *slide*, that there was virtually 100 percent consistency when the same person verbalized his knowledge of this same object eight weeks later, and that the average number of modifiers used in all verbalizations was .33, a relatively low figure. Since the verbalizations in this case were written, no data are available on hesitations. Ongoing work on tape-recorded narratives, however, shows signs of confirming the value of hesitations (or the lack of them) as additional evidence for codability.

We may contrast this highly codable 'slide' object with another object that appeared in the same film. Rather than showing a high percentage of agreement on naming, this object was called many diverse things (see Table 1). Consistency in the naming of this object was 65 percent.

Table 1

Name used	Percentage of persons using name		
structure	28	kiddy climb	< 1
tower	20	building	< 1
platform	17	monolith	< 1
jungle gym	12.5	bandstand	< 1
construction	5.5	set-up	< 1
scaffold(ing)	5	equipment	< 1
monkey bars	2	contraption	< 1
frame	1	set of bars	< 1
playhouse	1	swing-set	< 1
apparatus	< 1	maze	< 1
stand	< 1	practice pole	< 1
tree house	< 1		

That is, people who called it a particular name immediately after seeing the film used the same name eight weeks later 65 percent of the time. This and other observations suggest that, for items of low codability, consistency tends to be in the general area of somewhat more than 50 percent, while for items of high codability it is close to 100 percent. Presumably the reason that consistency is as high as it is for items of low codability is that many people remember what they called an item the first time. Earlier choices are likely to determine what is said on later occasions. The average number of modifiers used for this object was 1.39, as contrasted with .33 for the highly codable 'slide' mentioned earlier.

Particular events may also be of high or low codability. The categorization of events, in fact, seems to take place in a way that is quite analogous, in these respects at least, to the categorization of objects. Thus, with the event on the slide there was 86 percent agreement on the verb *slide*. (Other choices included *go, come, glide, float, shoot, swoosh,* and *take off*.) Usually a two-word verb was used, where the word just mentioned specified the manner of motion and a second word the direction. In 98 percent of the cases the second word was *down*. The relatively high codability of this event showed up also in the consistency with which the same person used the same word eight weeks later. Consistency was 83 percent for the word expressing manner of motion, and 91 percent for the word expressing direction.

We may contrast another event in the same film, the one involving the activity of the boy on an old abandoned fire truck. What he did, roughly, was to get on the truck in the rear and move across it to the front. The verbs used are listed in Table 2. Usually a two-word verb was

Table 2

Verb used	Percentage of persons using verb		
climb	39.5	investigate	1
walk	20	step	.5
play	17.5	bounce	.5
crawl	3	meander	.5
clamber	2.5	jump	.5
explore	2.5	pause	.5
scramble	2.5	fool around	.5
inspect	2	move	.5
made his way	2	mess	.5
go	1.5	rummage	.5
run	1	proceed	.5

used here also, the second element expressing the direction of motion, but with this second element also there was much less agreement (see Table 3). This time, consistency in expressing the manner of motion was 53 percent after eight weeks, and for the direction of motion it was 50 percent.

What is going on here can be visualized in terms of Figs. 3 and 4. The point labeled X in Fig. 3 is meant to represent the speaker's knowledge of a particular object, insofar as that knowledge is a unitary thing —a single, discrete piece of knowledge. The small circle above, to

Table 3

Second element used	Percentage of persons using second element		
on	26.5	across	2.5
through	26	along	2.5
over	17.5	forward	1.5
around	7	from back to	
to the front	6	front	1.5
the length of	4.5	with	.5
in	4		

which X is connected, is meant to represent what the speaker knows about X: its various properties, perhaps, but perhaps also an analogic kind of knowledge that cannot be accounted for in terms of propositions alone, and that might, for many speakers at least, appear in the speaker's consciousness as a mental image of X.

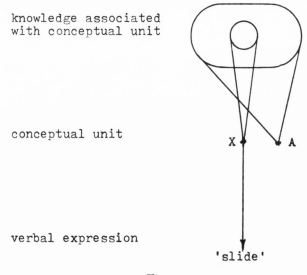

knowledge associated
with conceptual unit

conceptual unit

X   A

verbal expression

'slide'

Fig. 3

Let us suppose that the speaker has propositionalized an event in such a way that he wants to express X as one of the objects that participate in the event. He must, then, find a word or phrase that will make contact with or establish a corresponding X in his listener's mind. In this example let us assume that the listener has no prior knowledge of X, so that one result of the speaker's uttering the sentence he is about to produce will be to establish X as a new item of knowledge for the listener. He needs, then, to communicate his knowledge of X in such a way that the listener will have a sufficient idea of what X is like. That is, the speaker would like the listener to have an idea of X whose content will to some degree approximate the content represented by the small circle above X in the diagram. The listener is not likely to end up with a content as rich as the speaker's, but he needs to end up with a content that is sufficient for the situation. In order to provide the listener with such a content, the speaker must first interpret X as an instance of a category.

The point labeled A is meant to represent a category, from the point of view that a category can be considered a discrete conceptual unit. And the large circle above it, to which A is connected, is meant to represent the content of that category, which I will assume has both discrete and analogic properties. We can imagine that in the speaker's mind there are a very large number of such categories, and that the speaker's task, in categorizing his idea of object X, is to match the content of X (the small circle) as closely as possible to the focus of some category. For we may assume that the content of most categories, like the one represented by the large circle here, has a focus and a gradual fading away from that focus, just as do the color categories that have been the best studied in this respect. In other words, the small circle might be regarded as analogous to a color chip that someone is trying to match to a color category. The large circle represents the (often vaguely defined) boundary of a catgeory, and we may assume that somewhere within it lies a focus, analogous to the focus of the red category, for example.

In this case we are assuming that X is highly codable, which is equivalent to saying that X matches closely the focus of some category, in this case category A. X will then be interpreted as an instance of category A with a high degree of agreement, consistency, and lack of hesitation, and no modifiers will be needed. Let us suppose that in this case one major effect of this interpretation is that X can be called 'a slide'. When the listener hears it called this, he enters into his own mind a new unit, corresponding to X, whose content matches what is defined by the focus of the slide category in his own knowledge. Under the best of circumstances, where X is highly codable and where the content of the category in question is highly similar for both the speaker and the hearer, the speaker will have succeeded in communicating something very similar in content to what he started out with, namely the content of X. In many cases the communication will not be this effective, but very often discrepancies will be unimportant.

Fig. 4 shows what happens when codability is low. The item being

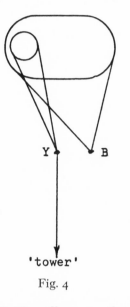

'tower'

Fig. 4

communicated is labeled Y. We will assume that in searching his category space for a category whose content has a focus closely matching the content of Y, the speaker has been unsuccessful. The best he has been able to come up with is category B, but the content of Y lies on the periphery of the category's content, and not near the focus. Let us suppose that category B provides the word *tower* for particulars that are interpreted as instances of it. The trouble is that by calling Y 'a tower' the speaker will communicate something whose content is like the focus of the tower category—a prototypical tower. But in this case the speaker has in mind a content that differs considerably from that focus, as is suggested by the placement of the small circle above Y at the edge of the large circle above B. This is the situation of low codability, where there is less agreement and less consistency in the categorization, where people are likely to hesitate, and where there is a greater use of modifiers.

The function of modifiers is easy to appreciate against this background. Fig. 5 illustrates the principle involved. An adjective or other modifier provides a content that intersects with the content of the

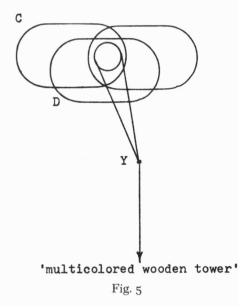

'multicolored wooden tower'

Fig. 5

original category. The area defined by this intersection is in a sense a new, ad hoc category, produced by the speaker for the specific purpose of communicating more accurately the content he has in mind. In this example we may assume that the speaker's dissatisfaction with categorizing Y as an instance of the 'tower' category has led him to use modifier C, whose name is 'multicolored', and modifier D, whose name is 'wooden'. The intersection of the content of C and D with the content of B defines a content that is closer to the content the speaker has in mind for Y. And the intention is that when the listener hears the phrase 'a multicolored wooden tower' he will form in his own mind a content that is closer to what the speaker was thinking of. More complicated modifier constructions can of course be used. If the speaker says 'a tall red and white platform that looked like a cattle loading platform except too high' he is creating an intersection, an ad hoc content, which even more narrowly delimits what he has in mind. I believe that the function of adjectives, relative clauses, and other modifiers must be understood in these terms.

It may be noted that the matching of the content of one's idea of an object or event with the content of a category must be an analogic procedure, like the matching of a color chip against an area of the spectrum. It necessarily involves comparison of one mental representation with another—of the content of a particular with the content of a category. This matching is not a matter of yes or no, but a matter of degree. A particular may be more or less codable, which is to say that its content may match more or less well the content of some category. Such a situation appears to demand that the mental representation correspond either in a continuous way or in some stepwise fashion to what is being represented. That, apparently, is the essence of analogic, as opposed to propositional representation.

Creativity

As was discussed briefly at the beginning of this chapter, many people, in recalling something they witnessed earlier or were involved in (even something they were told about), have the subjective feeling that they are reliving the original experience in a way that is not identical to that of the original experience but has something important in common with it. This kind of subjective experience is referred to as mental imagery. It need not, of course, be visual only; auditory and kinesthetic imagery, for example, are common enough. There is an old and still unresolved controversy over the nature, role, and importance of mental imagery in thought and language. There seem to be some real individual differences in imaging ability, which may have something to do with the disagreements that still rage in this area. (See Galton, 1907, for an early but still provocative discussion of individual differences, and Pylyshyn, 1973, and Paivio, 1974, for some modern controversy.) In any case, those whose imaginal experiences are strong tend to feel, as they are telling about something they have recalled, that they are describing a kind of replay of the original experience. Others apparently have less of this feeling, or even deny it altogether, claiming that they are conscious of only language.

It is important to realize that what is at issue here is the nature and significance of the conscious experience that results from recall, and that this question may or may not have a direct bearing on the fundamental issue of how knowledge is stored in subconscious memory. In considering the latter issue, one—but only one—of the possibly relevant considerations is the extent to which these subjective experiences of mental imagery that many of us have during recall should be taken seriously as clues to what is in memory. One possible view is that they should be taken seriously, at least to the extent that they show that memory has 'analogic' properties. Another possible view is that mental imagery is a secondary and misleading phenomenon that shows very little or nothing about how knowledge is actually stored.

Those who take the latter position (e.g., Pylyshyn, 1973) like to point out that imagery, whatever it is like, is unquestionably very different from the original sensory stimulus. Images, it is said—and in fact everyone who reflects on the matter ought to be willing to agree—are not like 'pictures', in the sense that the same interpretive processes that are applied during perception can be applied to them. Imagery, beyond doubt, is at least a partial *product* of interpretation, not a raw input. What is in memory, and thus necessarily what is recalled from memory into consciousness, must already have been filtered through perceptual processes. There seems to be no way in which imagery could be a direct copy of the original sensory stimulus. An easy way to demonstrate this to oneself is to look at a scene for a short time and then stop looking at it. After a brief interval, try to recall everything that was in the scene— the objects, relations, and events that it contained. You will find this quite a different experience from looking at the scene itself. In particular, I believe, you will not be able to 'individuate'—to pick out as discrete entities—objects or events that were not individuated while you were looking at the scene itself. Although I am not aware of psychological experiments specifically aimed at this question, it does appear to be at least intuitively plausible that the individuation of objects and events is something that takes place only while the stimulus is present. If it is not accomplished then, it cannot be accomplished later on. Of course it is possible that we will recall or introduce into our verbalization objects that were not present in the original scene. Memory may very well be constructive, in the sense that it adds things that were not there to begin with (cf. Bartlett, 1932; Münsterberg, 1909). But veridical recall —that which is derived from the original stimulus—seems not to allow individuation that was not accomplished when the stimulus was present.

But this is far from being the whole story. Individuation is not the only kind of interpretive process applied to sensory material. It is one thing to identify, for example, the presence of a certain discrete object within a scene. It is quite another to decide that this object is an instance of some category, for example, that it is the kind of thing that can be called an animal, or a dog, or a Dalmatian. Categorization appears to be a special case of a kind of processing that, for lack of a better term, I will call 'typing'. The basic idea is that we constantly find it necessary to interpret particular objects, situations, and events, each of which is a separate 'token', as instances of general types. And although it seems likely that *individuation* takes place only during perception, it would appear that *typing* may take place either during perception *or during verbalization*. Undoubtedly there is much typing that takes place at the same time an object is individuated. For example, at the same time that I pick out something in a scene as a discrete object I may also identify that object as an instance of the type (category) that may lead me to call it a dog. Or at the same time that I isolate a discrete event I may identify it as an instance of running. But, as we have in fact already seen with respect to categorization, a significant amount of typing takes place also during verbalization—while a person is actually talking.

I believe it is important in understanding how language works to realize that a lot of what goes on when we turn thoughts into words is in the nature of interpretation of the thoughts; that we do not simply transform deep structures into surface structures, where the deep structures already contain all the conceptual interpretation there is going to be. Talking about something recalled from memory is a creative activity, in the sense that the talker must at many points make choices that reflect a specific interpretation of his underlying thoughts. At the same time it is necessarily a distorting process, in that these choices are not likely to reflect the speaker's thoughts in a completely adequate way. He is likely to be left with the feeling that the words he uttered did not convey exactly what he had in mind. And in talking about the same thing on a later occasion he is likely to make different choices—to verbalize in at least a partially different way.

In summary, there appear to be two major kinds of processes involved in people's processing of the stimuli that come to them from the outside world: individuation and typing. While individuation probably takes place only during perception, typing may take place either during perception or during verbalization. The latter possibility makes of the use of language a more creative process than linguists have generally conceived it as being. So far, we have specifically considered the creative nature of categorization only. But two other kinds of verbalization processes were also discussed above: subchunking and propositionalizing. It is therefore of interest to consider whether those processes may also exhibit creativity in the manner in which they are applied during language use. Is there, for example, any evidence that speakers make choices regarding subchunking or propositionalizing while they are speaking, as appears to be the case with categorizing? If so, we could conclude that, like categorization, these kinds of interpretations are not necessarily a part of knowledge or memory, but may be a part of talking about what one knows and remembers.

Creativity in Subchunking

In talking about the same thing on different occasions, it is quite likely that a speaker will not perform all subchunking operations in the same way each time. The differences may be of several types. For example, given a particular larger chunk the speaker may break it down into one set of smaller chunks on one occasion, and into a partially different set on another. Occasionally he may even make use of different schemas on different occasions, so that the resulting conceptual interpretations are distinct. I will not try to illustrate such cases here, but will discuss only some aspects of the apparent fact that the different subchunks within a larger chunk are not all of equal status.

One of the scenes in the film showed the boy sliding down a slide. The subchunks within this scene that were verbalized at least once by someone included:

1. arriving at the slide
2. climbing up the back
3. reaching the top
4. standing at the top
5. hitching up his pants
6. sitting down
7. sliding down
8. landing at the bottom
9. jumping off
10. standing up
11. walking away

There was no one who mentioned all these events, and in fact only (1), (2), and (7) were mentioned very frequently. Fig. 6 shows the

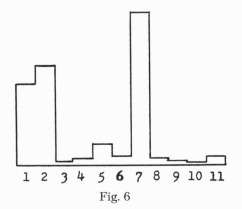

1 2 3 4 5 6 7 8 9 10 11

Fig. 6

relative frequency of mention. Nearly everyone verbalized (7), the sliding down. Somewhat more than half mentioned (1) and (2), the arrival and climbing up the slide. The other events were mentioned by only a few people each. It is tempting to attribute these differences in frequency of mention to a factor that might be labeled 'salience'. In so doing we would, of course, like to be doing more than simply giving a name to the observation. In particular, we would like to have independent evidence for relative degrees of salience among events (with respect to a certain population). I hope that sound evidence of this sort will eventually be forthcoming, but at the moment I can only make a few potentially relevant suggestions.

An interesting phenomenon occurred among the persons who described the film shortly after seeing it and were asked to describe it again after an interval of eight weeks. In the later descriptions the sliding-down event was still mentioned by almost everyone, while the arrival and climbing had decreased in mention from somewhat more than half to somewhat less than half. The remaining events, with one exception, failed to be mentioned at all. The exception was the walking away, which was still mentioned by a small minority.

What explanations are there for this attenuation in the verbalization of all the subchunks, with the exception of the sliding down? One possibility is that salience influences memory as well as verbalization, and that it was only the more salient events that were recalled after eight weeks. A variant form of this explanation might be that all that was remembered after eight weeks was that this scene was an instance of the 'sliding-down' schema, and that the schema itself then provided a kind of reconstruction of the event. By this view the schema would be most likely to determine mention of arriving, climbing up, sliding down, and perhaps walking away. The other events, being either peripheral to or altogether outside the schema, would not be so likely to be reconstructed. This explanation is in line with Bartlett's theory of memory (1932:197–214). Still another possibility is that after eight weeks people were less inclined to include minor details in their descriptions, regardless of whether or not they remembered them. Under conditions of lower motivation the tactic would be to verbalize only the more salient items. These various explanations are not mutually exclusive, and at this stage of our knowledge we might suspect that all these factors play a role. The main point to be noted now is that Fig. 6 seems to predict something about what will be mentioned in later verbalizations of this same scene.

The last possibility mentioned above, that one may choose to verbalize only the more salient items even though one may remember more than that, raises the question of the relationship between salience and summarization. Suppose we think of Fig. 6 as the profile of a mountain range, and that we imagine a fog extending through the area such that only the highest peak rises above it. In that condition the verbalizer would say only "He slid down a slide," and by that single statement embrace the entire scene. Imagine now that the fog partially lowers, so that the two next highest peaks also appear above it. The verbalizer might then say: "He next comes to a slide. He climbs up the ladder of the slide and then slides down." Or imagine that the fog has more or less dissipated, leaving some or all of the lowest peaks in view as well. Perhaps then the verbalizer might say: "Next the boy comes upon a slide. He climbs up the ladder of the slide, sits down, and then slides down the slide. He reaches the ground, stands up, and again continues walking in the same direction as he started." (All these examples are from actual verbalizations.) Subchunking, in other words, usually gives the speaker a choice of how much detail to include—how many subchunks to verbalize, and one cannot choose randomly but must be governed by priorities in terms of salience. If the situation calls for a minimum of detail, the speaker will verbalize only the most salient chunk. In such a case we are likely to say that he has provided a 'summary' of what was embraced by the larger chunk. By including increasingly less salient items he can provide an increasing amount of detail. It would be interesting to know what factors influence the speaker's judgment as to the amount of detail he finds appropriate to include.

What are the determinants of salience? Ultimately it will not be enough to say that the different chunks defined by a schema, or chosen in the breakdown of a larger chunk, possess different degrees of salience. Nor will it be enough to discover various, at least partially independent methods by which salience can be measured. A fuller understanding of this matter requires that we eventually establish what it is that makes one item more salient than another. Whatever the answer turns out to be, it seems likely to be a complex one; we cannot expect that only one simple factor is involved.

One factor is likely to be the information value of the item in question: its degree of unexpectedness, in the information theory sense. We can imagine that everyday experience has a kind of base line representing things we fully expect to happen. If life never rose above this base line, it would be totally monotonous. But some of life, one hopes, is not that way. There are things that happen, good or bad, that are to some degree unexpected, and to that degree salient. But there must be more to salience than simple unexpectedness. For example, the boy might not have been expected to hitch up his pants at the top of the slide, yet that event seems not to have been overwhelmingly salient. To achieve some high degree of salience, the event must somehow strike the speaker as interesting or relevant. Perhaps this is a matter of how the event reacts with the speaker's preconceptions as to what is important and what trivial, but it is hard to say much more on this point at present.

One might also suspect that involvement of the speaker's own ego is a relevant factor. For example, on another occasion a number of people were asked to describe an incident during which, among other things, a certain person was blindfolded. One of the verbalizers was that person himself, and he was the only one who mentioned that the blindfold was at first ineffective and had to be readjusted. Because of his own involvement in at first being able to see and then not being able to see, the readjustment was salient to him. The onlookers, however, had no involvement of their own at that point; none of them mentioned the readjustment, and probably few of them even perceived it. Finally, and this is related to the factor of unexpectedness, salience seems to have something to do with the extent to which one item entails others. Sliding down the slide was the most salient event in that scene because most of the rest was predictable from it. In order to slide down a slide one has to arrive at the slide, climb it, and so on. On that basis it is easy to understand why mention of this one event provides a good summary of the entire scene; it is all that needs to be known in order to know what else happened.

It would seem, then, that the way a speaker decides to break down larger chunks of content into smaller ones can differ from one verbalization to another, and is not algorithmically determined by 'what is known' about the material in question. Furthermore, the chunks into which a larger chunk may be broken down are likely to differ significantly in degree of salience. Thus, even if a hierarchical diagram of subchunking were adequate as a first approximation to a representation of how knowledge is stored, its nodes would have to be marked in some way to indicate their degrees of salience. And these degrees would presumably be related in some analogic way to the as yet little understood determinants of salience just discussed.

Creativity in Propositionalizing

I will close with an example that illustrates how, in verbalizing the same item from memory on different occasions, a person may make different decisions not only regarding categorization and subchunking but also regarding propositionalizing. The example I will use was already mentioned in Chafe (1976), but I wish to expand upon several points that were made there in a sketchy fashion.

Soon after seeing the film, one person described one of the scenes as follows:

> He picked up some hay and lifted it over the corral fence and into the corral. All of the animals eagerly went after and began eating the hay.

At the outset the speaker must have had in mind a chunk that included this whole incident (but that was, of course, only a subchunk at some lower level within the large chunk that included the whole film). Suppose we call this initial chunk C_1. On the basis of the division into two sentences, as well as the shift from one subject (the boy) to another (the animals), we can say that C_1 was first broken down into two subchunks, C_2 and C_3, corresponding to the two sentences. Within C_2 there were three minimal events, the picking up, the lifting over, and the lifting into. However, it appears that the last two were chunked together as against the first, since they share a common verb and object ('lifted it'). On that basis we can say that C_2 was first subchunked into C_4 (the picking up) and C_5, and the latter then further subchunked into C_6 and C_7. C_3 (expressed in the second sentence), contains two minimal events that can be labeled C_8 (going after the hay) and C_9 (eating it). This pattern of subchunking is summarized in Fig. 7.

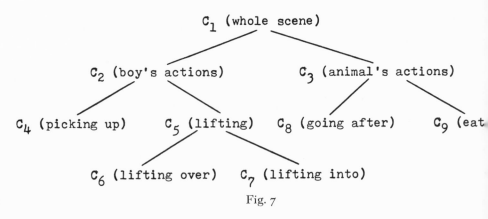

Fig. 7

In addition to subchunking, the speaker had to propositionalize each of the minimal chunks, C_4, C_6, C_7, C_8, and C_9. Let us focus on just the first of these. Fig. 8 shows one way of representing the propositional structure of the verbalization 'He picked up some hay'. The speaker chose to interpret this event in terms of an agent–patient structure, as-signing the role of agent to the object labeled O_1, and the role of patient to the object labeled O_2.

Having made this decision, the speaker went on to categorize O_1 and O_2, as well as C_4 itself. The unlabeled arrows pointing upward show the results of these categorizations. O_1 was assumed by the speaker to be already in the consciousness of the listener, and thus it is simply represented by the pronoun 'he' (Chafe, 1974). C_4 was interpreted as an instance of the category, which resulted in its being communicated with the words 'pick up'; while O_2 was interpreted as an instance of the category, which resulted in its being called 'some hay'.

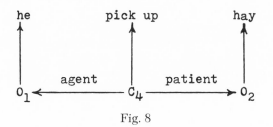

Fig. 8

Of interest is the fact that the speaker who produced the verbaliza-tion just described shortly after seeing the film, eight weeks later verbal-ized the same scene as follows:

He threw some hay over the top rail of the corral fence to the animals inside.

Several points may be noticed in comparing the two verbalizations. First, so far as subchunking is concerned, the second time the speaker imme-diately propositionalized the entire scene as a single chunk, rather than breaking it down in the manner shown in Fig. 7. Thus, in comparison with the earlier verbalization, he produced a summary. Second, he chose quite a different propositional format, as shown in Fig. 9. This format is more complex than any in the earlier verbalization, as if the lack of subchunking were compensated by the more elaborate propositional structure. The new format contains not only the roles of agent and patient, but also two roles that are indicated here simply with the arrows labeled 'over' and 'to'. The propositional structure, in other words, assigns roles to four different objects, O_1, O_2, O_3, and O_4. It should be noted in particular that the role assigned to O_4 (the animals), here a beneficiary role, is entirely different from the role assigned to O_4

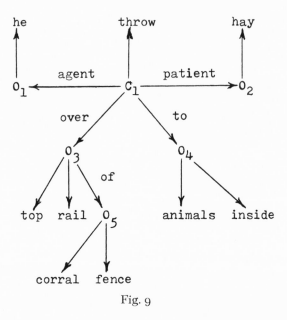

Fig. 9

in the earlier verbalization, where the animals were interpreted not as beneficiaries but as agents.

Starting with the same chunk from memory, C_1, the speaker verbalized it quite differently on the two occasions, both in terms of the subchunking process and in terms of propositionalizing. It is conceivable that his memory representation underwent some change, in propositional terms, during the eight weeks, so that O_4 shifted from an agent role to a beneficiary role. What is to my mind more intriguing and more likely, however, is the possibility that the memory representation contained no commitment to either of these roles—that it was of such a nature that either of them could be chosen. It is cases like this that make one doubt the adequacy of arrows like those labeled 'agent', 'patient', 'over', and 'to' in Fig. 9 for the representation of what is stored in long-term memory. And in fact this kind of evidence casts doubt on the adequacy of representations like Figs. 7, 8, and 9 to capture a speaker's underlying knowledge of an event. At best they seem to capture only certain decisions that were made during certain particular verbalizations. They show, not what was known about the event, but only some aspects of how it was talked about.

The speaker also made categorization decisions. As far as the event C_1 is concerned, he chose to interpret it in Fig. 9 as an instance of the category that resulted in its being called 'throw'. Whether he would have done this eight weeks earlier if he had chosen to verbalize this event directly rather than to break it down into smaller chunks, there is no way to know. For the several objects involved in C_1 there was little significant difference in their categorization after eight weeks, although a slightly different treatment was given to O_3. Whereas earlier it was called 'the corral fence', this time it was called 'the top rail of the corral fence'. In general one can say that the objects were high in codability, judging from the consistency with which the speaker categorized them. Nevertheless, we know from other examples that speakers are frequently inconsistent and hesitant in categorizing, and that many objects have low codability. Thus, the unlabeled arrows representing categorization in Fig. 9 are in principle the kinds of things that speakers may choose differently in different verbalizations of the same event. These arrows, too, need not represent what is stored in memory, but only what is decided on during verbalization. In sum, *none* of the arrows in Figs. 7, 8, and 9 need in principle represent what is known about this event, but only decisions as to how to verbalize it. What is known must be of such a nature as to allow multiple interpretations of these kinds. The most attractive conclusion, I think, is that what is known is not necessarily in a propositional format at all, but that it is in many cases in some analogic format that allows various propositional interpretations to be given to it.

The implication for linguistics is that there cannot be any such thing as a well-defined or autonomous semantic structure underlying a discourse (or a sentence). Talking is a creative process by which an underlying knowledge, to a large extent analogic in nature, is crystallized into propositional and linguistic structures. It is true that some, perhaps a great deal, of this crystallization will have taken place when the knowledge was first acquired. But much of it will not. And in order to explain things that we find in the use of language—such as inconsistency and hesitation in subchunking, propositionalizing, and categorizing, and even such a basic thing as the use of modifiers—it is necessary to recognize this as-yet-uncrystallized state of much of our knowledge. If we as linguists are interested in understanding how language really works, we will sooner or later have to expand our horizons to include these readily observable aspects of language use.

REFERENCES

Bartlett, F. C. 1932. *Remembering*. Cambridge: Cambridge University Press.
Brown, R. W., and Lenneberg, E. H. 1954. A study in language and cognition. *Journal of Abnormal and Social Psychology* 49:454–62.

Chafe, W. L. 1973. Language and memory. *Language* 49:261–81.

————. 1974. Language and consciousness. *Language* 50:111–33.

————. 1975. Givenness, contrastiveness, definiteness, subject, topic, and point of view. In C. Li, ed., *Subject and Topic*. New York: Academic Press.

————. 1976. Creativity in verbalization and its implications for the nature of stored knowledge. In R. O. Freedle, ed., *Discourse Production and Comprehension*. Hillsdale, N.J.: Lawrence Erlbaum.

Galton, F. 1907. *Inquiries into Human Faculty and Its Development*, 2d ed. London: J. M. Dent and Sons.

Goffman, E. 1974. *Frame Analysis: An Essay on the Organization of Experience*. Cambridge: Harvard University Press.

Hochberg, J. E. 1964. *Perception*. Englewood Cliffs, N.J.: Prentice-Hall.

Miller, G. A. 1956. The magical number seven, plus or minus two: some limits on our capacity for processing information. *Psychological Review* 63:81–97.

Minsky, M. 1974. A framework for representing knowledge. A. I. Memo 306. Massachusetts Institute of Technology Artificial Intelligence Laboratory.

Münsterberg, Hugo. 1909. *On the Witness Stand: Essays on Psychology and Crime*. New York: Doubleday, Page.

Paivio, A. 1974. Images, propositions, and knowledge. Research Bulletin 309. The University of Western Ontario, Department of Psychology.

Pylyshyn, Z. W. 1973. What the mind's eye tells the mind's brain: a critique of mental imagery. *Psychological Bulletin* 80:1–24.

Rosch, E. H. 1973. On the internal structure of perceptual and semantic categories. In T. E. Moore, ed., *Cognitive Development and the Acquisition of Language*. New York: Academic Press.

Schank, R., and Abelson, R. 1975. Scripts, plans, and knowledge. Proceedings of the 4th International Joint Conference on Artificial Intelligence.

New Directions in Phonological Theory: Language Acquisition and Universals Research

Charles A. Ferguson

I. Some Questions and Answers

My function in this series of lectures, as I understand it, is to discuss new directions in phonology as I see them from the perspective of the phonological research going on at Stanford. I am happy to do so, but let me acknowledge first that I will not be able to reflect the full richness of the phonological research there under the auspices of Linguistics, Speech and Hearing Science, and other departments. To give just one example, I will not be referring directly to the exciting seminar conducted jointly by Will Leben and Orrin Robinson in the summer of 1975 on models of phonology proposed to remedy shortcomings in the model of Chomsky and Halle's *The Sound Pattern of English*. The points I will make are my own, and my colleagues cannot be held responsible for them, but they will inevitably reflect the perspectives of the three research projects in which I am involved: Language Universals, Phonology Archive, and Child Phonology, which are supported at present principally by the National Science Foundation.

In recent years linguists interested in phonological theory have been asking new kinds of questions, questions that earlier theorists either had not thought of or had considered outside the realm of a general theory of phonology. The linguists who ask these questions feel strongly that phonological theory should provide answers, and they either attempt to find answers in current versions of phonological theory—and hence in their view help to confirm or give support to a particular theory—or suggest new models or modifications in existing theories that *will* support the answers. Accordingly, the kinds of questions being asked give good clues to what are likely to be new directions in phonological theory.

In order to make this point clear I would like to offer three examples of recent questions. The first was asked by the British linguist N. V. Smith. He wants to know why, in the development of a child's phonological system, there are well-documented examples of "the loss of a contrast which has already been established" (Smith, 1973:4). In other words, he wants to know why the phonological development sometimes seems to go backward instead of proceeding in a step-by-step differentiation and growth in complexity. The example he has used most often comes from his own son's development between the ages of two years and two months and two years and ten months. It is the boy's pronunciation of the adult words *side* and *light*. At the beginning of the period he pronounces them alike, something like [dait]. Several months later he differentiates them into something like [dait] and [lait], respectively. Still later they merge again as [lait].

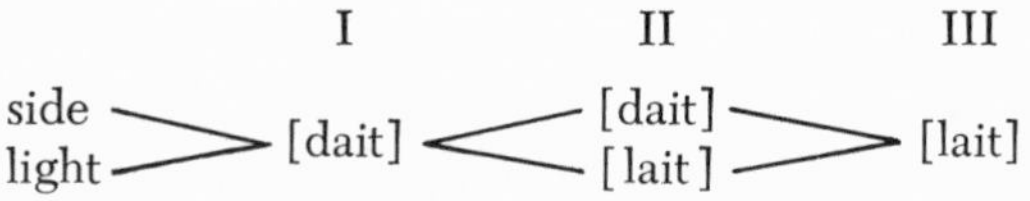

Roman numerals refer to successive time periods.

Fig. 1 (based on Smith).

This kind of question is new in that it focuses on the explanation of child language development as one of the functions of phonological theory. Smith says explicitly "The child's acquisition of phonology . . . is . . . of direct relevance for phonological theory" (1973:207), by which he means that the changes that take place in language acquisition offer evidence for the theoretical constructs set up to account for the adult language synchronically (1973:185). In fact, he even holds the view that the facts of "one nascent idiolect" are as relevant for phonological theory as "the facts of any other language, and to the extent that they have clear psychological validity, perhaps more relevant" (1973:185).

Turned around the other way, he is saying that phonological theory is valid only if it accounts for the facts of child language development. This kind of demand may not sound strange to us now because of the increasingly sophisticated investigations of child phonology in recent years, but just a few years ago such a demand would have been rejected almost out of hand by most linguists.

Be that as it may, what kind of answer does Smith find to his question about the phenomenon of 'recidivism', as he calls it? His model of child phonology includes (a) a set of unique lexical representations in feature matrices that are identical with the adults' surface phonetic system, and (b) an ordered set of 'realization rules' that are applied to classes of these representations to yield the child's output. Smith does not attempt to explain how this model is ultimately replaced by the adult model with its more abstract representations, but he seems quite certain that the feature system of the child's underlying representations does not change with development and that the set of realization rules at the age he studied is psychologically real or valid. Within this framework Smith finds his explanation for recidivism. The child, he claims, *has* all the distinctive features perceptually, but must gradually master them articulatorily, and the changes he makes in his realization rules reflect to a considerable extent his successive hypotheses on how to assign features in production.

In the case of his *side:light* example the child had distinct /s/ and /l/ in his lexical representations but his realization rules neutralized all alveolar consonants, including /t d s ʃ tʃ dʒ l r j/ to his |d|, with its voiced and voiceless positional variants. At this point the child pronounced both *side* and *light* as [dait]. He was producing the lateral [l] only in words in which all the consonants were liquids or semivowels, and these all appeared as [l], e.g., *lorry* → [lɔli], *yellow* → [lelo]. Next he began to pronounce the liquids and semivowels as lateral [l] also in the vicinity of coronal consonants, first varying freely with [d], then predominantly as [d]. At this point *side* and *light* were differentiated as [dait] and [lait]. Then the child, Smith thinks, hypothesized that the feature [continuant] rather than [fricative] was the crucial feature characteristic of /s/ and /ʃ/, and put into effect a realization rule that turned any /s/ or /ʃ/ in the vicinity of a coronal consonant into the lateral /l/, the only coronal continuant he could pronounce at that time, e.g., *see* → [li:], *shade* → [let], *side* → [lait]. At this point *side* was pronounced with [l] for the /s/, and *side* and *light* were once again homonyms, now as [lait], until at some still later time the boy could improve his realizations of /s/ and /ʃ/.

Smith's central point in this example seems indisputable. In improving his pronunciation of the sibilants, the child tried out a lateral production and stuck with it for a while even at the cost of some homophony involving laterals of other origins. Also, Smith's more general point in answering the question "Why recidivism?" seems well taken and instructive for phonological theory. He maintains that when a child seems to lose some articulatory ability in the course of his phonological development we should not assume that he has actually lost it but rather we should "invoke the psychological validity of the realization rules and the structural pressure of their longitudinal development" (1973:154). My reason for calling attention to the value of Smith's question and answer is not that I think his answer always works or that I think his model of phonology is correct. In fact, there are many cases of recidivism—or 'progressive phonological idioms', as they have been called by Moskowitz —that his explanation does not fit, including the example most often cited, Hildegard Leopold's *pretty* (Leopold, 1947; Moskowitz, 1973; Ferguson and Farwell, 1975), and the model as a whole is seriously inadequate in a number of respects. The question and answer are valuable for at least two reasons: the focus on discovering the nature and scope of phonological processes (such as those he is trying to represent in his realization rules) in human behavior, and the theoretical issues that his analysis has led him to reexamine.

Smith's concern for justifying and explaining his realization rules represents one of the new directions in phonology in that it focuses on behavioral evidence along with linguistic formalisms. In fact in his chapter 4, "The Nature of the Acquisition of Phonology," he spends twenty-two pages establishing the psychological validity of the realization rules and only six pages on support for them in terms of their formal linguistic properties.

Smith's discussion of the implications of child phonology for phonological theory touches a number of different points, and one is worth emphasizing as indicative of another new direction in phonology. Smith concludes that distinctive features, in spite of all their explanatory power, are not the only basic phonological units, but rather that syllables, phonemes, and other units also have psychological reality and make possible the statement of valid generalizations not capturable with distinctive features alone. The new direction is toward recognition of multiple units and greater complexity in phonological behavior as opposed to currently misapplied notions of simplicity and linguistic evaluation measures.

The second question representing an example of new directions is very different. The Soviet linguist T. V. Gamkrelidze recently asked "Why are /p/ and /g/ so weak in the stop systems of natural languages?" (Gamkrelidze, 1974, 1975). The phenomenon he is referring to is the tendency for /p/ and /g/ to be marginal or lacking in stop systems with voice contrast. The full set /p t k b d g/ is very widespread among the world's languages, but a number of languages have sets that are incomplete in one way or another, and the two commonest kinds of incomplete systems are /p t k b d –/ and /– t k b d g/. This kind of question is not new in a general sense, since one of the aims of phonological theory has always been to characterize the universal limits on sound systems of human languages and find explanations for the limits. The question does represent a new direction, however, in the sense that it is a very precise question, which requires reliable, comparable, accessible data from a large number of languages, preferably representing a systematic sampling of the world's languages.

Gamkrelidze's model of phonology is one in which phonemes of a relatively concrete, surface variety are basic units; distinctive features are also units with analytic autonomy; and markedness is a central concept. His model is very different from Smith's, perhaps most strikingly in its use of notions of relative frequency and relative markedness; he does not deal with child phonology. Phonemes are identified by presence or absence of particular features, although some features may be interpreted as redundant and hence not involved in the basic identification of phonemes. Markedness is not tied only to features but to clustering of features, and may vary in a scale along a particular feature dimension, such as place of articulation. See Fig. 2 for a typical Gamkrelidze diagram using arrows for markedness.

$$p \rightarrow t \rightarrow k$$
$$\downarrow \qquad \uparrow$$
$$b \leftarrow d \leftarrow g$$

Arrows point in the direction of more favored or less marked.

Fig. 2 (based on Gamkrelidze).

The relation between /ptk/ and /bdg/ in phonological analysis has usually been discussed in terms of correctly identifying the single feature that distinguishes them (e.g., voice, tenseness) or in describing the various articulatory, acoustic, and perceptual components or cues by which the feature is implemented (e.g., voice onset time, vowel duration, formant transitions). Linguists have shown very little interest in internal relations in the two series, and we are not prepared for a question about the differences between the *p–b* opposition and the *k–g* opposition and their linguistic relevance.

There can be no doubt that the phenomenon Gamkrelidze is asking about exists, and the demand that phonological theory provide an explanation seems reasonable. The data contained in many studies of child phonology development show an asymmetry between labials and velars in the acquisition of the voice distinction. In a number of ways, such as production errors and avoidance rules, children favor *b* over *p* but *k* over *g* (Ferguson, 1975b). Evidence for the disparity appears in the most unexpected places. The most likely explanation might be physiological—a consideration of relative ease of articulation—but a recent study by Saffran et al. (1975) found the same disparity in the perception skills of an adult male aphasic suffering from the syndrome 'pure word deafness' or 'auditory verbal agnosia'. The patient was given a variety of perception tasks to perform with both natural speech and synthetic speech stimuli. Although his spoken control of language was quite adequate, he had abnormal difficulties in identifying consonant differences in words and nonsense syllables. What is of interest to us in connection with Gamkrelidze's question is that he was overwhelmingly better in identifying *ka* and *ba* than any others of the series (*ga da ta pa*) and his errors were generally in the direction of identifying *pa* as *ba* and all the others (*ta da ga*) as *ka*. In some way that phonological theory at present does not explain, *b* and *k* are polar extremes in the phonological space of the series /p t k b d g/.

But let us return to Gamkrelidze's original question. His data on the tendency for /p/ and /g/ to be the gaps in phonological systems came from about thirty languages. Instead of looking for an explanation of the phenomenon, many linguists might doubt its reality, since the number of languages investigated was so small and the sample was quite possibly biased by the availability of grammars and informants, personal knowledge of the investigator, and consequent overrepresentation of particular language families or linguistic areas. Don Sherman of the Stanford Phonology Archive checked the phenomenon out on the 106 languages for which segment inventories were in our computer Archive at that time. Seventy-two had a voicing contrast in stops, of which sixty had the full /p t k b d g/ series. Of the twelve languages with incomplete series, seven lacked /g/ and four lacked /p/. Retrieval by phonetic segments as opposed to phonemically distinctive segments also agreed with the expectation: three languages lacked [g], one lacked [p], and all

languages in the sample had the remaining segments at least as allophones or marginal sounds. (Sherman, 1975, reports on this as well as
the data of a larger, noncomputerized archive, which gave comparable
results.)

Gamkrelidze's answer to his question is in terms of a scale of markedness. Certain feature combinations are more favored or optimal, i.e.,
'unmarked', than others. Thus in the series /p t k/ the velar end is the
least marked, the labial end the most marked; while in the voiced series
/b d g/, it is the labial end that is the least marked. Other things being
equal, a voiceless stop is less marked or more favored than a voiced stop,
but with the added scale of markedness that the combination of place of
articulation and the voicing dimension shows, this basic marking is
strengthened or weakened. Thus, /k/ is more favored over /g/ than
/t/ is over /d/, and /p/ is correspondingly less favored over /b/.
Gamkrelidze also applies this notion of relative markedness of feature
combinations to fricatives and other consonants, and he sees the deeper
explanation in terms of articulatory and perceptual constraints of human
physiology.

Gamkrelidze's answer may not be fully satisfying because it is not
worked out in enough detail and needs evidence of other kinds to
support it, but it is of interest in showing that the concept of markedness
can be further explored with promising results. Smith, on the other
hand, in his study of child phonology, was disappointed in his attempt
to make use of markedness, concluding "it would seem . . . impossible to
effect any interesting correlation between acquisitional phenomena and
marking conventions" (1973:201). Markedness is, of course, not a single
unified concept but a family of concepts intended to explain quite
different phenomena of favoring one alternative over another under various conditions in phonology and in grammar in general. It would be
interesting to have Smith check the /p g/ weakness phenomenon in his
own child phonology data. From the data as given in this book there is no
evidence for it at all, but the data were, of course, selected and analyzed
with other aims in mind.

Even more interesting than the novel view of markedness is an aspect
not realized by Gamkrelidze at the time he asked his question, namely,
the way his /p g/ phenomenon shows up in child phonology and speech
pathology. It is this kind of interconnectedness among phonological
phenomena that gives us hope that some day we may have a comprehensive general theory of phonology. One of the new directions in phonological theory construction is certainly the incorporation of data from

sources other than detailed phonological analyses of normal adult languages, and we should welcome it in spite of the additional knowledge and skills it requires of the phonologist.

The third question I want to cite is quite different from the other two in its focus on diachronic change. In 1971 the American linguist Alan Bell asked an old question in a new form when he wanted to know "Why are languages which lack CV syllables so rare?" Jakobson and Greenberg had both discussed the universality of CV syllable structure, and Greenberg had ventured a further related 'universal' that if a language has clusters of n consonants in a particular syllable type then it also has clusters of $n-1$ consonants in that position, except that $CV \rightarrow V$ does not hold (for citations of Jakobson and Greenberg, see Bell, 1971). The phonological theorist would be likely to ask the question "Why is CV a universal syllable type?" but Bell views the existence of particular types of syllable structure not as all-or-none, fully determined language states but rather as more or less likely outcomes of a variety of processes of language change. Accordingly he wanted the question really to be "Why are languages without CV syllables so rare that none are known?"

Bell's model of phonology is essentially that of generative phonology with two differences. First, he works only with the systematic phonetic level at which he assumes each segment is specified for the feature 'syllabic' and for its syllable adherence, i.e., what 'nucleus' it belongs to (Bell, 1971:114). Second, he adds the notions of language state and diachronic process in a Markov chain model in which it is possible to assign probabilities to the various processes that lead to a change of state. See Fig. 3 for an example of one of Bell's diagrams.

Finding the answer to the question was time-consuming and full of frustrations, but the final result was a much better understanding of processes of change in syllable structure and possible synchronic states as well as the development of a model that could be applied to other phonological questions. Bell used data from 144 languages plus another 25 for illustrating particular phenomena. He devised a new typology of syllable types that was more delicate and more revealing than existing ones: a parametric typology in terms of maximum and minimum numbers of segments in initial, medial, and final clusters. He proceeded to identify three main categories of processes that lead to change in syllable structure: cluster formation processes, cluster simplification processes, and word combination processes. Within each category he assigned relative probabilities to the processes included. This was done by estimating, calculating against the actual language data, and then correcting. Finally the relative weighting of the three main categories

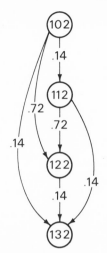

Fig. 3 (based on Bell). The numbers 102, 112, 122, 132
represent particular syllable types, and the figures
.14 and .72 roughly represent the probability
that one type will change to another.

of processes was expressed by constants that likewise were estimated and
adjusted against the language data.

The answer that emerged from Bell's computations was that the CV
syllable is not universal or near-universal by its inherent nature, but
because of the high probability of various processes that lead to it, or,
more exactly, by the high probability of the processes that lead away
from certain other heavily disfavored syllable structures. CV syllables
as such may disappear by vowel loss (and are more likely to do so than
CVC syllables, for example), the positions of occurrence of CV syllables
in a given language may be highly constrained, and even when there are
not distributional constraints the frequency of occurrence of CV syllables may be low. The explanation in terms of the summation of probabilities of alternative processes of change seems much more convincing.

This third question and answer certainly represent some new directions
in phonological theory. In particular I would call attention to the principled relationship between diachrony and synchrony and the use of
probabilistic models. In recent years we have seen renewed and increased interest in the theoretical foundations of sound change, and it
is becoming apparent how useful it is to regard every phonological state
as the outcome of processes of change or indeed as the manifestation of
changes in progress. Greenberg's state-and-process model, which was the

basis for both Bell's paper and Larry Hyman's very different recent paper on nasals (Hyman, 1975), provides an excellent starting point for a new direction in phonological theory. The use of probabilistic models as opposed to the traditional categorical models of phonology is also slowly invading the field. Several decades ago Martin Joos explained to us that linguistic structure and even linguistic change have no place for probabilities and frequency; what really matters is all-or-none (Joos, 1950). A generation of structuralists followed by a generation of generativists have by and large agreed with this position. Now, however, we have Labov and his colleagues demonstrating the linguistic relevance of variable rules, and Bell's question and answer suggesting the use of a Markov model for certain aspects of language change. It certainly looks as though at least some parts of phonology are following the path of many scientific disciplines toward quantification and calculation of probabilities for predicted outcomes.

In this lecture I have used three questions, one asked by a British, one by a Soviet, and one by an American linguist, in order to point to new directions in phonological theory, and although the topics were very different the three questions all point toward similar new directions: First, the broadening of the concerns of phonology to include in a central place such formerly marginal fields as child language development and speech pathology. Second, the abandoning of our high evaluation of certain narrow forms of simplicity in favor of much more complexly ordered models, which will in part require reliable data from large numbers of languages and the use of probabilistic models. Third, the focusing on behavioral processes in both synchronic and diachronic phonology as opposed to inventories of elements or the formal characteristics of rule systems. Finally, the cheerful adoption of a pluralistic phonology, i.e., willingness to make use of apparently conflicting or overlapping models, in the hope that the transitional probabilities of our science favor the reaching of a more stable state of phonological theory some time in the future.

II. Lessons from Fricatives

In the discussion period after yesterday's lecture, Sandy Schane asked a question, which was in effect "Why worry about child phonology?" Let us start with his question today. Schane acknowledged that the study of child phonology was of some intrinsic interest, but he was really asking "What does that have to do with the goals of phonological theory as many of us understand them?" or "What does that have to do with writing phonological components in the grammars of languages?" That made me realize that probably many of you had not experienced the impact of the book that Jakobson wrote back in 1941. I would like to start today by trying to relive for you the effect it had on some of us at that time. Although the book was largely wrong in detail, its impact was important and the kind of inspiration it gave can be just as great today, even though our goals in phonological theorizing may be somewhat different.

In 1941 Roman Jakobson wrote the little monograph entitled *Kindersprache Aphasie und allgemeine Lautgesetze* and published it in Sweden, in an out-of-the-way series, and in German (Jakobson, 1941/1968). Not many American linguists read it, and those who did read it had varying reactions to it. Some said it was nonsense. I can remember several distinguished American linguists saying that there are no such things as *allgemeine Lautgesetze* ('general sound laws'). Another reaction was that it was simply the truth: many people accepted what Jakobson said in that book as fact about how language is acquired as though it had been based on a solid body of data. Needless to say some of us did not sympathize very much with either of those two reactions to *Kindersprache*, but felt "This is great, this is fascinating, let us begin studying the phonological principles he is talking about and see to what extent they are true. Perhaps we will be led in new and important directions." And that is what we have been doing at Stanford, first with Ruth Weir's work (Weir, 1962) and then after my arrival in 1967, in the Child Phonology Project.

Now what were the claims Jakobson made in his little book? One of the first was that babbling is more or less random, or unstructured from a phonological point of view, that babies are likely to make any sounds at all when they babble, including those that occur in all sorts of languages, not just the sounds of the language they were exposed to, and that this is very different from the onset of true speech. In fact, he pointed out that sometimes there is even a period of silence, when the child stops babbling for a while before he starts true speech. In short, he made strong statements to the effect that in babbling almost any sound may be uttered, whereas true speech, when it comes, is very structured.

This leads to a second claim Jakobson seemed to make, that from the very first real utterances of the child the phonology is structured in exactly the same sense that adult phonology is structured. Not that the facts of the child's phonology will be the same in detail as the facts of the adult language, but that the nature of the structure is the same. Even if the child has only two words as a total active lexicon, those two words will have a phonological structure that in essence is the same as adult language. He meant by that, of course, that there will be distinctiveness —or 'contrast', as American phonologists often call it—i.e., there will be phonological oppositions used to distinguish lexical items. Also, there will be variations conditioned by position, or 'environment', i.e., there will be allophonic variation in both child and adult phonology. There will be limitations on distribution; phonotactic constraints such as neutralization, typical word shapes, and the like in both; and finally there will be subsystems and marginal phenomena in both. Here it is of interest that Jakobson points out that in child phonology marginal phenomena have an extra role in that the marginal material is sometimes the source of core material; that is, may move from the margin into the main body of the phonological organization.

At the time Jakobson wrote, the dominant position in the study of child phonology was that the child's mistakes in the acquisition of phonology were random, that there was no structure. Jakobson took the extreme opposite view, that true speech on the part of the child is organized in exactly the same sense that adult phonology is organized, and also—a further claim—far from being random or unpredictable, the 'mistakes' that the child makes approaching the adult phonology are systematic, lawful, rule-governed—whatever terminology you like to use. Patterns can be found and established for individual children, for whole languages, and even for all languages.

And that brings us to another important claim that is very explicit on Jakobson's part. Jakobson said that if you have the correct analytical framework of distinctive features and oppositions you will find that there is a universal order of acquisition. Children acquiring a language, no matter what the language is, no matter where it is or when it is, will follow the same general order of the acquisition of features and oppositions in relationship to the phonological organization of the adult language. That is an astonishing claim. Of course, when you look even at any two children acquiring English you find it does not seem to work very well, but put in Jakobson's terms, it was a claim that made sense, and it is this particular claim of Jakobson's claims that has perhaps been most widely either denounced or accepted as correct.

The universal order of acquisition was tied to another of Jakobson's claims. He said that the time when a particular sound or opposition is acquired by the child will be related to the distribution of that sound or opposition among the languages of the world. Let me use some examples of his to make his point clear. Since a sound like *t*, an apical stop of the *t d* sort, is practically universal in human language—almost every language has an apical stop—then that should be one of the first sounds acquired in the universal order of acquisition, no matter what the language. Or the opposite extreme, if a sound like the fricative Czech *ř* is very rare in the world's languages—there are very few languages that have a segment of that kind in their inventory—Jakobson would claim this is one of the latest sounds to be acquired by a child learning a language. If a child is learning Czech, the *ř* should be among the latest acquired of the sounds.

He made still another claim related to the universal order of acquisition. Sounds are not only always acquired in a given order but also are lost in the reverse of that order; in other words, the last one acquired is the first one lost, in the case of aphasia or other circumstances in which phonology is disappearing. So we can make an exact mirror kind of statement to our earlier examples: we can say the Czech *ř* will be among the first sounds lost with a Czech aphasic and a *t* or *d* would be among the last. Jakobson claims that there is one set of underlying principles that account for the universal order of acquisition, the universal order of dissolution, the relation between these and the distribution of sounds in the languages of the world, and so on. There is a set of underlying principles to which he gave the quaint name "Laws of Irreversible Solidarity."

Now I would like to talk about the kind of research we do at Stanford in relation to Jakobson's theories. Maybe at this point we can say what he said that was wrong and what was right, and give you some sort of feeling for the kind of research we might want to do under his inspiration. First, what was wrong? Babbling is not random, and it tends to improve in intonation; it develops toward clearer syllabic sequences in later stages, and among children who continue to babble along with true speech, there are cases where a certain sound appears more frequently in babbling just before it appears in true speech (cf. Kaplan and Kaplan, 1971). That was just one instance where Jakobson was wrong. In fact, since we are going to talk about fricatives today, let us note that although Jakobson said children babble almost any sound, they rarely babble voiceless fricatives, particularly those formed in the forward part of the mouth, *f s ʃ* and so forth (Cruttenden, 1970; Ferguson, 1975a). There is almost none of that in babbling. I suspect that if Jakobson realized how wrong he was on babbling, he would now extend his notion of structuredness to earlier years and claim that babbling is also structured and regular and systematic, although not quite in the same sense as 'true speech'.

Or perhaps he would say it has incipient structure or is preparing the way for full structure.

He was wrong about aphasia also, by and large. I know very few students of aphasia today who would accept his formulations as far as phonology is concerned. Aphasia is too complex a thing. Some of you here are taking courses in aphasia and would know this better than I. Aphasics can have many strange things go wrong in phonology or syntax, but they rarely seem to follow the nice orderly pattern that Jakobson would like.

How about cases in which Jakobson simply did not talk about things that were important, where you might say he was inadequate? He never talks about which positions certain sounds come in, beginning or end of a word, between vowels, and so forth. That turns out to be important, since there are different patterns of acquisition in different positions, sometimes quite unlike what Jakobson suggests, so that some of the rules are broken, so to speak (cf. Ferguson, 1975a; Macken, 1975). He does not even talk about such an obvious thing as clusters. Individual segments are not acquired the same way in clusters as they are as single segments. Jakobson also says almost nothing about perception vs. production. The examples he gives are almost all in terms of production: the child learns to make certain sounds or to make use of a certain opposition at a particular point in his development. Jakobson does not talk about whether the child has already mastered the sounds or oppositions in perception, or whether perception and production are learned the same way, or what the relation between the two might be at all. In fact, Jakobson pays almost no attention to what is meant by the notion of acquired: when a given sound, a given opposition, or a given feature is acquired, does that mean the child pronounces it in all the words where he should pronounce it, and does so with a pronunciation that is acceptable in the adult community, or just that he sometimes gets it right in some words or even makes a phonological opposition in his own speech, not commensurate with the adult phonetics? When Jakobson says stops are acquired before fricatives, does he mean all stops before any fricatives, or at least some stops before the first fricative? The lack of precision on this point is quite disappointing, because when it comes to trying to check Jakobson's predictions, which seem so remarkably clear and explicit, you find you really cannot. Almost always the actual data are too complicated to check out his predictions.

So then what *is* right about Jakobson's claims? Why am I still so inspired? Why do I still think Jakobson is so great that I want to go on doing research on child phonology inspired by him? Well, for one thing there *is* a surprising amount of order. In spite of the fact that individual children do differ in order of acquisition, in spite of the complexities I just alluded to, it is astonishing that overall there tends to be a kind of universal order of acquisition, and to a considerable extent it seems to reflect what Jakobson said. That is a fantastic achievement. I do not know of any other sphere of human sociocultural behavior where you can make that kind of nice precise prediction and find it confirmed; even though to some extent it is wrong and does not take care of many of the facts, it is successful enough to be inspiring.

Secondly, he is right in that there is a relationship between the order of acquisition and notions of markedness or frequency of occurrence in the languages of the world. What is predicted about *t d* and Czech *ř* is found to be true. When you study the acquisition of Czech by Czech children, the *ř* sound is among the last to be acquired. On the other hand, a *t-* or *d*-like sound is among the first to be acquired by any child.

This viewpoint of Jakobson's is so clear and insightful that it is possible to interpret apparently quite different new phonological theories and bring them into line with what Jakobson was saying. For instance, if you want to throw out phonemes and oppositions as the things learned, and say it is only features that are learned, as some theories of phonology might suggest, you can still reread Jakobson, and it will make sense that the distribution of the languages of the world and phenomena such as pathology are all related by some common principles. Or if you take a position like Stampe's, it can be done. His view of phonology is radically different from Jakobson's: he does not basically predict a universal order of acquisition—although recently he is moving a little closer to that. He talks about the child's being born with a finite number of unordered natural processes, and as the child grows up he must progressively suppress them or limit their operation or order and reorder them until he eventually achieves the adult phonology, but Stampe is still basically following Jakobson's line that there are underlying principles—natural processes, if you will—that account for the interrelationships of acquisition and other kinds of phonological behavior (Stampe, 1969).

I think it must be clear to you what I mean by what I call the Jakobson vision. His vision was that somehow at the bottom of all kinds of phonological phenomena, no matter where we look, whether it is speech pathology or language change through time or the way children acquire language, at the bottom of all phonological phenomena there are some general principles that hold; it is the job of the phonologist to discover them, and you can get at them no matter where you start. You can study speech pathology or language acquisition, or write descriptive grammars, or study the phonological history of families of languages, or whatever, and somehow you will be getting at the same basic, underlying principles. That is what Jakobson was saying, that is the vision that captured my imagination, and even if Jakobson was wrong in many details, and even if phonological theory itself keeps changing, I think that his vision is still as compelling now as it was in 1941.

Now what do we do in the way of research on child phonology at Stanford? Other places do important work but Stanford's is what I want to talk about. We do lots of kinds of things. Let me hasten to explain that we do not spend all our time studying children's fricatives, although that is what I am talking about today. One feature of our approach is not just to do our own isolated little experiments and then try to generalize on the basis of those experiments. We prefer to make use of work from very different lines of research. For example, we go through in detail the diary studies done by others in the past, as psychologist or linguist parents of particular children followed their phonological development through time, and we do some longitudinal studies ourselves. We look at large-scale studies where investigators have checked thousands of schoolchildren to see what sounds they are pronouncing satisfactorily in English, and we have done some cross-sectional studies. We want to try to incorporate findings from that kind of research in our thinking. There are also some carefully worked out psycholinguistic experiments where the research design is intended to be foolproof, where you have control groups and all that machinery, and you have randomized everything. We want to find out what those studies have to tell us, and we do a few of them ourselves.

If you are going to investigate fricatives, we first need longitudinal data. We have followed seven English-learning children through a period of about a year, beginning at an age when they had at least one fricative, on that fairly lengthy process of fricative acquisition. We now have tape recordings and transcriptions of these seven children through that period of time, and we are writing up that body of data from a number of points of view. We also carry out some psycholinguistic experiments of our own kind: we have about 28 children, whom we put through various kinds of perception and production experiments on particular hypotheses. In some instances the number of subjects or the number of trials is too small for fully convincing statistical results, but we still find these experiments one of the most fruitful sources of information about how children acquire phonology. Suppose, for example, we think, because Jakobson or some current phonological theory suggests it, that such and such must occur in such and such a way. We devise a test to see if in fact that is what happens, and so we have that kind of specialized information about particular aspects of fricative acquisition from 28 kids—unfortunately not including the seven we followed in our longitudinal studies. Finally, I tend to be suspicious, no matter what kind of general linguistics research is involved, if we look at only one language. I have always been suspicious of efforts of finding universals by looking deeply at one language. I do not deny that it can be done, but I myself am nervous about that kind of approach and so we always like to have at least two languages, preferably a much larger number. So, in addition to studying English-speaking children and their acquiring of fricatives and other sounds, we also study Spanish-speaking children and hope to add some Cantonese-learning children before long. There are enough Spanish-speaking children in the neighborhood of Palo Alto so that we can have a number of children to follow longitudinally. By this time I think the attrition rate has gotten the number down to only four children from whom we have data for a number of months, fewer children than we would like to have, but nevertheless a good bit of data and again with specific psycholinguistic testing of particular hypotheses.[1]

I think that is enough to give you a feeling for the kind of data that we look for and how we go about obtaining it. I might add that we ourselves do not do any testing of pathological cases or deviant phonologies, but it so happens that Dave Ingram, Mary Louise Edwards, and others who have been associated with our project have in fact done some of the same things with children whose phonologies are deviant, and they relate those findings to what we are doing, so that there is a connecting link between our own Stanford-sponsored work and work with speech pathology.

Now why fricatives? One reason is that they are late in acquisition; as I said a few minutes ago Jakobson said that children will in general acquire stops before fricatives. (Have you ever tried working with a child a year and a half old, trying to get him to do psycholinguistic tests of one sort or another? You can realize why we long for the mature two-and-a-half-year-old so we can work with fewer handicaps.) Also, fricatives present a number of special problems. They do not seem to be acquired quite so neatly and directly as stops are, and so in that sense the

---

1. At the time this paper was given, only four children were participating in the study; later one child returned and another was added. By the completion of the study, complete data had been gathered from six children over a nine-month period.

study of them should be more revealing. Finally, Jakobson made a number of predictions about them and we can check them out, or at least use them as a starting point. I assume that you all know what the fricatives in English are, but let me set down the symbols f v θ ð s z ʃ ʒ. Unfortunately when we started the study we did not include the affricates tʃ and dʒ along with the fricatives, so for some tests we have data on the affricates, and for others we do not.

Now what are the predictions that Jakobson made? First, as we have said several times, he predicted that stops would be acquired before fricatives. He also predicted that this would be true in each place of articulation, i.e., if there is both a stop and a fricative in a given place of articulation in any language the child would acquire the stop first. Also, he implicitly makes the claim that voiceless fricatives would be acquired in principle before voiced ones, because voiceless fricatives are somehow less marked or more favored among the world's languages. A claim that he made quite explicitly was that s would be the first fricative to be acquired. He gave a number of reasons why that would be so, and you can imagine what those reasons would be in terms of distribution in the world's languages, and so on. There are some complicating factors, since he would acknowledge that a labial stop would often be acquired before an apical stop, but he maintained that the s would be acquired first among the fricatives.

You remember that Jakobson also insisted on the systematic nature of the relationship between adult phonology and child phonology. Accordingly, he made predictions about the kinds of substitutions children will make for adult sounds. In the case of fricatives he predicted that the commonest substitutions would be stops, as would be expected from the order of acquisition. Finally, since Jakobson viewed acquisition in terms of adding oppositions, he claimed that as a particular opposition—or the distinctive feature that implements it—is acquired, the feature will tend to spread rapidly throughout the system. In other words, when [± continuant] or [± voice] is acquired it will tend to spread across the board to phonemes already acquired, insofar as the new opposition is relevant.

Those were some of his predictions. Now, what are the facts when you look at our acquisition? In part, Jakobson is right. It is true in general that stops are acquired before fricatives, and it is true in general that voiceless fricatives are acquired before voiced, but it is not true that s is always acquired first. More children learning English acquire f first. Some children do acquire s first, and that brings up a point that I will come back to, that there is more individual variation than linguists would like to consider.

Let us look at the order in which fricatives are acquired. In general *f* *s* *ʃ* are acquired first, then *v* *z*, and finally θ ð ӡ. This is a rather strange order in some respects, and raises a number of interesting questions. Let us just note that it agrees only in part with Jakobson's predictions.

Next, what are the most common substitutions for the fricatives? You remember Jakobson would predict stops. The most common substitutions are these:

Adult sound	Child's substitution
f	*s*
v	*b*
θ	*f, s*
ð	*v, d*
s	— (distortions)
z	*s*
ʃ	*s, t*
ӡ	*d*

These are not the only substitutions by any means; many others occur, but these are the commonest ones. A lot of questions are raised for the Jakobsonian viewpoint: For example, why do we have a *b* as substitute for a *v* but *s* as substitute for *f*? While this pattern holds for English-learning children it is not true for our Spanish-learning children. The Spanish-learning children have a great tendency to produce *p* as a substitute for *f*, which is relatively rare with children learning English. And for those of you who do not see any connection between child phonology development and phonological theory in general I would call your attention to this question: Why is it that when speakers of some languages try to pronounce an *f* in a foreign language that they do not have in their own language, they produce a *p* as a substitute for the *f*, while speakers of other languages do not do so? For example, speakers of Philippine languages typically substitute *p* for *f* in English. In the same way here, both Spanish and English have a *p* and an *f*, and yet English-learning children by and large do not substitute a *p* for an *f*, while Spanish-learning children, at least in our experience, very often do so. It seems to me that there is some kind of fundamental phonological question here; I would assume the most likely explanation is that there is something about the phonological systems of Spanish and English that is a determining factor in having one pattern in Spanish acquisition and another in English.

We could talk about these substitution rules at some length. It turns out there is a series of possible substitution patterns: avoidance, deletion, stop, continuant, correct fricative. Let me talk about the first one. Children avoid pronouncing certain sounds that for one reason or another they think they cannot pronounce properly. They are perfectly happy to imitate wrongly or make substitutions for some sounds, and other sounds they just will not choose to speak. We found this out in connection with children pronouncing word-initial stops. A given child would fluctuate in pronunciation between p and b, but saying predominantly p, and had no productive contrast between p and b. Yet, if you looked at the words that particular child was using, almost all the ones he had in the $p–b$ category were words that began with b in the adult language, and he was avoiding words that begin with p in the adult language. At some level he was saying, "There's a difference between these two things and I am going to choose this one." So, in a primitive way the child begins to acquire voicing opposition. If we had time, I would like to talk a little more about what I call avoidance rules, or saliency rules, because I think these are a part of adult phonology as well. If I asked all of you to write down particular sounds that you avoid, either in English or in some other language you have learned, you would probably be able to mention a few, particularly certain clusters or certain combinations with stress. Also, there are particular words you avoid, not only particular sounds, but particular lexical items. This avoidance is a part of all phonological systems in my view. It is a phenomenon particularly evident with fricatives: many children in the early stage of their acquisition of fricatives characteristically either avoid producing all words with fricatives or avoid one class, for example, all f's.

Then some fricatives are deleted. Instead of having a substitute, the word is said with no sound in the place where the fricative should be. This is done more often with voiced fricatives than with voiceless ones, and there are other kinds of limitations to it; nevertheless, it is a very common phenomenon.

Then we have the stop and continuant substitutions. 'Continuant' is a loose term here by which I mean to indicate less closure and less friction noise than a fricative, for example, a w for an f. The Smith child referred to yesterday used a w substitution for an f in the early part of his acquisition of fricatives.

Now the order I wrote is not an arbitrary order; Ingram (1975) claims that as any child goes through the process of acquiring fricatives he follows this order of substitution patterns, although no one child ever goes through the whole sweep of possibilities. Thus, in acquiring a fricative a child always avoids before he deletes, deletes before he has a stop, and has a stop before a continuant. For example, a given child first avoids words with *f*, then may substitute *w* and finally go to *f*, or he may first delete *s*, then have a *d*, and finally go to an *s*. Our data do not bear this out completely, but to a surprising extent. This is of particular interest in speech pathology, since in deviant phonologies some of these early patterns may persist very late.

I said earlier that Jakobson did not talk about position or 'environment'. In the case of fricatives this is important because it turns out that fricatives are more easily acquired between vowels or after vowels than stops are, so that in word-final position a child may acquire fricatives before he acquires stops. This tells us something about the nature of fricatives (Ferguson, 1975a).

Also, Jakobson did not discuss clusters, but the patterns of acquisition of fricative clusters are likewise instructive. Let me take one example, clusters with *s*. Three common kinds of initial *s*-clusters occur in English: *s* plus stop (*sp- st- sk-*), *s* plus nasal (*sm- sn-*), and *s* plus 'glide' (*sl- sw-*). The first question is whether the child treats each cluster as a sequence of two segments—as the phonologists assume the adult does—or as a singleton of special characteristics. The best evidence for the singleton hypothesis comes from children's pronunciation of *sw-*. It is amazing how often the *sw-* cluster is handled as a single unit by children acquiring the language, and is represented by an *f*. The frication of the *s* and the labiality of the *w* combine in the *f*, however you want to phrase that in your brand of phonology. I think we have a lot to learn about the acquisition of clusters. If I understand Sarah Hawkins's research correctly, even schoolchildren as old as twelve years of age who seem to have the whole cluster system of English do not have the same temporal relationships between parts of the clusters that adults do (Hawkins, 1973). Apparently in the long and gradual acquisition of the temporal characteristic of clusters, they seem to follow quite a different path from combinations of single segments.

Let us take *sp-* and *sn-* clusters as examples of two major types. With *sp-* clusters, the commonest pattern is the deletion of the *s* and pronunciation of simple *p*, and as the *p* gradually acquires an *s*, the *p* is typically lengthened and often less aspirated than the *p* found elsewhere, so that there is an opposition between *p-* and the reflex of *sp-*, but not in terms of successive segments for /sp/. It is as though the child is doing the best he can to pick out this and that characteristic of the *sp-* cluster until he finally gets everything into it. With initial *sn-* what characteristically happens is that the child first says just *n*, then *n* with a voiceless onset, that is, the child gets the voicelessness of the *s*, and then puts it into the *n* first before succeeding with the full *s* onset. These developmental sequences, like Jakobson examples, help us to predict; they show the incredible degree of pattern in the acquisition of phonology and suggest facts of underlying structure in adult phonology.

I would like to make a point about individual patterns of acquisition, individual strategies or paths toward acquisition. I said that most children acquire *f* first, before *s*, but not all children do. A very good example of another way of acquiring fricatives is Hildegard Leopold's, where her first fricative was ʃ, and it came up in a funny way. Her family played a kind of game with a toy train: as they pulled the train along, I think the parents said "choo-choo" or "sh-sh" to imitate the sound of the steam. In any case, she began referring to the train game as ʃ and then extended the meaning to movements of similar kinds, to many things that had nothing to do with trains. Similarly they said "sh!" to her, meaning 'be quiet', just before she went to sleep, so that her ʃ came to mean 'Go to sleep' and probably was related also to English *sleep* and German *schlafen* in that bilingual family's use. In any case, she had a pair of ʃ homonyms. These items are so marginal that people might argue that they have nothing to do with real fricative acquisition, which blossoms much later, but that is not true. The ʃ stayed along as her first continuant, and in final position after a vowel it comes to be the representative of any final fricative and some nonfricatives; for example, adult final *f*, *s*, and ʃ are represented by her final ʃ. It is the only fricative she had in her system for a long time, and the final ʃ is in complementary distribution with her initial [j] which represents another set of sounds altogether, these two functioning in some sense as two parts of the same unit (Ferguson, 1968). It is this kind of phenomenon, incidentally, that makes me unhappy with Smith's notion that the child has no phonological system of his own, but only a system of realization rules to get from the adult input to the child's output. In many senses, the child does have his own phonological organization.

Now let us talk about the perception and production of fricatives. It is generally assumed that children learn how to perceive an opposition before they know how to produce it afterward. That sounds like a very reasonable assumption, that before a child learns how to make an opposition he learns how to recognize it and identify it. Now, of course, some of you who take a position along the lines of the so-called motor theory will question that assumption, saying that in order to perceive a sound difference you have to be able to make the relevant articulatory movements yourself. But in general most linguists probably make the assumption of perception before production. First, I would like to make the point that infants apparently can discriminate some speech-sound differences. The article most people refer to that began a whole sweep of neonate experimentation, Eimas and associates (1971), showed that children as young as one month of age (when you cannot ask for their intuitions, you have to measure their nonnutritive sucking responses and the like) could apparently react differently to *ba* and *pa*. Even if there are some problems with that particular experiment and its claims, I think the literature in general suggests that at a very early age children are able to make certain very precise discriminations among special sounds. The research literature suggests not only a different kind of processing for speech and nonspeech material but even the possibility of some very specific built-in feature detectors, of the kind we have been so surprised in the past few years to find in visual perception. The point I want to make here is that this one aspect of perception comes very early in the development of child phonology, but it is not the same as what Shvachkin has called 'phonemic perception', that is, the ability not only to discriminate between two different sounds but also to sort lexical items on the basis of containing them, store the lexical items appropriately, and use the sounds consistently for recognition of the lexical items. This kind of linguistic perception can be tested before the child is able to produce the sounds at all, as well as at any later period in the development. Testing of this kind is relevant for evaluating Smith's claim that at a very early age the child has the perceptual system complete and that phonological development is essentially perfecting production. At Stanford we have used the Shvachkin technique of testing perception, in the linguistic sense of perception, in the early stages of language acquisition. Let me summarize our work in one or two sentences for our purposes here.

It is generally agreed that children at a relatively early age, although not necessarily prespeech, are able to differentiate among *l*, *r*, *w*, and *y*, but are not able to reproduce those oppositions consistently until much later. The situation is much more complicated than that—there are all sorts of individual variations—but let me just say that it is pretty clear that liquids are perceived as different relatively early, but produced correctly relatively late. If all sounds went like that we could be much more sympathetic with Smith's position. However, fricatives do not work that way. We did some Shvachkin tests of fricatives with our children. These tests are a real nuisance. (You make little toys and name them *mak, bak,* or the like, and you get the child convinced that one thing is really called a *mak* and another a *bak*, and then get him to give you evidence that he correctly identifies and remembers the two names. Unfortunately sometimes children do not pay attention, or deliberately do what you do not want, because that is what they think you're after, or adopt some irrelevant strategy such as always choosing the first one mentioned.) Nevertheless, we are quite convinced that the linguistic perception of fricatives is not early, as is the perception of liquids. In some of our tests it comes at about the same time, sometimes even the production for a given child is a little ahead of the full mastery of perception for a particular opposition. Now presumably this means that the relationship is complex and difficult to tap, but it certainly goes against the notion that perception always precedes production by some great interval in the system. Fricatives are a very good place to test that, because fricatives happen to be a place where perception and production are developed relatively late, and so we have this clear demonstration that it is not true that the perceptual always precedes the productional by great intervals.

I would like to make a final observation: much child phonology research is relevant, among other things, to speech pathology. One little example is that individual differences in early phonological development are so great that we may be able to use some of them as diagnostic devices to predict whether a given child is going to have something wrong with his later phonological development. I will mention two illustrations: If an English-learning child (as opposed to a Spanish-learning or Tagalog-learning child) substitutes *p* for *f* the chances are that he or she is going to be a slow phonology learner. If an English-learning child has a lot of reduplication in the earliest stages as opposed to a moderate amount, then again the indications are he is likely to be a slow phonology learner. In this respect our findings may not have anything to do with phonological theory in the narrow sense but with the usefulness of linguistics to society: a careful phonological description of a child's language behavior at an early time may turn out to be very useful in predicting pathologies or individual lines of phonological development.

III. Universal Nasal Processes

Today I would like to talk, not along the Child Phonology line of research at Stanford, but along the line of Language Universals research and our Phonology Archive. First, I should explain that this lecture will be dedicated to two members of the faculty here this summer, professors Robins and Schane, because the former wrote a paper some years ago on nasalization in Sundanese, which has been reprinted and commented on in many ways (Robins, 1957), and the latter has written at considerable length on the status of nasalized vowels in French and more general theoretical problems related to that (e.g., Schane, 1968).

I will talk about three universal nasal processes. Before we get to the first one, let me say a word about nasal consonants in general. *Languages have nasal consonants.* That is the kind of statement one would like to make in universal, all-or-none terms. It would be very satisfying to say that *all* languages have nasal consonants, but if I try to get away with a statement like that there will be a specialist in American Indian languages who will speak up and point out that there are a half dozen languages in the Northwest Coast area, of several unrelated families, that in fact lack nasals. It is no help to learn that some of them are known to have had nasals not so long ago and the nasals changed into voiced stops: the fact is that some languages in the world just do not have nasals. Nevertheless, the statement is a good way to start to talk about nasal universals, somewhat in the same philosophy as some of the comments made in connection with Alan Bell's question in the first lecture. It is still a universal-type statement if you can say 'in almost all situations', as long as it then becomes part of some more general framework in which you can specify the conditions under which it will not happen or some several dimensions along which you can predict varying probabilities. In any case, languages in general do have nasal consonants, and I would like to make a few observations about them. The number of nasal consonants is typically no greater than the number of positions in the basic obstruent series in the language, that is if you have labial, alveolar, palatal, and velar obstruents there will be no more than four different kinds of nasals as far as place of articulation is concerned in the language. Once again there are a handful of exceptions, although actually not one that clearly breaks that rule without a questionable line of analysis (Ferguson, 1966).

Another observation may be along the lines of which nasal is preferred to another, that is, which is more favored or less 'marked'. If we were going to use the Gamkrelidze arrows to show which is preferred we could write

$$n \rightarrow m \rightarrow \eta.$$

n is the most favored, or at least marked, and then m a very close second to that, but still second for a number of reasons, and the η a very poor third, and after that the list really tapers off very rapidly so that palatals, retroflex, and other kinds of nasal consonants are much less preferred. We could say many more interesting things about nasal consonants, but that is enough at this point (Ferguson, 1975c).

Now we will get to the first of the nasal processes; I call it Nasal Spread. What I would like to assert is that in every language there is some evidence for the fact that the nasality of nasal consonants spreads to the surrounding vowels. This is a universal process in the sense that there is always a *tendency* for nasality to spread in this way although the extent and the details vary from language to language. Those of you who care about experimental phonetics and the physiology of speech production will be able to hazard some reasons for that: it is a question of the timing of the velic opening vs. other articulatory movements that have to be made, and this kind of process belongs with other kinds of familiar phonological processes of assimilation where a characteristic of one stretch of speech spreads over into surrounding sounds. Let us pause a while and look at this phenomenon.

It is the kind of phenomenon that phonologists do not pay much attention to by and large, but I would like to discuss it a bit. Suppose we imagine two languages with identical phonologies in terms of inventories of phonemes, and rules, and so forth, except that one has a lot more Nasal Spread than the other; that is, in one there is just a little bit of nasalization of vowels next to nasal consonants and the other has a lot of it, although it still does not affect the phonemic status or the nature of the rules or inventories involved. I think we would feel that there is a significant difference between these two phonologies, that we have put our finger on something that characterizes two languages as different from one another (one thing that linguistics is trying to do is to achieve better means of characterizing the differences between languages of the world). Here, it turns out, if we examine the degree of Nasal Spread in different languages the degree may be very different, and unexpectedly so. For example, look at English, American English in particular. There is a considerable amount of Nasal Spread, generally from the nasal consonant to the preceding vowel and more with some vowels than with others, and more depending upon which consonant follows the nasal and so on, but there is so much Nasal Spread that we must put English toward the high end of the scale. On the other hand, look at Swedish: it has as many nasal consonants as English has and is not so drastically different phonologically from English, but there is almost no Nasal Spread (some, to be sure; you remember we agreed on a conspiratorial working assumption that all languages have Nasal Spread). Swedish has very little, and I suggest that one of the significant differences between the Swedish and English phonological systems is degree of Nasal Spread. Some people have hazarded the guess—a quick and easy guess—that facts like this have to do with whether there are distinctive nasal vowels in the language. There is something to that as a guess, I am sure, but let us think of some languages that have nasal vowels and see if there is the same kind of variation in Nasal Spread among them. In French there is very little Nasal Spread, that is, when you have a nasal consonant next to an oral vowel that oral vowel does not get much nasality attached to it, some but not very much. It has very little nasalization compared to the vowel in a corresponding position in English, next to a nasal consonant; but if we look at a language like Hindi, which also has distinctive nasal vowels, there is quite a bit of Nasal Spread involved under these conditions, so that languages apparently differ systematically or in patterned ways in the degree of Nasal Spread.

Another thing I would like to observe: several degrees of vowel nasality are recognizable, at least in phonetic terms. Bengali is a favorite language of mine for examples. It has seven oral vowels and seven nasal vowels, and the contrast between oral and nasal vowels is neutralized next to nasal consonants under a variety of conditions. The interesting observation I want to make here is that the vowel next to a nasal consonant—where the opposition is neutralized—is often more heavily nasalized than a distinctively nasal vowel elsewhere. People who like neutralizations to come out with the unmarked member are troubled by that kind of phonology, but in any case that is the way Bengali works. The point to be made here is not the phonological status of nasalization in Bengali, but simply that it is fairly easy to discern three levels of nasalization: zero nasality, phonemic nasality, and nonphonemic nasality, of which the last is the greatest in this language, as it so happens. In general, it is fairly easy to recognize two levels of nasality in addition to nonnasal, and those who have listened to both French nasal vowels and Portuguese nasal vowels can notice that the French sound more strongly nasal than the Portuguese. I do not know exactly what the difference is. Decades ago Henry Sweet said it had to do with pressure in the pharynx (Sweet, 1877:8, 211; 1913:468). Finally, people whom I respect tell me that in Chinantec there are three levels of nasality where there is really a distinctive function involved—oral vowels, nasalized vowels, and supernasalized vowels—no matter what kind of analysis in terms of underlying nasal consonants, etc., may be adopted (Merrifield, 1963). In short, there is a tendency for nasality to spread to neighboring vowels, and this important phenomenon comes in measurable doses in various ways in different languages (Clumeck, 1975; Ferguson, 1975c).

The second process I call Nasal Loss. By this I mean the process by which consonants drop out of languages. Once again we can consider this a universal process. Where you have clusters involving nasals there is some tendency in every language for the nasal consonants to drop out of them, and where the nasal comes at the end of the word there is some tendency for the nasal to drop. Just as we saw that Nasal Spread was part of a family of assimilation processes, we can regard Nasal Loss as part of a whole family of weakening processes, including cluster simplification in general and erosion of consonants in final position.

You might find that a little misleading, because you might think I mean that nasals are particularly weak and likely to be lost, but nothing could be further from the truth. In fact, homorganic nasal obstruent clusters are among the world's most frequently occurring clusters. For example, if a language has any medial clusters at all, it is likely to have one consisting of nasal followed by oral stop in the same place of articulation. Similarly, single nasals are not at all rare at the end of a word, in fact, the other way around. If a language has any final consonants at all, the chances are it has a final nasal. If we watch languages losing final consonants, the chances are they get rid of obstruents first, leaving only *s*, a couple of liquids, and *n*, and then it is just the *n*, and then finally the *n* goes, so that when I am talking about nasal loss here I am not saying that nasals are weak and very likely to be lost. No, very often they get lost *after* other things, but Nasal Loss is nevertheless a universal process in that it tends to happen, and when the conditions are favorable enough, it gets carried through.

Let us talk first about the characteristic way in which nasals get lost at the end of a word. Suppose a language has *m*'s, *n*'s, and ŋ's, all as possible final consonants. One way you could imagine final nasal loss taking place would be for each of them to get a little bit weaker, but keeping a three-way contrast, until finally all the final nasals just fade away. In fact, however, languages never seem to work that way. What happens instead is that there are mergers. Instead of the nasals getting weaker, the number of contrasts keeps decreasing and what tends to happen is that *m* becomes *n* and *n* becomes ŋ, and finally ŋ becomes a nasal vowel. This is pretty certainly what has happened in the history of French and more spectacularly in the history of Chinese dialects, where, although there are exceptions here and there, generally the route has been for a gradual merger of nasal endings with the final stages being velar nasal and nasal vowel before complete disappearance of nasality (Chen, 1973; Ruhlen, 1973; Ferguson, 1975c).

It is fun to look around for a language in which final vowel loss is happening, where the process is working itself out before your eyes. Spanish is the language I have in mind. There is only one possible nasal in final position in Spanish. It is difficult to get speakers of Spanish to produce the contrast between final *m* and final *n*. In teaching English to Spanish speakers you get the students to bring their lips together and say a nice clear final *m* and the next minute they are again saying *n* for *m*. This is a very deep-seated neutralization in Spanish. Millions of Spanish speakers have only an *n* in final position, but other millions of Spanish speakers have gone a step further and have ŋ in final position, and still other Spanish speakers have a fluctuation between *n* and ŋ or fluctuation between a final ŋ and a final nasal vowel (Cedergren and Sankoff, 1975). We see a very good example of this regular process of Nasal Loss in final position.

It would be very nice if once again we could say "That's the way final nasals always get lost." Unfortunately, that is not always the way final nasals get lost, although it may represent one of those universal statements that are valid if you put them in a larger framework. Let me offer one counterexample to show that this is not the way it always works. At almost any period, starting some centuries B.C. and coming down to the present time, Greek has been losing its final *n*; in fact Greek has been trying to lose its final *n* for over two thousand years: it almost makes it every once in awhile, but the speakers pull the *n* back into the language because they know how to read or write or because on occasion they speak a more formal variety of Greek, which has it, or whatever, so that the final *n* is still there in present-day spoken Greek, at least some of the time. Now we would expect the loss of final *n* in Greek to happen the way we said it generally tends to happen—that is, the *n* becomes a velar nasal, then a nasal vowel, and disappears. I think you can look in vain among present-day Greek dialects to find someplace where utterance-final *n* is pronounced like a velar nasal, or where the final *n* has become a nasalized vowel. Instead what happens is that people just drop the *n*; they just drop it altogether, it's gone. It is either all the way there or all the way not there, and many words vary, having two forms, under some circumstances with *n* and under others without.

So here we find there are at least two ways you can have a final Nasal Loss, but one way is clearly dominant, and occurs over and over again, and the other way occurs in a much more limited number of languages under different sets of circumstances. Seeking to understand why Nasal Loss occurs one way in one language and another way in another is an example of what phonology is all about.

What happens to Nasal Loss in clusters? If you have a cluster consisting of a nasal consonant followed by a nonnasal consonant, there is a definite sequence to the loss of the nasal and a definite preference as to where it disappears first. It depends on whether the following nonnasal consonant is voiceless or voiced. (It also depends on whether it is a fricative or a stop, and other things.) In general the nasal consonant disappears (and affects the preceding vowel) first before voiceless consonants and only later, if at all, before voiced consonants. In fact, there is very different treatment between clusters with a voiceless consonant and clusters with a voiced consonant. Frequently, for example, instead of Nasal Loss in the voiced cluster, you have some kind of assimilation resulting in a geminate nasal consonant, or something else takes place. Whatever the details are, and there are many, depending on the language, what is really striking is the difference between what happens before a voiceless consonant and what happens before a voiced one. The evidence comes from changes through time not only in languages but also in child phonology. The way children acquire nasal clusters, in English and other languages (English is best documented) is very different in a cluster that has a voiceless consonant from one that has a voiced consonant. To call on Smith's data again, his child dropped the nasal before the voiceless stop particularly in the early stages, but before the voiced stop the nasal stayed and the voice stop dropped, and that is a very common thing in child language development.

Nasal vowels as separate 'phonemes' or lexically distinctive segments come into languages almost always as the result of the interaction of Nasal Spread and Nasal Loss. That is, if in a given language nasality is spreading far to the vowel system and the vowels are becoming fairly heavily nasalized, and also the other kind of weakening process is coming in so that final nasals are lost or nasals in clusters are lost—if those two processes match in just the right way, you will have one or more nasalized vowels, without a surrounding environment conditioning the nasality. So one useful way of looking at the coming into existence of distinctive nasal vowels in a language is to see it as the interaction of the universal processes of Nasal Spread and Nasal Loss.

I am not concerned here with what phonological level this is happening at—whether it is happening at the most surfacy kind of level or several notches deeper. What I am concerned with is the nature of the processes in general, whether in some particular language it may have gone only so far that there are still morphophonemic alternations around that give you a nasal consonant in some sort of abstract notation, or whether it has gone still further and there are no such alternations around so you are forced to have a nasal vowel at an underlying level, or whether you do not use that kind of terminology or analysis at all. What I am looking at is simply the process of coming into existence of nasal vowels in languages. They seem to be the result of Nasal Spread and Nasal Loss in various kinds of overlapping interactions (Greenberg, 1966; Ferguson, 1966, 1975c).

I made some comments in the beginning about nasal consonants; now let me make some about nasal vowels. *Some languages have distinctive nasal vowels.* If there *are* nasal vowels in a language, we can be sure there will be no more nasal vowels than the number of oral vowels in the language. Bengali, for example, has seven oral vowels and seven nasal vowels, which is a maximum system in terms of the number of nasal vowels in relation to the number of oral vowels. Very often you find systems with fewer nasal vowels than oral vowels. If there *are* fewer nasal vowels, you can be sure one will be some kind of [a]. You might find a really rare exception, but if the nasal vowels come into the language by the route we are talking about, which is almost always the way they come in, then the language will have at least one [a] vowel. The frequency of occurrence of nasal vowels relative to the frequency of oral vowels is very low, incredibly low. In Bengali, which has an equal number of oral vowel and nasal vowel phonemes, if you count occurrences in running texts you will find at most 1/20 as many nasal vowels as oral, and with some nasal vowels as low as 1/50 the number of corresponding oral vowel occurrences. Finally, we could observe that in most languages with nasal vowels, there are morphophonemic alternations with nasal consonants.

Now we have arrived at what I regard as an interesting question, and one of the reasons I have been doing all this talk about processes. Suppose someone asked you as a linguist or phonological theoretician or whatever, why, when we have many languages in the world that have, say, five-vowel systems, say /a e i o u/ (there are hundreds of such languages), do we not have any languages in the world that have instead as a vowel system /a ə ã ɔ̃/ and /ɑ̃̃/ with second-degree nasalization. We just said we could have two degrees of nasalization and we know about distinctive use of vowel length. Why couldn't we have a system of this kind? In fact, why couldn't we have a nine-vowel system with length and double length, and nasality and double nasality? That would work perfectly well as far as bearing information loads and identifying items in the lexicon are concerned; everything would work fine. There is no obvious reason you could not have a phonology of that sort to do what a language has to do, and yet we all know that is a very unlikely phonology. We can answer the question along different lines. Someone asked after the first lecture: "What did Bell mean by looking at inherent nature vs. processes?" I would like to look at the question both ways.

First, you could give an answer based on 'inherent nature'. I do not want to use that phrase if it turns people off, but you could give an answer that says the system would not work for good articulatory and perceptual reasons. People who have done experiments with the ability to perceive nasal vowels have found unambiguously that it is harder to distinguish vowel-quality differences among nasal vowels than among oral vowels. Similarly, while nasality by itself is quite easy to perceive, to recognize two degrees of it would put a strain on our perception apparatus. Thus perceptual problems would account for the tendency to merge and neutralize nasal vowels more than oral vowels, and for some of the other characteristics of nasal vowels we talked about, such as their lower frequency with respect to oral vowels. Or you could use the same approach from an articulatory point of view and you could probably show that it is harder to produce nasal vowels: not only do you have to put the tongue in the right position but you have to do something with the velic opening. I don't know, but I am suggesting that you could find answers along the line of the inherent nature of nasal vowels to explain why we have vowel systems of the kind we have instead of other easily imaginable vowel systems based on nasality.

You could also give an answer based on the process point of view. Where do nasal vowels come from? In almost all cases they come from Nasal Spread and Nasal Loss in clusters and in final positions. That means there are never going to be more nasal vowels than oral vowels to begin with because they come from oral vowels by nasalization. What is more, they are going to be less frequent in occurrence because their origin is oral vowels followed by a nasal, and there will be fewer instances of that than oral vowels not followed by a nasal in a given language. So the total result is going to be, once again, fewer occurrences of nasal vowels. I would like to agree, I think, with whoever asked that question the first day, and say that both are legitimate ways of looking at the question "How do you characterize language states in general?" or "What is universally true about how a language must work?" Both approaches are important, and in some important fundamental sense they must be the same thing. They are not unrelated; they must have the same underlying principles, Jakobson's Laws of Irreversible Solidarity, if we only knew what they were.

The third process is Nasal Syllabicization, a clumsy name for the tendency for nasal consonants to become syllabic. We all know that some consonants can become syllabic although it is usually vowels that are syllabic, and we can even make some principled statements about which consonants are more likely to do this than other consonants. One might be inclined to say offhand that liquids, *l*'s and *r*'s, are more likely to do this than *n*'s and *m*'s. This sounds like a reasonable kind of statement because it would agree with dominance orders or sonority scales or whatever, in which liquids are somehow more sonorous than nasals are more sonorous than fricatives are more sonorous than stops. Scales of that sort account for certain facts of distribution, certain changes, and so forth. It would be pleasant if it turned out that you would be more likely to get liquids than nasals becoming syllabic consonants. Interestingly enough, if you check it out with languages it turns out not to be so. In over sixty languages where we could get good evidence of the occurrence of syllabic consonants, only three languages had liquids that were syllabic consonants but not nasals. Many had both, and many had nasal syllabic consonants and not liquids. Obviously, whatever order or preference list is involved here, it is not the one we have for sonority. That makes us a little unhappy because I at least was raised to believe that Sanskrit was the language you should pay attention to for things like that; Sanskrit does have syllabic *l*'s and *r*'s and does not have syllabic nasals although some people reconstruct earlier stages of Indo-European where there were syllabic nasals as well. I am not talking about phonemically distinctive syllabic consonants, whatever that may mean. I am just talking about the existence of syllabic consonants at a systematic phonetic level, or whatever you want to call it, in a given language, so that English, for example, has syllabic nasal consonants, regardless of what kind of phonological interpretation you want to give them—as in my pronunciation of the *on* in *button*. And it is quite clear that languages are more likely to have syllabic nasals than to have syllabic liquids.

Which is the most likely nasal consonant to become syllabic? I think given what I have said so far and our personal experience with languages, we probably are not able to make a reasonable guess. If you guess *n* you are wrong. Maybe it is a good time to point out that English syllabic nasals are not very typical of syllabic nasals around the world. Just as we tend to think of all nasal vowels as working the way French ones do, since French is the language with nasal vowels that is most at hand, we tend to think of English syllabic nasals as the norm. However, by and large French nasal vowels are just on the edge of 'normality', they are not typical of nasal vowel systems around the world, and the same thing is true of English syllabic consonants. For example, English syllabic consonants generally assimilate to the preceding consonant, not the following consonant, but most languages are the opposite. In English, it is more likely that *n* will become syllabic rather than *m* or *η*. To put it impressionistically in terms of my own behavior, I am more likely to have a syllabic *n* in *button* than a syllabic *m* in *open* or a syllabic *η* in *broken*. If you look at enough languages to keep a proper score, *n* is definitely the *least* likely of the three nasal consonants to become a syllabic nasal; *m* is by far most likely to become syllabic, and *η* and *n* are relatively close to one another, but *n* is clearly in third place. This conclusion is the result of looking with great care at some 65 languages that have syllabic nasals, and it constitutes a universal statement in the sense we have been using, that is, not exceptionless, but illustrating the way languages fundamentally work (Bell, 1970).

It should now be clear that if you want to look for universal processes of this kind, or even if you want to look for generalizations about possible language states, the only way to do it is to have reliable, comparable, accessible data around that you can turn to and get answers. Strangely enough, linguists traditionally do not like that. If, for example, we want to know when it is most likely for an *n* to become syllabic what we apparently prefer to do is think about languages that we know, go to our own file cabinets, 3x5 cards, or whatever, call up a friend on the phone and say "Hey, Joe" or "Hey, Sue, do you know any languages where *n* becomes syllabic under such and such circumstances?" Or if we get really serious we go to the library and look up some grammars that we think might have syllabic nasals in them. I know of no other scientific discipline that operates in that strange way. Somewhere we should have information of this sort in books and articles, put in a comparable format where you can get at it, so you can ask the librarian or the archivist or the computer and the reply will be "Oh, yes: there are 66 languages that have syllabic *n* under these circumstances and they are A, B, C, . . . and four of them have interesting exceptions." It would seem obvious that we could work much faster at getting to an understanding of phonological systems if we had that kind of thing available. That is why we set up the Phonology Archive at Stanford.

That was the thinking in back of the project, but actually getting it started was not easy. It is not just that linguists do not like the idea, for whatever historical reasons in the development of our discipline, but there are some real practical difficulties. Some we deliberately did not pay much attention to. For example, if you ask most linguists about the feasibility of a phonology archive, they say you cannot do it because the published grammars and articles are not reliable, they are just full of mistakes. Our response to that objection has always been something like this: "Then why do we go on publishing them? Presumably, we have a body of published descriptions of languages; if they are no good, then why are we in the business at all? There must be something there—some parts of the information must be reliable. We don't have to go and check every single fact every single time we want to find one." On that basis we decided to use only published sources. Sometimes we have them checked by linguists who know the language well and can add comments, but basically it is published documentation, not individual interpretations of a particular native speaker or particular linguist. Thus, the sources are publicly available for any user of the Archive to consult and evaluate.

Also there is the question of what theoretical interpretation you are going to have. Different linguists want to ask very different questions about phonology. I am sure that the way I put some of the material in my lectures here has been very different from the way you have heard some other phonologists put questions, and what is more, ten years from now, or twenty-five years from now, they are going to ask very different theoretical questions from the ones any of us are asking now. So the question is how to put things into the computer or the archive, so that people of different theoretical persuasions can get at them. That is not an easy question to answer. We did not want to have an archive that would be good just for our theory, if we had one; or just for a current, widely accepted theory; or even for what the theory is going to be ten years from now. We wanted to put in observable data that we all agreed on, which would be grist for anyone's theoretical mill, so to speak. That is asking a lot, but we worked for two or three years to come up with a format that we think would do it, and the Archive is now operational.

I would like to make a final point or two, about the kind of questions you want to ask. There is a great tendency for all of us to ask pseudo-questions or red herrings. I will now reveal my own biases since some of you here can accept the red herrings about which I get upset and some of my questions seem pointless to you. Let me give some examples of what I mean by pseudo-questions. "Is nasality a feature of segments or is it a prosodic entity of some kind?" That is the kind of question people ask seriously. I do not deny their right to ask it, but it is the kind of question I would regard as a pseudo-question or a red herring as far as our Archive would be concerned. It is my own bias that any feature in phonology might function either as a segmental feature or as a prosodic entity of some kind. Now to be sure, stopness is much more likely than stress to be a segmental feature, and stress is much more likely to be some kind of prosodic feature. But there is no knowing. For example, we tend to think about [± voice] as a segmental feature; in fact, one day at a staff meeting of the Universals Project at Stanford I made the mistake of saying "I don't know of any languages where a given morpheme or word is plus voice or minus voice throughout— whose voicing really works as a kind of accent," and Joe Greenberg, as he always does, came up with an example: "How about Yambe in New Guinea?" It turns out that Yambe really does work that way, and I was happy to have an example for adult language, since the phenomenon is well attested in child phonology.

In the very early stages of acquisition when they are trying to master the notion of voicing, there are a number of children who will extend it over the whole word. For example, Hildegard Leopold's *pretty, ticktock*, and some other words she said voiceless or whispered throughout, while most of her words were not devoiced that way. She had either plus voice or minus voice for whole words until she mastered the feature and got it localized down into segments. So even an apparently segmental feature such as voicing can, in some instances, function prosodically. Nasality is a good example—it is right in between. When I think about Bengali, one of the really fine languages on the face of the earth, with its seven oral vowels and seven nasal vowels, it is really quite debatable whether nasality is a prosody or not, because there are severe prosodiclike constraints on its occurrence. For example, you can have sequences of vowels and semivowels in the language, up to seven in a row, but they generally have to be all oral or all nasal, and we have already mentioned the neutralization of nasality in vowels next to nasal consonants. I suspect that in every Indo-Aryan language there are some reasons for wanting to regard nasality as prosodic and some reasons for wanting to regard it as segmental. My concern would be not to decide once and for all, as some linguists would like to do, whether nasality is really a prosodic feature or really a segmental feature, but rather to find out the nature and extent of the variation in segmentality or prosodicity of nasality in different languages, the conditions under which it may be one or the other, and so on. And that is the kind of information that somehow has to be available in the archive, not obscured by premature decisions of coding.

Another red herring kind of question would be "Is this a major class feature?" Linguists tend to get preoccupied with what the features are that really divide all segments into major classes such as consonants and vowels, true major features. Nasals are particularly interesting in this connection. What major class do they belong to? I would say they may belong with both liquids and stops. They belong with liquids in the sense that they may become syllabic, as we said a while ago, and they do a lot of other things that liquids do; they belong with stops in that they tend to share a place of articulation features and other kinds of phenomena. Nasals just do not fit that neatly into one major class. Arabic is a good illustration of that. Most varieties have *m* and *n* as nasal consonants, and are these a separate class of nasals or do they belong with the liquids *l* and *r* or with obstruents *b f t d*, etc.? There is one principled way of answering that question that is of considerable interest. In Semitic phonology there are constraints on the co-occurrence of phonemes within a given root, depending on how close they are phonetically. If you have a *b* as the first consonant of the root, you cannot have a *b* as the second, and you are not even likely to have an *f*, whereas you can have a *t* or *d* very well as the second consonant. The roots are typically three consonants long and there are severe co-occurrence restrictions on root consonants in Semitic in general and in Arabic in particular (Greenberg, 1950). Now if you calculate the phonologically similar classes as found by looking at what can occur with what in a given root, you will find that the *m* clearly belongs with the *b* and *f*: the frequency of co-occurrence is very low for this compared to the co-occurrence of one of these with consonants outside that class. But if you look at *n*, *t*, and *d* there are no restrictions whatsoever, they occur quite freely, but *n* does not co-occur with *l* and *r*. This is why Cantineau, the Arabic phonologist, said *n* does not belong with *t* and *d* in Arabic, it belongs with the *l* and *r*, whereas *m* belongs with the *b* and *f*; and once having looked at it this way, he found a lot of other phonetic evidence that made sense (Cantineau, 1946). It is that kind of classification that one might miss if one were setting up things like major class features in constructing an archive. Major class features are for the user of the archive to construct if he wants to, on the basis of the material he can get from the archive.

IV. What Is Phonology?

Today I would like to sketch a beautiful, detailed, explicit model of what phonology is and provide a satisfying set of methods for finding out more about it, and the lecture would be called "Models and Methods." Unfortunately such a session would take more time than we have and require a more intensive intellectual effort than I can provide.

In lieu of that I will just ramble on in a fairly unstructured way about models and methods, and call the lecture "What Is Phonology?" The word *phonology* is ambiguous in that it means either the study or the thing studied. I mean both, and it will generally be clear from what I say whether I am referring to the study or the object of study.

What is phonology? I do not want to give a formal definition, but we at least have to agree informally in order to know what we are talking about. I would say that the study of phonology is the study of sound systems in human language, or, better, the *systematic* study of sound systems in human language. If you like the word *scientific* with a capital S you can say the scientific study of sound systems in human language; I do not care one way or the other on that point. The object of the study is just that—sound systems in human language. Now how old is the systematic study of phonology? When did it start? We could pick 1957 or 1921 or any other landmark. My view is, however, that it started at least as far back as the second millennium B.C.

I am thinking of the study that must have gone into creating the first more-or-less alphabetic systems of writing, at the eastern end of the Mediterranean. I cannot imagine how people could have thought up writing systems of that kind without their having done some systematic study of sound systems of human language. There is no way you can accidentally stumble on the alphabetic principle. You have to do a lot of thinking and introspecting, listening and experimenting, before you come up with it, and I think that the invention of alphabetic writing reflected both of the principal goals of the study of phonology, as I see them. Those two principal goals are: (1) to achieve a better way to characterize or represent particular sound systems, showing how any one particular sound system differs from another or all other sound systems; and (2) to characterize sound systems in general, that is, the nature of sound systems in human language, the universal constraints on them, their universal properties, and so forth. Those early alphabet inventors were doing both those things, that is, they were figuring out a way to characterize their own particular language (or languages, because actually the alphabet got used right away for different varieties of the same language and even different languages), and they were also trying to figure out how language works in general. Now, of course, this is only speculation because they did not write it down and say so; I am just asserting that they could not have done what they did without having those goals. If we want explicit written evidence and not just circumstantial evidence that people were doing phonology, then we probably do not have to go back quite so far, maybe the fifth century

B.C. or something of that sort. For instance, we could take the universal favorite Panini; everyone says he was a great phonologist, and I think he was. He really cared about how a sound system works. It is a little hard to be absolutely sure that he was interested in how sound systems work in all human language, and not just in how the Sanskrit system works, but I am willing to give him the benefit of the doubt. I think he was doing both things and doing them very explicitly. Of course he had predecessors and colleagues; whomever you want to credit with the first explicit study of phonology, it is way back in time, and we are still now slowly building on what was found in the past about how sound systems work.

Now we have to have some justification for talking about phonology all by itself. Is phonology autonomous in some sense? As you know, people sometimes quarrel over whether phonology is autonomous, or for that matter whether syntax is autonomous or other things are and I want to reply both yes and no, in a fairly commonsense way. Phonology is not autonomous in the sense that people do not make sounds in isolation from the rest of language; particular people make sounds in particular words on particular occasions in particular constructions that mean particular things; apart from that you do not have sound systems. Sound systems do not make sense outside of language use and in that sense the study of phonology can never be completely autonomous. On the other hand, it does turn out in a very commonsensical way that we can give some analytical autonomy to phonology. Wherever we may want to draw the line in our theory, we have to give some autonomy to phonology. We all know the person who has learned to speak a foreign language so fluently and so well that he is more at home in that language than he is in the one he started with, and yet he still speaks the second language with a terrible accent. We have all met the linguist or phonetician who learns to pronounce the language so well that you cannot distinguish his pronunciation from that of a native speaker, yet he cannot construct two sentences in the language properly. It is possible to see a kind of commonsense autonomy in which phonology is somehow separate from the rest of language even though it always appears in language use.

Now another issue. Phonology is more complicated than we think. That sentence is really enough for the whole lecture today. Phonology is more complicated than we think, and the more we find out about it the more complicated it turns out to be. I do not think that is a bad thing at all. In fact, I tend to make good value judgments about it. The more you study phonology the more beautiful and the more awe-inspiring it turns out to be. I do not mind at all using a religious word when I say the attitude of a phonologist to phonology is reverence. The more you study human phonologies the more fascinatingly complex and orderly and impressive they turn out to be. I would like to make that point very explicitly at the beginning, just because, time after time, we find ourselves slipping back into wanting to make phonology simpler. There is a great tendency to want to make everything as simple as possible, and although I am not in favor of multiplying entities unnecessarily, I *am* in favor of recognizing not only that phonology is very complex but that the deeper we look into it the more complexity we will find.

How do people acquire phonology? Children do not learn phonologies as such, that is they do not directly learn oppositions or phonemes or features or rules or whatever it is that phonology consists of. Children learn how to say things. They learn words and how to put them in constructions that mean things on appropriate occasions. But in some marvelous mysterious way, while they are doing that, they sort out this other machinery that is there and gradually begin to operate with features and rules and so on. I think it is very important to remember this point. Jakobson talks about acquiring oppositions; that is in some ways a bad metaphor. It is not as though the oppositions are there, and the child learns first this opposition and then that one. The *words* are there and the child learns the words, and in some wonderful way the child hypothesizes about the phonology; he organizes phonological regularities from the words he is learning. I would rather change the metaphor a little bit and say that the child *learns* words and things like words, but he *constructs* a phonological system.

Now why do I insist on that backwards way of saying it? After all, I am interested in phonology, and presumably the child does in some sense acquire it. I would say we were forced to put the metaphor in that backwards way at Stanford when we kept studying how children acquire language. We looked for such things as oppositions and phonemes and familiar entities of that sort, but what we found was strangely different. Suppose you want to find out whether a child has a p–b opposition, a very reasonable thing to look for. One thing you could do would be to look around and see if he has a minimal pair. In very young children with fewer than fifty words total vocabulary that is not so easy to do, and you must often settle for other evidence. What we found out was disconcerting. Usually you cannot answer the question in a simple, direct way. For example, if you look at how particular words beginning with labial stops are pronounced, one word may begin pretty consistently with a p—or very close to p. Another word, a different lexical item, may vary all over the place, sometimes pronounced with a *p*, sometimes with a *pʰ*, sometimes with a *b*, and so forth; another word is sometimes pronounced with a *b*, sometimes with a *β* and perhaps still another is pretty consistent with a *b*, so it turns out that almost every word has its own phonological characterization and its own phonological history.

Facts like that finally led us to realize, against all our intentions and all our training and background, that something similar holds true even in adult phonology, that at the basis of an individual adult's phonology is really something like the phonologically unanalyzed phonetic shapes of whole words, no matter how much phonological order the individual may put into it. All of us make some use of phonetic shapes of whole words unphonologized. We can all repeat a new word we have never heard before, maybe one in another language, blurt it out, not following some of the phonological rules we have in our language, and finally say it again with awareness and note, "Oh yeah, that ends in such-and-such a way." Let us say you come from a part of Texas where you pronounce *thing* [θæŋ] although you pronounce *sing* [sɪŋ] (people tell me there are parts of Texas like that). It is perfectly possible that you could discover, when you are age 45 or so that *thing* does not rhyme with *sing*; suddenly you notice it. You have been saying it all your life, but you have not become phonologically aware of it; it has not been explicit. Maybe that is not a very convincing example.

Let us consider TOT, the tip-of-the-tongue phenomenon. When you try to remember a word, you know what it is, but you cannot get it out —somebody's name, for example, or a word you do not use very often. There are some ways in which you try to get access to it in a phonologically oriented way. It is true, that certain segments may come to you, but it is also possible that the strangest, most extraneous kind of phonetic information comes to your mind. To take a very obvious example, the position of stress in the word may come to mind. You may not be able to recall any of the segmental material upon which you would presumably base your phonological rule of stress placement, but you still remember the stress on the word. It is obvious that at the early stages children have whole phonetic word shapes and only gradually do the word shapes get phonologically analyzed by the child. As we grow older we keep adding phonological organization until the phonetic shapes of the words become relatively unimportant, but we still have those, too, somewhere underneath.

As the child continues to grow his phonology develops and he makes more complex organizational hypotheses about the sounds he uses, largely out of awareness. The child shows by his behavior that he has some sort of productive rules. He pronounces something aspirated or stressed or nasalized or long depending on the conditioning environment. As the child is doing all this he is also getting into a network of social variation in the use of the language. The people talking to the child are speaking different regional and social dialects and situational and functional registers depending on where they come from and what the occasion is, e.g., talking to a child or to an adult. The child is taking in all that kind of data at the same time and hypothesizing about it. It is a different kind of hypothesis making; he has to say, "my [æ] is his [ɛə]" when it is Uncle Joe who is talking to him; he has to make all kinds of generalizations of this sort about the language he hears and speaks. Again, some of this variation is just learned as whole word shapes, some is phonologically organized, and so on, but there is a whole network of social variability in pronunciation that the child is acquiring, and that is an important part of acquiring the phonology of any language.

In our own society we eventually learn how to read and write, too; that is still probably not true of most people in the world, but it is increasingly true, and this is so important we just cannot brush it aside. It is part of the social variability business, too, but it has such a tremendous impact that as phonologists we have to recognize it. As soon as a speech community begins to write and read its own language, the spelling representation begins to affect the speakers' phonology. Examples are legion, but linguists prefer to ignore them, pretending there is only an occasional spelling pronunciation. That is not the way it is. We begin to add to our phonetic/phonological representation—if you want to use that word of words—a written dimension in addition to all the other stuff we are already loading it down with, and that enriches or complicates the kind of phonological knowledge or competence we have.

All of this can eventually get awareness added to it. All these wonderful phonological hypothesizings are done at first basically out of awareness. The child cannot talk about it. But as the child gets older, he gets to the point where he *can* talk about it. I am sure that some of you, especially if you have tried to teach reading or the first grade, have had the experience of watching the child discover what you mean by saying two things end the same way or begin the same way. Maybe you have had the same frustrating experiences I have had, talking to a reading teacher or a reading specialist who says, "This child can't make [or can't hear] the difference between *b* and *p*." I want to say, "What do you mean? This child is in the first grade; when he says *ball* or *Paul* he knows what is meant, he says it right and reacts consistently when others say it. What do you mean by saying the child can't do that?" The reading teacher, however, *does* mean something. It turns out that if you try to get the child to tell where the difference is between *ball* and *Paul,* the child has no idea—he may not even know whether the difference is at the beginning of the word or the end of the word. The child has not yet acquired the awareness of segmentation, which is a prerequisite for learning how to read (Mattingly, 1972). We are so used to written representation that we think the segmentation is natural and consciously accessible. Awareness of the sort of phonological organization we have in our heads is something that grows gradually and has its own patterns of growth, differing from the growth of phonological organization as a rule. It is also worth noting that individuals differ a lot in the degree of phonological awareness they have. It is rather pleasant to think that it is phonologists and linguists who have the greatest awareness. Maybe, in fact, that is all the study of phonology is: making more precise or explicit the phonological awareness we can have inside our heads.

No two of us have exactly the same phonology. We each learn a different set of vocabulary items from different people around us under different circumstances; we do our internal phonologizing in different ways; and we reach different levels of phonological awareness. As a result, every one of us has a unique phonology. That is something that is very hard to persuade linguists of; I know, since I have tried on a number of occasions, and the resistance is very strong. I say something like, "We all have a different phonology and it doesn't make sense to say that a child acquires English phonology by age X"—and a little later (once after almost two hours of talking about it) one of the linguists present says, "Yes, but there *must* be a time when the child *really* has acquired the phonology of the language"—so I really have not made the point. It is strange that we do not mind this when we are talking about lexicon; everyone admits that no two of us have exactly the same vocabulary, and that we do not use the words we have in common in exactly the same way. Phonology is like that too. There is, of course, a great deal of overlap among individual phonologies in a speech community, and I would suspect that the amount of overlap is roughly comparable to that in lexicon. The overlap makes it possible to construct an impressive set of common phonological rules, but we must not kid ourselves, for example, that we all speak *the* phonology of English. We all speak our own phonologies, and the way we organize them internally happens to overlap a lot. Studying the nature of these overlappings is interesting and important in itself, and it is a necessary part of learning how phonological systems work.

Let us move to the question of phonological change. When a change

in the phonological behavior of a speech community takes place—
and this is happening all the time—it must start with particular sounds
in particular words said by particular speakers on particular occasions,
and then it may spread from some sounds to other sounds, or from the
same sounds in some words to the same sounds in other words, or from
some groups of speakers saying those sounds in those words to other
groups of speakers saying the same sounds in those words or different
words; it may spread from one occasion of use to another. It just does not
happen that a sound change takes place in all words for all speakers for
all occasions. So any model we have of phonology has to account for this
complicated way that phonological change takes place in a speech community. There is no model of phonology currently available that really
can do justice to these facts about phonological change.

How do we explain the changes that take place anyway? Which kinds
of change are possible and which are not possible? What constraints
are there on sound changes and what explanation can we offer for them?
I would hazard a guess that there are at least three quite different kinds
of constraints or explanations. One I call *phonetic*, and by this I mean
things that have to do with the physiology of speech production and
speech perception. A lot of the changes are explainable in these terms or
along this dimension. I do not know where to draw the boundary line in
this fairly peripheral kind of processing—but presumably we want to
draw it somewhere before we get to the cortex. In any case, it has to do
with the way nerves and muscles and all the rest operate in both perception and production. I think *phonetic* is as good a word as any for
that.

For another kind of constraint or explanation I use the word *cognitive*
—a poor choice, perhaps, but *cognitive* already has so many meanings I
guess it will not hurt to use another one. By cognitive constraints or explanations I refer to the kind of processing that goes on, let us say, in
the central nervous system. But I am not concerned with the physiology
at the moment; I am concerned with identifying the kind of constraints
that are true not only for sound systems but also for other kinds of human
cognitive behavior, including processes of classification, hierarchization,
and so on, which are not limited to phonology but appear elsewhere in
language and for that matter in nonlanguage kinds of behavior.

Finally, the third kind I call *social*. I take it as a universal assumption
that in all societies social groupings tend to be reflected by language use.
Also in all speech communities some people tend to change their speech
to talk more like other people or less like other people, depending on
social factors. These universal kinds of social constraints are an important factor in phonological change.

The characterizations we make, the definitions for phonology we use, must include processes of change and must include ultimately these three kinds of dimensions, what I am calling crudely *phonetic, cognitive,* and *social.*

Now I would like to run through some characteristics of the study of phonology in the future. I think this is what I am supposed to talk about —New Directions in Phonology. As it so happens some of the 'new' directions are very old, but some may be really new. Let me run through a list of characteristics of phonology and methods of research that typify the new directions.

First, phonology is *polysystemic*—a good working term, I think. I say that with considerable reluctance because I was raised in a tradition that said—what arrant nonsense!—phonology is a unified system even if you have some fairly distinct little subsystems. While that is a good and insightful notion, I think it is basically wrong. Years ago when I was studying Bengali I noticed, as any phonologist studying Bengali would notice, that the stem vowels of the verbs alternate in highly regular ways, between i~e, e~æ, u~o, o~ɔ, and a~e, depending on the suffix. Part of the conditioning seems to be phonological and part morphological, but if you are a little imaginative in constructing the underlying representations (or their equivalents in other theoretical frameworks) it can be completely phonological. So that within the verb system all verb stems have an automatic vowel alternation such that you only need to posit five underlying vowels. There are seven vowel qualities, but you do not need to talk about seven vowels in analyzing Bengali verb stems. But those seven surface vowel qualities are identified by any Bengali with the seven distinctively different vowels in the nonverbs of the language, which are all over the place and do not alternate so neatly. I remember a Firthian analysis of Bengali verbs that really irritated me because it insisted that there were only five vowels in the verb even though there may be seven vowels elsewhere in the language. I said, "That's crazy; anybody knows there are seven vowels in the verb, along with some regular alternations." Somehow we have to get both those facts strongly and importantly in any phonological description of Bengali. It is not accidental or superficial that there are only five stem-differentiating vowels in the verb system and seven vowels elsewhere, and that the seven surface vowels of verbs are phonetically identical with the seven vowels that contrast elsewhere. The interlocking systems must somehow be captured in a way that I cannot feel any current phonological theory does. That is one example of polysystemic analysis.

It would take too long to give an autobiographical list of sins where I feel I have forced something into a single system when it was many systems, but I think we increasingly have to reckon with interacting systems within our phonologies. In child phonology we often have to recognize different systems in initial position and final position, or different systems of chronological layering. In whole languages there can be vocabularies of different origins that differ in phonology or in marginal phenomena of baby talk, or animal calls, and some that in some respects are similar to core phenomena in a system, but in other respects work quite differently.

I am not offering just a recapitulation of Firthian phonology by any means, but Firth and his followers at least had their eyes on some important characteristics about phonology when they made fun of American linguists' squeezing everything into a segmental, monosystemic framework.

Second, phonology is *variable*. The fact of variation has to be included systematically in any type of phonological theory. And if we need a nice example we can take a Labovian variable, so that we all know what we are talking about. It is a part of the competence of any speaker of New York English that the degree of post-vocalic *r* in his speech will correlate with the degree of carefulness of speech, social class, and some other social factors, and it is interesting to study the patterns of such variation. The pattern of this variation in New York is different from the pattern elsewhere, so to that extent it represents regional dialect variation. Also, it differs by social class, so that it is social dialect variation. Finally, the variation depends on degree of formality and who the addressee is, so it is registral variation. Some way of handling geographical and social dialect variation as well as register variation has to be built into our understanding of phonology and the kind of model we have of phonology.

An interesting kind of variation is the modification of pronunciation adults make when talking to children. A simple example again out of my own experience: I spoke with a very marked Philadelphia accent when I was growing up, and as I grew older and went to the university some of the features of the Philadelphia accent were cancelled out or modified, toned down a little bit. When I was quite young you could tell after a sentence or so that I came from Philadelphia; when I was older you might have had to listen to quite a number of sentences and focus very carefully on my pronunciation of 'short *a*' or some other special feature before you could figure out that I did indeed come from Philadelphia. It would seem then that I had gotten rid of those early Philadelphianisms, or toned them down. But when I was talking to my own children when they were very young, I found myself reinstating many of those Philadelphianisms that I thought had vanished. Not that I intended to; in fact I was dismayed to find I was doing that. Then I observed that a lot of other people do the same kind of thing, and it seemed clear that stored away somewhere in my competence was a set of rules that said, as it were, "Suppress certain phenomena in ordinary conversation but throw a switch and let them up and out again in certain situations." And this is not a strange peculiar property of Philadelphians, or of linguists, or of Ferguson. It is a phenomenon that is found in all speech communities on the part of all speakers. We all do it, and it belongs somehow in our theoretical framework of phonology.

An example that I have used over and over again (e.g., Ferguson, 1972) is the difference between [r] and [γ] in Christian and Muslim dialects of Arabic in the city of Baghdad. The Muslim dialect has a contrasting r and *gamma;* the Christian dialect also has a contrasting r and *gamma,* so they have the same inventory of phonemes, so to speak, but there are many words in Muslim Arabic with an r that have a *gamma* in the Christian Arabic. By no means all; there are some that have r also in Christian Arabic. It is also true that many Christian speakers can switch to the Muslim pronunciation, so that if a group of Christians are speaking to each other freely, and a Muslim walks in, they may all switch over automatically to speaking Muslim Arabic, which is the dominant variety. What does this mean? It means that the Christian Arab in Baghdad has a set of lexical items in his repertoire that are labelled "pronounce *gamma* if there are Christians there, but pronounce r if there are Muslims there." He also has a set of lexical items that are always pronounced with r, and another set that are always pronounced with *gamma.* Now that is an incredibly complicated thing to do, yet people do it largely out of awareness—although every Christian will recognize right away as soon as he hears the *gamma* in a certain word that he is speaking with a coreligionist. The signal is there. That kind of variation is not strange and peculiar—only the example is strange because it is not familiar to us—the phenomenon is a part of all languages, all speech communities, all phonological systems; it has to do with the way phonological systems function.

The third thing is that phonology has *multiple basic units.* It is fun to argue about which is *the* basic unit: is it the distinctive feature or the phoneme, the opposition or the segment. Those are all good candidates, and one can think of many others; but I think the more one seriously tries to represent what is going on in phonological systems the more one is driven to recognize that one cannot get along with just one or two basic units. There is a whole list of basic units that we have to find. It is quite clear in some languages that a unit like the word plays an important role in the phonology, and you cannot do without it; that is you cannot derive it from other kinds of units in the same system. Linguists tried to get along without syllables for a long time; I was raised in the tradition that said syllables were not really of interest to linguists; you could always characterize them by sets of abbreviations of segmental units. Then it turns out that in many languages you have to have syllables as the unit in which phonological rules work, and that the syllable is basic in child language processing (e.g., Fudge, 1969). I am sure you are familiar with the studies (e.g., Gleitman and Rozin, 1973) that show that in teaching children to read it works better, by and large, to teach them in terms of syllables rather than phoneme-length segments. All I am saying is that we have to have many more levels, units, and components in our phonology than we ever dreamed. We have to have units larger as well as smaller than the distinctive features of phonemes.

Now a fourth characteristic, and this is not so much a characteristic of phonology as it is a current bias of mine. Given our present primitive understanding of how phonology works, I think we always have to look at phonological phenomena in at least two ways: as the organization of elements and relations, and as processes. Sometimes those two ways of looking at things are easily translatable, one into the other; and sometimes it is quite clear that some things are better, more helpfully, more conveniently stated in organizational terms or in processual terms, but sometimes there is an important insight in doing it both ways, and sometimes it is not clear which way is better. So for the time being I have adopted a policy of trying to say everything both ways. In a way it is reminiscent of Hockett's talking about item-and-arrangement, process, and so on (Hockett, 1955). One of the great things generative phonology has done for us is to give us the notation X→Y/Z for the notion that X becomes Y under condition Z; it is a wonderful kind of notation and turns out to be useful and suggestive in many ways.

We should not lose sight of the fact that we can use the same notation and conceptualization in talking about synchronic processes in which there is no real time involved, and diachronic processes in which there *is* real time involved. We can talk about processes with this notation and conceptualization if they are within the same system and if they are between systems. Let me give just one example of this last point. When we talked about substitution rules in child phonology development, that was going outside the system. We were not talking about processes in the same sense linguists usually talk about phonological rules. We were talking about the processes relating to the adult model and the child's output. So we have a kind of four-way classification that is between synchrony and diachrony, between within-system and across-system. What is fascinating about making lists of phonological processes from different languages and in those four categories is that hundreds, perhaps thousands turn out to be the same. They do not all turn out to be the same. Some of them will happen in only one or several of the four categories but not in the others, but that is what is fundamental about understanding phonological processes. We have to find out which of these processes are common across the board and which are not, and try to find explanations of why that should be.

Just one more characteristic of phonology—it is likely to put less emphasis on distinctive vs. nondistinctive, or phonemic vs. phonetic. I did not say we were abandoning the notion that features of distinctiveness have some particular role in phonology, but we have in general tended to emphasize that idea so much that we have lost important information about how phonological systems work. Again, we were forced to recognize this in doing child phonology studies. We found out we could understand what we were doing only if we looked at extreme phonetic detail before we could phonologize. In opposition to some people who are saying emphatically that we must draw the line ever more carefully between phonetic and phonemic interpretations of child language development, I would say no, we must practice more erasing of that line here and there to understand how some of the phenomena work, although we must somehow do it without losing the important content of distinctive function.

Now just a few words about method. How do you find the data? How do you get the facts in phonology? I am a proponent now, as I think I have been as far back as I can remember, for all four ways that people use, and I am particularly opposed to people who say only one of those four ways is the right way to do it. The first way is introspection. "Say it to yourself and try to figure out what is going on." It is easy to downgrade that and to note that you can always kid yourself. Introspection has lots of problems. Psychologists have discovered and rediscovered that time and time again. It is a tricky approach to use to find out about human behavior, but still there are many things to be found out by introspection that cannot be found out in other ways, and introspection has provided some of the most insightful and instructive work in the whole field of phonology. Another way is the old-fashioned structured elicitation of the anthropologist. "Tell me a folktale would you, and let me get it on my tape recorder." Of course, it is easy to put that down too. The situation is unnatural, and what you get is going to be distorted.

The critics ask why not at least get into a conversation with the informant. I will just repeat the argument I used for introspection. In spite of all the difficulties of doing it that way, some of the most important work in phonology has been done that way, and it is still a very intensive way to get the kind of data we want and need in phonology.

The third way is naturalistic observation. We are finally getting better at that. We are finally getting to the point where we observe real language in actual use and have a record of it in reliable form. I think that is great. I do not know that I have to defend that method here. There are some people who would say, maybe you do not even want to do that. I remember an argument in which someone said that ordinary, sloppy, casual, quick conversation is the worst place to start; it is the farthest removed from the norm. First you have got to get super-careful pronunciation in just the right way, and then you can write the rules when you get back to the other one, maybe. This represents two points of view, essentially the same ones that Hockett characterized a long time ago as clarity norm vs. frequency norm. Finally, there is another method, which an increasing number of people are using these days and which we have to learn to do better: carefully designed experimentation to get the data we need in such a way that even nonlinguists will be convinced that the material is valid and reliable.

In addition to predicting the use of all four methods, I think that phonologists will tend to be more sensitive in certain ways than many have been in the past. First they will be more sensitive to physiological phenomena. It is all very well to hypothesize and speculate about the nature of phonological systems, but we can no longer afford to do so in as much ignorance as we have often shown about human anatomy and physiology. Also we will have to be more sociolinguistically sensitive. Phonologists have made incredible blunders by failing to cope with sociolinguistic factors, and we are still wasting a lot of time arguing about noncomparable data because we are sociolinguistically insensitive to the limitations involved. I like all four methods of getting data, and I would like all four to be done with physiological and sociolinguistic sensitivity; I do not see how any one can really quarrel with that. We are in favor of virtue.

I would like to say at least a word about whether I think the prognosis for phonology is good, bad, or indifferent. We should stop and take a look at the field and see whether we are really getting anywhere. Is it going to turn out that this field does not really exist or that phonology has to mark time while some other branch of linguistics moves ahead?

No, I have high hopes for phonology. I think the prognosis for phonological theory is excellent; I feel more optimism about phonology at the present time than I do about syntax and semantics. Needless to say, in every branch of linguistics the theoretical positions are in disarray; that is, there are alternatives that seem to be mutually exclusive. You try one alternative for a while and it turns out to be very disappointing; you try another and it does not seem to work any better. But let us realize that in the field of phonology we have an enormous amount of data from all kinds of languages, and we have a degree of sophistication in phonological analysis that we have never had before. We have ways of asking questions about phonology that have become a matter of course, although a few years ago they were not known. I would say that the future of phonology is very bright indeed. The patient is not in serious condition, but on the way to good health, and maybe we should not talk about its being a patient at all.

REFERENCES

WPLU = Working Papers on Language Universals
(Stanford University)
PRCLD = Papers and Reports on Child Language Development
(Stanford University)

Bell, Alan. 1970. Development of syllabic nasals: the case of the Bantu noun class prefixes *mu-*, *mi-*, and *ma-*. *WPLU* 2:B1–B18.
————. 1971. Some patterns of occurrence and formation of syllable structures. *WPLU* 6:23–137.
Cantineau, Jean. 1946. Esquisse d'une phonologie de l'arabe classique. *Bulletin de la Société de Linguistique de Paris* 43:93–140.
Cedergren, Henrietta J., and Sankoff, David. 1975. Nasals: a sociolinguistic study of change in progress. In Ferguson et al., eds. (1975), *Nasálfest*, pp. 67–80.
Chen, Matthew. 1973. Cross-dialectal comparison: a case study and some theoretical considerations. *J. Chinese Ling.* 1:38–63.
Chomsky, Noam, and Halle, Morris. 1968. *The Sound Pattern of English*. New York: Harper & Row.
Clumeck, Harold. 1975. A cross-linguistic investigation of vowel nasalization: an instrumental study. In Ferguson et al., eds. (1975), *Nasálfest*, pp. 133–53.
Cruttenden, Alan. 1970. A phonetic study of babbling. *British Journal of Disorders of Communication* 5(2):110–17.

Eimas, Peter D.; Siqueland, Einar R.; Jusczyk, Peter; and Vigorito, James. 1971. Speech perception in infants. *Science* 171:303–306.

Ferguson, Charles A. 1966. Some assumptions about nasals: a sample study in phonological universals. In J. H. Greenberg, ed., *Universals of Language*, pp. 53–60. Cambridge: MIT Press.

———. 1968. Contrastive analysis and language development. *Monog. Series on Lang. and Ling.* 21:101–12.

———. 1972. Some requirements of a theory of language behavior. Presidential address, L.S.A.

———. 1975a. Fricatives in child language acquisition. In Luigi Heilmann, ed., *Proceedings of the 8th Int'l. Congress of Linguistics* (Bologna-Florence, 1972), pp. 647–64. Bologna: Società editrice il Mulino.

———. 1975b. Sound patterns in language acquisition. In D. P. Dato, ed., *Developmental Psycholinguistics: Theory and Applications*, pp. 1–16. Georgetown University Round Table 1975.

———. 1975c. Universal tendencies and 'normal' nasality. In C. A. Ferguson et al., eds., *Nasálfest*, pp. 175–96.

Ferguson, Charles A., and Farwell, Carol B. 1975. Words and sounds in early language acquisition. *Language* 5(2):419–39.

Ferguson, Charles A.; Hyman, Larry M.; and Ohala, John J., eds. 1975. *Nasálfest: Papers from a Symposium on Nasals and Nasalization.* Stanford, California: Language Universals Project, Department of Linguistics, Stanford University.

Fudge, E. 1969. Syllables. *J. Linguistics* 5:253–86.

Gamkrelidze, T. V. 1974. Sootnošenie smyčnyx frikativnyx v fonologičeskoj sisteme. Moscow: Institut Russkogo Jazyki, Akademija Nauk SSSR.

———. 1975. On the correlation of stops and fricatives in a phonological system. *Lingua* 35:231–62.

Gleitman, Lila R., and Rozin, Paul. 1973. Teaching reading by use of a syllabary. *Reading Research Quarterly* 8:447–83.

Greenberg, Joseph H. 1950. The patterning of root morphemes in Semitic. *Word* 6:162–81.

———. 1966. Synchronic and diachronic universals in phonology. *Language* 42(2):508–18.

Hawkins, Sarah. 1973. Temporal coordination of consonants in the speech of children: preliminary data. *J. of Phonetics* 1(3):181–217.

Hockett, Charles F. 1955. *A Manual of Phonology.* Baltimore: Waverly Press.

Hyman, Larry. 1975. Nasal states and nasal processes. In Ferguson et al., eds. (1975), *Nasálfest*, pp. 249–64.

Ingram, David. 1975. The acquisition of fricatives and affricates by normal and linguistically deviant children. In A. Caramazza, and E. Zuriff, eds., *The Acquisition and Breakdown of Language*. Baltimore: The Johns Hopkins University Press.

Jakobson, Roman. 1941. *Kindersprache, Aphasie und allgemeine Lautgesetze.*

Uppsala. Trans. by Allan R. Keiler: *Child Language Aphasia and Phonological Universals*. The Hague: Mouton, 1968.

Joos, Martin. 1950. Description of language design. *Journal of Acoustical Society of America* 22:701–708.

Kaplan, Eleanor L., and Kaplan, George A. 1971. Is there any such thing as a pre-linguistic child? In John Eliot, ed., *Human Development and Cognitive Processes*. New York: Holt, Rinehart and Winston.

Leopold, Werner F. 1947. *Speech Development of a Bilingual Child: A Linguist's Record*. Vol. II: *Sound-Learning of the Two-Year Old Child*. Northwestern University Humanities Series, Vol. 11. New York: AMS Press.

Macken, Marlys A. 1975. The acquisition of intervocalic consonants in Mexican Spanish: a cross-sectional study based on imitation data. *PRCLD* 9:29–42.

Mattingly, Ignatius G. 1972. Reading, the linguistic process and linguistic awareness. In J. F. Kavanagh and I. G. Mattingly, eds., *Language by Ear and Eye: The Relationships between Speech and Reading*. Cambridge: MIT Press.

Merrifield, William R. 1963. Palantla Chinantec syllable types. *Anthropological Linguistics* 5.5:1–16.

Moskowitz, A. I. 1973. Acquisition of phonology and syntax: a preliminary study. In Hintikka et al., eds., *Approaches to Natural Language*, pp. 48–84. Holland: Reidel Publishing Co.

Robins, R. H. 1957. Vowel nasality in Sundanese: a grammatical study. In *Studies in Linguistic Analysis*, pp. 87–103. Oxford: Blackwell.

Ruhlen, Merritt. 1973. Nasal vowels. *WPLU* 12:1–36.

Saffran, Eleanor M.; Marin, Oscar S. M.; and Yeni-Komshian, Grace H. 1975. An analysis of speech perception in word deafness. *Brain and Language*, in press.

Schane, Sanford. 1968. *French Phonology and Morphology*. Cambridge: MIT Press.

Sherman, Donald. 1975. Stop and fricative systems: a discussion of paradigmatic gaps and the question of language sampling. *WPLU* 17:1–31.

Smith, N. V. 1973. *The Acquisition of Phonology*. Cambridge: Cambridge University Press.

———. 1973. *The Acquisition of Phonology: A Case Study*. Cambridge: Cambridge University Press.

Stampe, David. 1969. The acquisition of phonetic representation. *Papers from the Fifth Regional Meeting of the Chicago Linguistic Society* 5:443–54.

Sweet, Henry. 1877. *A Handbook of Phonetics*. Oxford: Clarendon Press.

———. 1913. *Collected Papers*. Oxford: Clarendon Press.

Weir, Ruth H. 1962. *Language in the Crib*. The Hague: Mouton.

Index of Names

CURRENT ISSUES IN LINGUISTIC THEORY

Edited by Roger W. Cole

A state-of-the-art survey of a wide spectrum of sub-disciplines within linguistics by some of the most prominent contributors to linguistic theory of our day. The areas covered include phonology, syntax, semantics, discourse theory, sociolinguistics, and historical linguistics. Taken together, the eight essays in this volume do more than exemplify a number of the most interesting approaches being taken in linguistics today: they point the directions in which the discipline is likely to move in the coming decade.

Noam Chomsky, in the opening essay, argues that the goal of linguistic theory must be to develop universal grammar as a theory of the abstract properties of grammar. In "The Sociology of Language: Yesterday, Today, and Tomorrow," Joshua A. Fishman reviews the influence of the Whorfian hypothesis on sociolinguistics in the fifties and sixties, the influence of bilingualism at present, and the significance of language planning for the future. Charles J. Fillmore carries the discussion of lexical semantics away from more formal approaches into the realm of discourse theory and concentrates on the implications of text comprehension for semantic theory. In an essay titled "Semantic Domains and Componential Analysis of Meaning," Eugene A. Nida, Johannes P. Louw, and Rondal B. Smith describe a novel approach to lexicology with important implications for semantic theory. Writing on historical linguistics, Henry M. Hoenigswald argues that, despite attacks on some of the